There's Sunshine Awaiting You

"I love Jennifer Campbell's heart, love, and passion for Jesus and His never ending love for each one of us. Jennifer's words of encouragement have ministered, encouraged, and challenged me numerous times since we first met. I love that in spite of all she has walked thru and dealt with, she constantly focuses on the good. She's real, she's honest, she speaks life and truth, and above all else, I know her greatest desire is to share the message of His hope and encouragement to all she comes in contact with. This book will be one that I will pick up and read over and over as a reminder of Jesus' great love, care, and strength for not only myself, but for so many reasons. I am cheering Jennifer on because that is what encouragers do, and I believe in her. Read this book, and apply the truths of her heart to where you are on the journey."

Dusty Wells
Author, Blogger, Encourager, Music Biz Guy

"Jennifer never fails to fully communicate the love of Jesus in her writing. She has been a faithful member of our *SGN Scoops Magazine* team for many years, and we are thrilled that she has taken the step of releasing a volume of her own. Articulate and compassionate, Jennifer is eager to share her faith with the world."

Lorraine Walker
Editor, *SGN Scoops Magazine*

"Jennifer Campbell is a kind, gentle soul with a heart of gold. I have had the privilege and honor of knowing her for more than twenty years. Jennifer has grown into an amazing woman of God. It is a joy to watch and see how the Lord is using this gentle giant. Her love for Jesus is contagious. She has a tremendous burden to lead people to the saving knowledge of Jesus Christ. She has used her experiences of traveling the world for reaching out to people from different cultures and personally giving them the Gospel. She talks with them, shares meals with them, sings with them, and most of all, she prays with them. Just like the Helen Steiner Rice's poem, 'Strangers Are Friends We Haven't Met Yet,' that hangs on her wall, Jennifer genuinely cares about everyone. No one is a stranger to her. To know Jennifer is to love her. She inspires me to become a better witness for the Lord. This honest, pure, heartfelt book is filled with wonderful stories and testimonies. It truly reveals Jennifer's sincere passion to be the hands and feet of Jesus Christ. She is a bright light in this world!"

Karen Peck Gooch
Karen Peck & New River

"What an honor and privilege it is to speak on behalf of Jennifer Campbell. Having known her for a number of years, I have always been inspired by her genuine smile and godly presence. Now having read portions of her book, *There's Sunshine Awaiting You*, Jennifer has fully exposed her love for God, and her desire to spread the Gospel to every land. This book will certainly ignite a fresh love for God in you by sharing that love with all people."

Terry Williams
Priority Worship; Director, Florida Worship Choir & Orchestra

"This is a must-read for every believer. Within these pages, Jennifer shares her story, and her story begins with her miraculous birth. In this autobiography, Jennifer shares with passion her gratitude for her Savior, her love for family, and her desire to help grow the body of Christ."

Angela Hester
Lifelong Friend

"Whenever Jennifer opens her mouth to speak or to sing, or when she takes to her computer to write, Jennifer is a communicator. And there really is only one subject she desires to communicate: the Lord Jesus Christ. Thank you for always pointing us to the sunny side of the street!"

Evie Tornquist Karlsson
Evie Music

"I praise God for His grace toward me to see Jennifer's ministry, humiliation, and deep valley experiences, not closely, but indirectly from far away. God has elevated Jennifer and set her as a model and inspiration to many others in the church after she has successfully overcome many problems and has been made as a cleansed precious pearl. A good Christian life is worth more than a thousand messages. Jennifer's writings are like a candle in the darkness for many people, encouraging them through faith, as per Acts 1:8 & Mark 16:15."

Praveen Kumar
Pastor, Bethesda Indo-Kuwait Ministries, Kuwait and India

"Jennifer has always had such a positive, sweet countenance that radiates when she shares Christ! I am grateful for those who provide a little sunshine in a dark world, and it is a privilege to watch Jennifer shine!"

Sheri Easter
Jeff & Sheri Easter

"Jennifer is a sweet child of God devoted to writing her heart in song and now her new book. She has dedicated her life to following Christ and encouraging others. She has blessed many souls through her ministry. I'm so proud of her first literary effort, *There's Sunshine Awaiting You*."

Marcia Henry
Songwriter

"Jennifer and her dad served God in our church with praise and worship songs and the Word of God in the summer of 2018. I was touched by their passion for Jesus and their passion for the lost. When Jennifer and her dad shared their testimonies, songs, and the Word of God with us, God touched all of us and their words are still remembered today. We were glad to have them among us in Romania. Jennifer's godly joy comes from a sincere heart. She is full of passion to spread the Gospel of Jesus Christ everywhere in this world, like in the book of Acts 1:8. I would like to encourage you to read Jennifer's book, for I believe God will use it to touch you, encourage you, heal you, and your life will change. Please get a copy of this book and read it with joy."

Peter Rong Makur
Pastor, Spiritual Revival Baptist Church, Bucharest, Romania

There's Sunshine Awaiting You

When You're in the Sunset,

There's **Sunshine** *Awaiting You*

JENNIFER CAMPBELL

Foreword by Ken Campbell

Dedication

To my loving parents, You loved me before I was born. Words can never fully express my gratitude and love for you both. You were the first ones to tell me about Jesus. You gave me a foundation like no other. I have built my hope on the solid Rock because of your godly influence in my life.

Dear Daddy, You are a prime example of God's unconditional love. You are a blessing to my life in so many ways. You are my travel buddy, teaching colleague, kitchen companion, and faithful friend. Only God could have given me such a loving father. It is a joy to "do life" with you. Even with all of our amazing adventures, there is no greater honor than standing by your side, proclaiming the excellent name of Jesus Christ. No matter my age, I will always be your little girl. I love you, Daddy.

Dear Mama, I wish you were here to read this book. I miss you so very much. You were my encourager, my confidante, and my friend. You loved Daddy and me unconditionally. Best of all, you loved Jesus with all your heart. I can only imagine the smile on your face when you stepped into the presence of the King! When our hearts were broken, your heart leaped with joy. Until the moment I see you again in Heaven, I pray I will continue to make you proud. I love you, Mama.

Above all, to Jesus Christ, I am alive because of You. You deserve all of the glory, honor, and praise. You are my best friend. I love You so very much, Jesus. I worship and adore You, my Savior and my Lord.

There's sunshine awaiting you,
Just wait and see.
'Cause in the lowest valley,
He sends you to your knees.
And when you just can't go on,
This is what God says.
When you're in the sunset,
There's sunshine awaiting you.

—Jennifer Joy Campbell

Contents

Foreword

"But the fruit of the Spirit is love, joy, peace, longsuffering,
gentleness, goodness, faith, Meekness, temperance:
against such there is no law." (Gal. 5:22–23 KJV)

"Moreover it is required in stewards, that
a man be found faithful." (1 Cor. 4:2 KJV)

The foreword of a book is frequently written by a prominent individual or celebrity. When Jenny asked me to write the foreword for her new book, she said that she wanted someone who was most familiar with the author. As her earthly father, I have probably been in the best position to observe the stories and events contained in the pages of this book. It is my privilege to travel the road of life with the person I admire and the person I most respect, the author of this book, my daughter.

The Bible describes a number of characteristics that should be manifest in the life of a Christian believer. They are called the fruit of the Spirit. For almost four decades, I have seen these fruits consistently and abundantly evidenced in Jennifer's life. From the very beginning, I can assure you that our life has frequently been more of a battlefield than a playground. I will not recount the events you are about to read, but I will say that the doctors were already giving a discouraging report the day before she was born. When she was born lifeless, my wife and I held hands and prayed, "Jesus, help." We did not pray anything else. We did not want God to think that we were trying to impress Him with any kind of fancy words. Our confidence had to be in God alone.

I know the real Jennifer. We have lived under the same roof

for more than thirty-seven years. We have traveled together around the world to more than fifty countries and territories. We have the privilege of sharing the Gospel of Jesus Christ as laborers together in God's field of ministry. Jennifer's webcast, *Be Encouraged*, is seen each week by thousands of people around the world. In spite of illness and tragedy, she has pressed on toward the prize of God's call upon her life. Motivated by love for those who are lost, she has patiently and meekly continued to reach out to those who often respond with personal insults and rebellious rejection of God's grace.

When the road has been rough, Jennifer has responded with gentleness and faith. On more than one occasion, she has faced critical health issues with complete confidence in Christ. As a steward of God's talent and blessings, she has been so very faithful. Many times, her attitude has been, "We may not be the greatest, but God knows that we are willing." The Bible records many occasions where attempts were made to silence the servants and messengers of God. Many times, the situations may seem hopeless with the light growing dim, but remember, "When you're in the sunset, there's sunshine awaiting you."

Ken Campbell

Introduction

"May these words of my mouth and this meditation of my heart be pleasing in your sight, LORD, my Rock and my Redeemer." (Ps. 19:14)

Writing has always been a passion of mine, from the very first moment I could hold a pencil in my hand. Beginning with the composition of rudimentary letters to my mom and dad as a child, gradually working through the creation of numerous essays, stories, poems, and speeches throughout my childhood, I have always had a desire to write.

When I was fifteen years old, I wrote my first song. That same year, I became a feature writer for a nationally known gospel music magazine. In college, it seemed writing lengthy compositions on various topics more closely resembled a pastime rather than an assignment for me. I wrote several hundred papers during my six years of undergraduate and graduate school. Thousands of words written, yet there is one thing that has always been missing in my repertoire of written words.

Until now, that is.

I have dreamed of writing a book for more than thirty years. Not just any book, mind you, but the particular book you are reading this very moment.

Ecclesiastes 3:1 says, "There is a time for everything, and a season for every activity under the heavens." I am so grateful to God for allowing me to publish my first book during this season of my life, for His timing is always perfect.

I pray this book will encourage you and inspire you. Above all, I pray God will use the words in this book to minister to your heart and to remind you that Jesus Christ loves you more than you could ever possibly imagine.

As you meet my beloved family and journey with me to foreign lands, I hope you quickly realize I would be nothing without the grace of God. As you will discover in the pages of this book, I owe my life to Him.

God allowed me to write a song a few years ago titled, "Thank You, Lord."

Chorus:
Thank You, Lord,
For Your boundless love.
Thank You, Lord,
For everything You've done.
I raise my hands in worship;
You're the One whom I adore.
Standing humbly in Your presence,
I praise and thank You, Lord.[1]

This song is my prayer every single day, as I could never thank the Lord enough for the multitude of ways He has rescued me. I pray He will continue to open doors for me to share my testimony with others. My passion in life is to proclaim the Gospel of Jesus Christ. He deserves all of the glory!

When you turn to the last page of this book, I pray you emerge as a different person. Whether you are a follower of Jesus Christ or someone who is hearing about Jesus for the very first time, my prayer is that God will use the Gospel message found within this book to change your life.

Jennifer Joy Campbell

Chapter One

Jesus, Help

"Hear my prayer, LORD, listen to my cry for help."' (Ps. 39:12)

On January 2, 1982, a premature baby girl entered this world in the midst of what seemed like a hopeless situation. The doctors focused on doing what they could for her mother, who was having complications from the labor and delivery. This little girl had no chance of living a happy, normal life. She was born without a heartbeat. Born nearly eight weeks early, the doctors gave up hope for her survival. They told the parents they were sorry, but their newborn did not make it.

Still, this baby's parents did not give up hope. They knew God was faithful. Struggling to cope with the situation, they did not rely on some eloquent prayer written with formal language. They did not call on the doctors. They called on Jesus Christ. They simply prayed, "Jesus, help."

As her parents prayed, the little girl began to cough like a small kitten. The doctors were amazed, yet some of them said she would likely have limited cognitive ability, even if she did survive. Her parents did not care. They wanted her to live regardless of the challenges she might face.

At the tender age of seven days old, this premature baby had heart surgery. Even so, her parents continued to pray, having faith God would heal her body and make her whole. After spending many weeks in Shands Neonatal Center in Gainesville, Florida, the parents of this baby girl were finally able to bring her home.

The doctors said she may have developmental challenges, but God had other plans. Once during a doctor's appointment, her parents told the doctor she could read, at the young age of two. He did not seem to believe them, thinking she could only read books she had memorized. They handed her one of his medical journals and while she could not comprehend them fully, due to her young age and the advanced nature of the text, she read the words effortlessly.

Now, at the age of thirty-seven years old, she has since completed six years of college with honors, earning her Master of Science degree in English education with a 4.0 GPA. Obviously, the doctors were wrong. God had His hand on this little baby from the very moment she was born. Jesus heard her parent's cries for help and He answered them.

My name is Jennifer Joy Campbell. That little baby girl was me. I was born lifeless. God raised me up and gave me life. I can tell you with full assurance that God still performs miracles. I thank Him every day for what He has done for me. Hebrews 13:8 says, "Jesus Christ is the same yesterday and today and forever." The same One who worked a miracle in my life will do the same for you. He will never change, nor will His love for you and me.

Have Faith

If we have faith as small as a mustard seed, we can command mountains to move (Matt. 17:20). My parents had great faith. In spite of their vast knowledge of the human body, the medical world determined I would not live. With humble faith, my parents called on Jesus to help them in their time of need. He heard their desperate cry for help and answered their prayers.

When I was born, my mom and dad did not offer up a ceremonious prayer. They did not gather an army of pastors or deacons. There was no music played. Instead, two people humbly prayed, "Jesus, help." They believed this promise to be true: "'For

where two or three gather in my name, there am I with them'"
(Matt. 18:20). My parents joined in faith and spoke the name
above all names, Jesus Christ. Because of the miraculous power
of Jesus Christ, I am alive today. He deserves all of the praise.

The apostle Paul wrote, "He who began a good work in you
will carry it on to completion until the day of Christ Jesus" (Phil.
1:6). God began working in my life even before I was born. He
knew my mom and dad would endure one of the biggest trials of
their lives on the day I came into the world. He also knew He
would complete the good
work He had begun in my life.
My parents prayed and had
faith, and God answered by
completing the work He had
set out to accomplish.

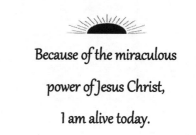

Because of the miraculous

power of Jesus Christ,

I am alive today.

In Mark chapter five, we
read of a woman who had
such strong faith that she
believed she would be healed,
if she could just touch the hem of Jesus' garment. She had
suffered from "bleeding for twelve years," and the medical care
she received only worsened her condition (Mark 5:25–26). One
day, she heard about Jesus, and "she thought, 'If I just touch his
clothes, I will be healed.' Immediately her bleeding stopped and
she felt in her body that she was freed from her suffering" (Mark
5:28–29). She had such great faith; she knew she did not even
need to speak to Jesus, but only touch His clothes.

There was a large crowd gathered around, yet "Jesus realized
that power had gone out from him. He turned around in the
crowd and asked, 'Who touched my clothes?'" (Mark 5:30). His
disciples criticized His question, telling Him there were many
people around Him, so it would be virtually impossible to know
who had touched Him. Still, Jesus wanted to acknowledge the
woman who displayed such great faith.

If you have ever been to a huge metropolis, such as Paris, France, you know just how crowded a busy thoroughfare can be. In Times Square in New York City, for example, up to 450,000 people pass through each day. Of these hundreds of thousands of people, if someone accidentally bumped in to you, there would likely be no way of knowing who it was. Likewise, Jesus was in a very crowded area and He was a highly sought-after individual. People pressed in to see Him. The likelihood of finding the woman who touched His clothing was slim to none, yet "Jesus kept looking around to see who had done it. Then the woman, knowing what had happened to her, came and fell at his feet and, trembling with fear, told him the whole truth. He said to her, 'Daughter, your faith has healed you. Go in peace and be freed from your suffering'" (Mark 5:32–34).

Jesus Christ loves you more than you could ever truly imagine.

Jesus was omniscient, so He knew exactly who had touched His garment. He knew power had gone out of His body. He was not upset or angry when He asked who had touched Him. He simply wanted to speak to the woman who had such strong faith. He knew her life story. He knew about her medical condition. Why did Jesus heal her body? Because she had absolute faith, that Jesus would heal her infirmities.

Jesus said her faith had healed her (Mark 5:34). He did not say she had done enough good deeds to receive healing, or tell her she had prayed long enough. He did not even tell her she had to donate money to a local charity or church. All she needed to possess was genuine, sincere faith. Because of her great faith, Jesus cleansed her body and restored her health.

Likewise, my parents had faith that God would restore my life. As my mom and dad prayed, "Jesus, help," they did not need to use a particular recitation or book of prayers. This prayer was the cry of their heart, when they could not utter any other words. Sometimes we pray long, deep-rooted prayers. Other times we are too disheartened to pray. There are even times when we are only able to allow God to hear the cries of our heart. In these moments, we need to open our hearts to Heaven and have solid faith that God will intervene on our behalf. The impossible becomes possible when we pray. I am living proof that God will perform a miracle when we pray.

God does not require pomp and circumstance. He only requires childlike faith. Whatever you are going through, Jesus wants to help you. No situation can place you beyond the reach of Jesus Christ. He can heal the sick, mend broken hearts, and restore shattered lives. He is the friend who is "closer than a brother" (Prov. 18:24). Put your trust in Jesus today. Reach out for the hem of His garment!

Jesus Christ loves you more than you could ever truly imagine. He will help you, just as He helped me the day I was born. He continues to help me every day of my life. Call on the name of Jesus Christ. Every single time you need Him, Jesus will answer your cry for help.

God Is Our Refuge

Have you ever found yourself in a frightening situation? One of my most feared creatures is a snake. When I was a child, I was riding my adult-size tricycle in our backyard, only to look down and see two or three snakes slithering below me. I pedaled faster than I ever had before, praying I would be out of their reach before being struck by one of these reptiles. Another time, we were heading out the door on our way to church one Palm Sunday morning, only to find two black snakes slithering across our kitchen floor. Somehow, my dad managed to capture them both and remove them from our home safely. Apparently, they had found their way through a pipe fitting, which my dad promptly secured. Even with this alarming detour, we still made it to church on time. Incidents like these are wonderful reminders of how God always protects us from harm, no matter what Satan tosses into our path.

When I was younger, my dad and I set out for my first whitewater rafting excursion. We hopped in our brand new orange and black, two-person inflatable boat, excited about this great adventure. As we floated down Raven's Fork Branch in Western North Carolina, I could only think about how I wanted to do it all over again. Floating through the rapids was exhilarating. The beautiful scenery of the Great Smoky Mountains National Park and the refreshing cool water on a warm summer day made for a truly incredible experience.

On our second trip down the river, though, a branch or some other sharp object in the river punctured the bottom of the boat. The rapids continued to drag us over the jagged rocks, which was anything but a joyride. Soon, my dad decidedly jumped out of the boat, stopping this perilous ride and getting us ashore safely.

On another Carolina excursion, my parents and I went for a rafting trip down the Oconaluftee River, which runs straight through the town of Cherokee, North Carolina. The first part of the trip was remarkable. The second part was terrifying. My inner tube flipped over abruptly, leaving me nose down in the water. My mom screamed. I heard fierce splashing, as if someone was racing toward me. All I could think about was the advice my dad had given me when he said, "Nose and toes."

He had recently gone on a whitewater trip down the famed Nantahala River and the guides had shared this life-saving advice with him. When you are in a river filled with rocks and rapids, the goal is to keep your nose and toes above water at all times. This is to avoid getting your feet stuck below debris lurking underwater, which would result in the swift current pulling you forward, causing you to drown.

Yet here I was, face down in the water, somewhat stunned by the blow my knee took from a rock beneath the water's surface. It seemed as if my life flashed before my eyes in an instant. Soon I got my bearings and put my head above water. What seemed like minutes were likely only seconds. In no time at all, my dad was by my side to make sure I was okay. A fisherman rescued my inner tube. After catching my breath, I hobbled to the river's edge with blood dripping down my leg from where the rock attacked my knee, relieved to be back on dry ground.

Looking back, I am grateful to God for His protection during both of these hazardous whitewater incidents. I can see how these experiences stand as valuable life lessons. Sometimes, we are coasting through life, sailing smoothly above the rock-riddled rapids. We may perceive the situation as if nothing could spoil the serenity we feel when everything runs according to our plans. Then, all of the sudden, something comes along to rip a hole in our boat. Life spirals out of control, just as our raft began to travel wildly over the jagged rocks. Similar to the way my dad pulled our inflatable boat to safety, our Heavenly Father will bring us to safety if we call on Him.

Although my short-lived whitewater adventures are somewhat of a blur, I distinctly remember calling on the Lord for His protection. While it was not an eloquent prayer or even a verbal prayer at all, I had assurance God would keep me safe from all harm. He has always proven faithful in my life, and I knew He would be with me even in the middle of the river. Like the rocks I encountered, many dangers surround us daily. We must put our trust in Jesus Christ, for He is the only One who has the power to save us. He is the source of lasting hope.

Perhaps you feel as if your life is turning upside down, just as my inner tube flipped over in the river. You may be trying to come to terms with an unfaithful husband or wife. Addiction could have you in its clutches. Guilt, regret, or despair may be filling your mind. No matter what battle you may be fighting, there is nothing too hard for God to handle. Jesus said, "'In this world you will have trouble. But take heart! I have overcome the world'" (John 16:33). Jesus will help you climb every mountain and overcome every fear. He will reach down and pull you out of the low place in which you find yourself. He will rescue you, just as my dad rescued me in the river. Jesus is our Heavenly Father. He always looks out for His children. He loves us so very much.

There could be doubt in your mind as to whether Jesus will be there for you every time you need Him. You may be dealing with bitterness toward a parent, grandparent, or another loved one who abandoned you when you were young, or even a spouse, family member, or friend who has left you as an adult. People will often disappoint you, but Jesus Christ said He "'will never leave you nor forsake you'" (Josh. 1:5). Nothing on earth can separate you from the love of Jesus Christ. The apostle Paul wrote, nothing in all creation "will be able to separate us from the love of God that is in Christ Jesus our Lord" (Rom. 8:39). No tragedy, no sickness, no form of evil on this planet can take away the unconditional love of the One who created us in His own image.

Jesus Christ loves you so much that He gave His life for you (1 John 3:16). He wants to be your Lord, your Savior, and your help in times of trouble. One of my favorite scriptures is Psalm 46:1: "God is our refuge and strength, an ever-present help in trouble." He will always be with you through every trial you face in life, calming your fears and reminding you that everything will be okay. Whenever you need help, call on the name of the Lord. Jesus Christ will be your helper.

Chapter Two

Shine His Light

"Let your light shine before others, that they may see your good deeds and glorify your Father in heaven."" (Matt. 5:16)

Psalm 37:4 says, "Take delight in the LORD, and he will give you the desires of your heart." One of my greatest desires has always been to tell other people how Jesus Christ saved my life. There is no greater joy than sharing my testimony of His miraculous power. To have the opportunity to introduce someone to the amazing love of Jesus Christ is like the icing on the cake. My prayer is that God will use me for His glory. Every year, God overwhelms me with even more opportunities to fulfill this lifelong dream.

When I was four years old, I sang my first song in public at a revival in Atlanta, Georgia. I sang the song, "He's Still Working on Me," penned by my dear friends, Joel and LaBreeska Hemphill. Looking back, I know my parents chose the perfect song for me to sing, for God began working in my life at a very young age and He is still working on me.

While I did not realize it at the time, this is the moment God began preparing my heart for ministry. I sang throughout my childhood, as my dad ministered in word and song at many revivals and churches across the southeastern United States. Whether we were getting ready in a hotel room, a bedroom in a pastor's home, or even in a room positioned behind the platform inside the sanctuary, we prayed for God to use us to spread the Gospel message. God always blessed every service.

Without fail, I sang everywhere God opened the door, from

the county fair to the local nursing home. Some of my singing engagements as a young person were quite difficult, such as the times I sang at the funerals of my two baby brothers who were born prematurely. Sometimes, I have even sung about my best friend, Jesus, in some unlikely places, such as the teacher talent show at the public school where I teach. No matter where God gives me the opportunity to sing, one thing always remains true: I sing for the Lord.

For ten years, I was a member of a youth organization that places a focus on the importance of agriculture and leadership. Even within this predominately secular group, I found opportunities to minister, whether it was to lead the blessing over a meal, share devotions as chaplain, or sing a song about the Lord at the annual banquet. While I proudly wore my official jacket at many different events, I wore my faith in Jesus Christ even more proudly.

Regardless of where I am, I have never been shy about telling others about Jesus. Soon after I began teaching, I served as the Recording Secretary on the Executive Board for the Florida Council of Teachers of English. This position, along with my position as Public Relations Chair and Social Media Manager, represent a combined twelve years of volunteer service to this organization. In addition, I served on the National Council of Teachers of English (NCTE) Middle Level Section Nominating Committee. I received the NCTE Leadership Development Affiliate Award in 2009. I have given presentations at numerous county, regional, state, and national education conferences in the areas of English, ESOL, reading, and mathematics. Although these experiences have served to make me a better educator, the most rewarding aspect of these conferences has been the opportunity to share Jesus Christ. Whether I am speaking to a conference attendee, venue employee, or one of the textbook vendors, it seems God always gives me opportunities to share the Good News, even in the midst of a secular education event.

Witnessing is part of my DNA. My passion is telling others about the eternal hope we have in Jesus. I am constantly on the lookout for opportunities to encourage someone, and prayerfully, introduce them to my best friend. My life revolves around my personal relationship with Jesus Christ. Romans 1:16 says, "For I am not ashamed of the gospel, because it is the power of God that brings salvation to everyone who believes." I am not ashamed of Jesus Christ. While I publicly profess that I am a Christian, I prefer saying I am a follower of Jesus Christ. I am not indebted to any particular religion, but to the One who gave His life for me. He is my closest friend, even before my family whom I love very much. I place Jesus Christ first in my life. He is my Lord and Savior, who has given me abundant life, matchless grace, and boundless love.

When people ask if you are a Christian, do you hesitate and try to sidestep the question? Are you embarrassed or afraid of what they might think about you, or do you promptly proclaim that He is the Savior of your soul? I pray you are quick to tell someone what Jesus Christ has done for you. We need to be ready and willing to share the love of Jesus with everyone we meet, even if it means losing a friend or two along the way. We cannot afford to be ashamed. I often encounter people who do not seem to understand my love for Jesus Christ, even to the point of responding with derogatory remarks. Nevertheless, I continue to declare His wonderful name everywhere I go.

During my elementary school years, I briefly attended a private Christian school. Even at school, I passed out Gospel tracts to my fellow classmates. As a young child, my parents taught me the importance of sharing the Gospel with others. I handed out tracts at youth club meetings, at the county fairgrounds, and in many other locations. Having parents who were proud of me for sharing my faith was a huge encouragement to keep doing what I was doing. How grateful I am to them for encouraging me to live out what the Scriptures tell us to do. We need to follow the example of Paul, who "proclaimed the kingdom of God and taught about the Lord Jesus Christ—with all boldness and without hindrance" (Acts 28:31). Paul was not ashamed. He did not let anything stop him from sharing the message of the Gospel, not even imprisonment, riots, or persecution. He knew his mission in life was to tell others about the redeeming grace only found through Jesus Christ. Likewise, we need to be bold and unashamed!

Luke 9:26 says, "'Whoever is ashamed of me and my words, the Son of Man will be ashamed of them when he comes in his glory and in the glory of the Father and of the holy angels.'" Jesus Christ paid for our sins. He paved the way for us to have eternal life in Heaven. If we are ashamed of Him, then Jesus will be ashamed of us when He returns to this earth. Imagine disappointing the very One who gave His life for us. I pray I will never disappoint my Lord and Savior. I strive every day to live a life that is pleasing in His sight. Will I make mistakes along the way? Of course, we all make mistakes.

Do not be ashamed of the Gospel. Shine your light and live your life for the cause of Christ!

Nonetheless, I pray I shall never be ashamed of the One who saved me, healed me, and loved me so much that He gave His life for me.

Jesus gave His life, so we could have an eternal home in Heaven. No human being on earth could ever come close to matching the amazing love of Jesus Christ, nor could they bestow upon us such a priceless gift—the gift of salvation. We need to shine forth the light of Jesus, so others around us will find the unmerited favor God extends to everyone who believes that Jesus Christ is Lord. It is our responsibility to share the Gospel with the world. Do not be ashamed of the Gospel. Shine your light and live your life for the cause of Christ!

Two Quarters

As a young person, I regularly volunteered to sing at two different skilled nursing facilities in our local area. I was not only the one who strived to be a blessing to others, but I often received a blessing myself. One day at the Surrey Place Care Center, I led a few hymns on the upright piano, which sat in the corner of the common recreational area. Afterward, one of the caregivers told me one of the residents wanted to speak to me. I promptly went over to this woman, never expecting the impact this encounter would have on my life.

The woman motioned for me to hold out my hand. She placed something in my hand, with her palm facing downward, so I could not see the contents within my own palm. She told me my singing had blessed her and thanked me profusely for coming to cheer them up. I graciously thanked her for her kind words and told her it was my pleasure. After letting her know I would pray for her, we parted ways.

Two quarters—that was what the precious lady placed in my hand. Before leaving the facility, the caregiver told me the woman who gave me the quarters told her about it beforehand, saying she wanted to bless me, since I always came to bless the residents with music. She informed me that the sweet resident did not have any wealth on this earth, and that the two quarters could possibly represent the only cash she had in this world.

Immediately, I was reminded of the widow's offering. Jesus watched a poor woman place two small coins in the offering. Other people gave large amounts, looking down upon this widow due to her meager contribution. However, Jesus expressed the value of her gift when He said, "'Truly I tell you, this poor widow has put more into the treasury than all the others. They all gave out of their wealth; but she, out of her poverty, put in everything—all she had to live on'" (Mark 12:43–44). This woman held nothing back. Proportionately, she gave a larger percentage than those with great wealth.

The lady at the nursing home may have only given me two quarters, but this offering represented so much more than monetary value. I am humbled that God would allow me to experience such a pivotal moment in my ministry at such a young age. For this dear woman essentially gave all she had to the work of the Lord.

Through the years, I have met people who gave their all and others who did not want to share their wealth, not even with their own family. Regrettably, some people are not only lovers of people and things, but some people actually love money itself, so much so that they strive daily not to spend one dime, even though their bank account is laden with thousands, or even millions, of dollars. Jesus said, "'It is easier for a camel to go through the eye of a needle than for someone who is rich to enter the kingdom of God'" (Mark 10:25). This does not mean the wealthiest people cannot enter Heaven, but it does mean we need to ensure our wealth does not blind us to the fact that there are people less fortunate than we are. While it is important to make investments and reserve some wealth for necessities, we should really invest in God's Kingdom.

There is no point in hoarding our riches, for we cannot take it with us. Jesus shared this advice with others: "'Go, sell everything you have and give to the poor, and you will have treasure in heaven'" (Mark 10:21). This does not mean you literally have to sell everything you own and live on the street somewhere, but it does mean you should be willing to help individuals in need. Everywhere you go, you will find people who are hungry or hurting. Some of them have made poor decisions, yet they are human beings who deserve a second chance. Although some people pass them by without even acknowledging them, God loves the homeless people on the street. A cup of coffee, a sandwich, or a warm blanket could be the avenue by which they discover God's love in a tangible way.

In Rome, Italy, I saw an elderly man pull a container of half-eaten watermelon out of the garbage can, dump it on a dusty ledge inside Termini Station, and eat it with his soiled fingers. In New York City, I have seen homeless people retrieve drink cups out of the trash receptacle, and then proceed to drink the remaining fluid inside. Others have been grateful to receive a pack of peanut butter crackers out of one of our backpacks while we were on vacation. Such a small gesture, yet when it comes with a Gospel tract, it could prove to be a life-changing gift.

Whether God calls us to give a little or to give a lot, we should never hold anything back.

Even in the United States, I have been in a home where one of the members of the family had to go to the corner store to buy some milk, so they could serve peanut butter and jelly sandwiches for dinner when my parents and I were their dinner guests. While I truly enjoy peanut butter and jelly sandwiches, the mere fact that they were unable to keep a basic staple such as milk on hand regularly was difficult to fathom.

When we visited the island nation of Haiti, I observed people who were fraught to sell beautiful handmade baskets for mere pennies. Having traveled to many different countries, the anxiety displayed by these vendors was on a level I had never witnessed before. You could see the desperation in their eyes, inferring that every dollar earned would be the source of food on the table for their family.

People are suffering around the world. Even though we cannot afford to provide financial assistance for everyone, we can pray for them diligently. Whether God calls us to give a little or to give a lot, we should never hold anything back. We need to give our all for Jesus. He gave His all for us. Help the people around you. Pray for the hurting. Share the blessings God has bestowed upon you with others. As Jesus profoundly said, "It is more blessed to give than to receive" (Acts 20:35 KJV).

Breaking the Box

In the Gospels of Matthew and Mark, we read of one particular woman who gave all she could. Mark 14:3 says, "A woman came with an alabaster jar of very expensive perfume, made of pure nard. She broke the jar and poured the perfume on his head." She did not just "think outside the box," as the popular saying goes. She broke open the alabaster box and poured out the contents on Jesus' head.

While it was customary back then to anoint someone with a drop or two of essential oil when they entered your home, no one would have literally thought to pour this potent liquid on someone's head. This perfume comes from the spikenard plant found in the Himalayas, and is created by crushing and distilling the roots of this plant to create an amber-colored essential oil.[1] In other words, the perfume she used was not your average perfume found at the local drug store. It was quite expensive and was not something typically poured out so freely. Jesus' disciples knew this all too well.

The disciples said, "'This perfume could have been sold at a high price and the money given to the poor'" (Matt. 26:9). Besides the monetary cost, the scent of this perfume was strong and may have lasted for up to ten days. One or two drops would have been adequate. Because of customs in place at the time, the disciples did not see the need for such drastic measures.

Nevertheless, this woman did not just want to give a little; she wanted to give a lot. She wanted to be extravagant because

God had shown extravagance in His love for her. This woman knew the One she anointed was worth it all. Jesus was the priceless treasure, not the perfume she poured on His head.

The cost of the perfume she used was more than three hundred denarii, which would have been equal to the average person's yearly wages. What would your husband, your wife, your family, or your friends say if you spent a year's wages all at once? Just imagine! One decision and every penny you worked so hard for over the course of the entire year is gone. Yet she did not hesitate to give all she had to our Lord.

The Bible says she "broke the jar and poured the perfume on his head" (Mark 14:3). It does not say she stopped to think about what she was doing, or that she poured a little bit first and then slowly drained out the rest of the container. She came there on a mission. She had no doubts, no fears, and little concern for what others might think. She knew she was in the presence of the Lord God Almighty and she wanted to give her all to Him.

Jesus recognized the greatness of her kind gesture. Jesus asked, "'Why are you bothering her? She has done a beautiful thing to me'" (Mark 14:6). Jesus did not tell her to sell the perfume to give to the poor. Instead, He said they would always have the poor with them, but they would not always have Him with them (Mark 14:7). Shortly thereafter, Jesus gave His life for the forgiveness of our sins. The woman's action was in preparation for His burial.

The woman gave the equivalent of a year's salary to prepare Him for the difficult task ahead of Him. Yet Judas Iscariot agreed to hand over Jesus to the chief priests for only thirty pieces of silver (Matt. 26:14–16). By comparison, this could be as little as twenty dollars worth of silver today. Conversely, the woman essentially emptied her pockets in an effort to show her love for the Savior. In doing so, she found favor in the Lord's sight.

Jesus said, "'She did what she could'" (Mark 14:8). Jesus did not say she did too much or that she should have done more. He said she did what she could. She gave all that she had to give. She held nothing back. She boldly broke open the alabaster jar and poured all of the perfume on Jesus' head. Jesus recognized the magnitude of her generous deed.

Jesus said, "'Truly I tell you, wherever the gospel is preached throughout the world, what she has done will also be told, in memory of her'" (Matt. 26:13). This woman's boldness and compassion for Jesus is still a story shared more than two thousand years later. All because she disregarded the opinions of others, ignored the rebukes from Jesus' disciples, and broke open the box for Jesus.

She may have had a little trepidation, worried that other people might criticize her actions. Her concerns were valid, as individuals often fret about what people will say about them. They alter their conversations just to be more in tune with what other people want to hear. Concerned that people will squirm in their seats when they mention the name of Jesus, they may avoid mentioning the precious name of Jesus in order to find acceptance. Christians may attempt to be non-offensive, but then they lose the priceless opportunity to tell people what Jesus Christ has done in their lives.

Many churches want to be what the world is seeking, rather than introducing the world to the One whom we should be seeking.

Sadly, I have even seen churches cater to the desires of the world, highlighting secular music, magicians, and comedians. From bingo games to masquerade balls, they are striving to be like the world at an ever-increasing rate. Many churches want to be what the world is seeking, rather than introducing the world to the One whom we should be seeking. According to God's Word, we should not "conform to the pattern of this world" (Rom. 12:2). The church and its members must be proclaiming the Good News, not trying to get in the world's good graces.

The Bible declares that we are to boldly go into the whole world and preach the Gospel (Mark 16:15). We must tell other people about the infinite grace which comes from knowing the one true God. We cannot just sprinkle in a few scriptures or encouraging words here or there like the disciples thought the woman should have just used a small amount of perfume. We need to pour it all out, declaring the name of Jesus, for He is worthy of all of our praise!

There is no cost too great. The most valuable thing in the entire world is a personal relationship with Jesus Christ, the Lord of lords and King of kings. Nothing should come between us and witnessing to someone in need. Salvation is a priceless gift from God that we should share with everyone we meet.

We need to get outside the box, pick up the box, and break it open for Jesus. I encourage you to be a bright light in this world of darkness. Disregard the opinions of others and focus on the One who truly matters, Jesus Christ. By holding nothing back, you can live a life according to the will of God. I challenge you today to tell someone about the everlasting love of Jesus Christ! Be bold, stand firm, and break open the box. Let the light of Jesus shine forth!

Chapter Three

The Music in Me

*"My heart, O God, is steadfast; I will sing
and make music with all my soul." (Ps. 108:1)*

How fitting it is that my dad is playing a beautiful medley of worship music as I begin writing this chapter. In our household, there is nothing out of the ordinary about my dad or me playing the piano at the break of dawn or even in the wee hours of the night. I always want to play the piano. In all honesty, I would rather play the piano than sleep. Those who know me well know that I play the piano every single night before I turn in for the night. Even if we arrive home in the middle of the night from a long-distance trip, I still play the piano. Why, you ask? Because playing the piano is one of my favorite things to do.

Of course, my desire to play the piano has little to do with a manufactured instrument composed of eighty-eight keys and more than ten thousand parts, even though it is exquisitely beautiful in appearance and produces complex melodious sounds pleasing to the ear. My longing to play the piano stems from my deep-rooted love for the Lord Jesus Christ, for my dad and I firmly believe music is for worshiping the one true living God. When I sit down at the piano, I am not trying to imitate someone else, nor am I attempting to bring glory to myself. Every note, every chord, and every stanza is for lifting up the lovely name of Jesus Christ.

Music is not something I do, but part of who I am. Music is a piece of the fabric of my life. My parents played music for me as a baby in the womb. They are the ones who introduced me to the gift of music, and they always ensured I had musical instruments to play, such as my beautiful Gemeinhardt flute that was a birthday gift one year. When I was not playing music, I was listening to music. Vinyl records and cassette tapes transformed into compact discs and now I meticulously select songs for inclusion on my MP3 player. Even when I was younger, I would carry my blue and pink cassette player outside, where I enjoyed playing with my friends, listening to songs like "Imagine If You Will" by the Perry Sisters and "The Friendship Company" by Sandi Patty.

When I look back at my childhood, I praise God for a family who believed music should be an integral part of life. Not only that, but they also understood that music was primarily meant to glorify God. My Grandma Ethel, my dad's mother, sang with her sisters as the Cumberland Mountain Sisters for many years, performing at the Museum of Appalachia and other music festivals in the southeast. She used to teach me to play the autoharp, the instrument she played with the group. I inherited her autoharp and will cherish it always as I strive to carry on the family's musical tradition, along with my dad. My dad and I both play the piano, and my dad is a talented organist. We play other instruments as well, including the drums, guitar, and mandolin.

Of course, my family's musical heritage extends beyond my immediate family. My Uncle Larry played the guitar, banjo, and other instruments. He once wrote a song titled, "Don't You Know He Loves You?" This song has such a tremendous message concerning the love of Jesus. My Aunt Jewell played the piano and organ, and my Uncle Tom played the harmonica and saxophone. My Cousin Joan has played the upright bass, sousaphone, and accordion. Several other relatives picked and sang their hearts out at family reunions and church services through the years as well. I guess you could say we would have had one large family band, if we could have gotten everyone together at the same time, in the same place!

Music has even been an important part of the Christmas season, for my mom and I would always trim the tree while listening to Evie's Christmas classic, "Come On, Ring Those Bells." My dad still plays his beautiful arrangement of "O Holy Night" on the piano every December. Of course, things have changed since I was a little girl, as I have now learned to play this same incredible arrangement myself. My love for it is so great that it has become a mainstay in my piano repertoire, a song I play throughout the year.

Growing up, scarcely a weekend went by when we were not either singing at a church or gospel concert, or attending a gospel music event. There were all-night sings, Suwannee River Jubilees, and so many other venues. My musical heritage was comprised of a wide array of gospel music greats, including the Brooklyn Tabernacle Choir, Lari Goss, the Happy Goodman Family, the Hoppers, Karen Peck and New River, the Hemphills, Jeff and Sheri Easter, Betty Jean Robinson, and many others.

In 1997, I wrote my first cover story for *SGN Scoops Magazine*, a national southern gospel music publication. When conducting interviews for a feature, I often ask, "What was your first recollection of gospel music?" Personally, I have no idea how I would answer this question. Music has been a very important part of my life even before the day I was born and has continually been an integral aspect of my life.

During my childhood, my dad recorded and produced two hundred albums for various gospel singing groups and soloists. I had the joy of playing the drums for quite a few of these sessions, which was such a special opportunity. Because our recording studio was located within our home, I had the privilege of observing dozens of talented vocalists and musicians walk through our front door and into our lives. Many of these individuals dedicated to the cause of Christ quickly became a part of our family. One family in particular left a lasting impression on my heart.

The Singing Crisps were a gospel singing family from Dalton, Georgia, whose family harmony was truly exceptional. Their devotion to the Lord was evident, in that the father of the group often ministered on the weekends with his family, and then arrived home early in the morning, stepping off the bus and straight into the local carpet factory where he worked. Their heart for ministry extended beyond the platform. When I celebrated my sixteenth birthday, they came to our farm and sang at my All-Day Singing and Dinner on the Ground. How special it was to have them also attend my high school graduation. These dear friends may have entered our lives through our recording studio, but they soon became an extension of our family.

Music meant to glorify God and lift up His excellent name has a priceless value that will last forever.

Other gospel singing groups, such as the Joint-Heirs, were such a blessing in multiple ways. As soon as all of the headphones, microphones, and various levels were precisely set, they removed all of the recording equipment and bowed down on the floor, earnestly crying out to God to anoint their voices and save the lost as they declared His glory through song. How humbling it was to see these young men so devoted to the Lord and His call on their lives. God honored their dedication. They recorded five projects with us and distributed some twenty thousand albums in the United States and Europe.

I have so many fond memories of the years my dad spent recording gospel music for other groups and soloists. Each time a new artist would enter our home, they were more than a client. They were new friends, fellow members of the family of God.

More often than naught, my dad would make homemade pizzas, and my mom and I would prepare fresh garden salads and a sweet dessert for our guests. Our studio was more than a business; it was a ministry.

Because of the blessings bestowed upon us, we have also been able to record our own original songs, as well as songs that have ministered to us personally. When I was a teenager, I recorded my first album, *He Will Stand By You*. The title cut was one of the first songs I ever wrote. The chorus of this song says, "If you stand by Jesus, He will stand by you. If you follow in His footsteps, you'll be surprised what He can do."[1] I can honestly say that God continues to surprise me every single day. I am always humbled when I hear the intricate arrangements and orchestrations my dad creates in our studio even today. We continue to record songs in-house to lift up the name of Jesus Christ, many of which we distribute freely online to people around the world. We are grateful to God for the opportunity to create music to magnify His holy name.

When it comes to music, my dad and I have a special place in our hearts for music that blesses the name of the Lord. My dad and I were discussing our first recollections of the Brooklyn Tabernacle Choir recently, and it seems I have been listening to their music for approximately thirty years. Music such as theirs has helped mold me and shape me, allowing me to realize the importance of the Holy Spirit's anointing upon music. Beautiful melodies and well-written lyrics are well and good, but without the anointing of the Holy Spirit, a song meant solely for entertainment has no eternal value. On the contrary, music meant to glorify God and lift up His excellent name has a priceless value that will last forever. That is why music written in praise to our Savior and Lord will always be dearest to my heart.

I began singing publicly at the young age of four years old. I started to learn to play the piano when I was eight years old. I took piano courses in college, even though my major was

English. Additionally, I taught piano lessons for several years to two sweet siblings in our church. Their precious grandmother, Helen, wanted to ensure they learned how to play the piano, as she knew it would provide them a lifetime of enjoyment. Through the years, they grew out of needing piano lessons, but we simultaneously became closer and now they seem like part of my extended family—and it all started with music.

As a child, I fondly recall riding down the interstate, listening to my dad's *Preach the Word* and *Great Is the Lord* cassette recordings. Sometimes, we would be on the way to a musical evangelistic opportunity previously scheduled with a pastor. Other times, God would lead us to a particular church. My dad would speak to the pastor before the service and more times than not, the pastor would ask us to sing one or two songs, or even conduct the entire service. If they asked us to sing more than a couple of songs, I would have the opportunity to sing a solo as well. It was in moments like these that my heartfelt desire to share the Gospel through song began to flourish.

Although I do not feel very gifted as a vocalist, something inside me prevents my inadequacies from reigning supreme. While I have my own shortcomings in the musical talent department, I know God is more than enough. Thousands of people sing better than I do, but what matters is not my *ability*, but my *availability*. You see, I am always willing to sing anywhere God opens the door, whether the crowd consists of two or two thousand.

Words will never be able to express my gratitude for the way my parents raised me. They encouraged me to accept Jesus Christ as my Lord and Savior. My mom and dad are the reason music is a part of me. The absence of music in my life would be almost like the absence of oxygen. It is an essential part of my life, which I cherish greatly. Through music, I can express praises in my heart that I could never convey through mere words. Music is a gift from God. In return, I give all of my music to Him.

Ministry Not Entertainment

One of the most remarkable music-related memories I can recall was an event my parents and I coordinated. We hosted the Old Tyme Gospel Sing on the Friday night after Thanksgiving for many consecutive years. This event was in conjunction with a family-oriented agricultural event at a large music park.

I still get goose bumps when I think about the very first Old Tyme Gospel Sing. That night, torrential rain fell along with frigid temperatures, especially compared to the average fall temperatures in the Sunshine State. In spite of the inclement weather, there was standing room only inside the Music Hall. People were standing in crowds out on the porch, trying to hear the music. Many campers came to escape their tents, drenched with rainwater. While they were simply seeking shelter, some of them left with something much greater. For at that first gospel sing, I distinctly recall hearing stories of people finding Jesus Christ as their personal Lord and Savior for the first time in their lives.

This wonderful news validated every phone call made, every mile traveled, and every moment spent planning this event. My mom worked especially hard to organize such a large event. We did not spend our own time and money to bring glory to

Music is a gift from God.

In return, I give all of

my music to Him.

ourselves, nor did we exert so much effort to provide an evening of frivolous entertainment. We knew the priceless nature of bringing the Gospel to a secular event. We understood the importance of keeping admission free, allowing everyone to attend. Above all, we prayed for God to bless the music, so attendees would not only hear the melodies of the songs, but that they would also listen to the lyrics of the songs. The purpose of every song was to bring glory to God, and to draw people close to Him.

The groups and soloists we invited to sing knew they were there to minister, not to put on a show. Before each concert, we gathered backstage with the singers and musicians, joining hands and calling out to God to anoint the service. We viewed it as a church service, not simply a concert. We knew without His anointing, there would be no reason for even one note to echo through the musical venue that evening.

Sadly, even people in many churches today do not realize the need for God's anointing upon each service. They come to church for entertainment as opposed to encouragement. With all of the programs and tight schedules, there is little room for the Holy Spirit to work in their midst. If the pastor leads the congregation in a beloved hymn at the end of the service for an altar call, causing the service to dismiss at 12:05 instead of high noon, then the pastor may become the subject of the local town gossips. Congregants are often displeased when the choir sings one too many songs or if the praise and worship segment of the service requires them to stand for a few minutes.

Unfortunately, these individuals have missed the point of music all together. I am always puzzled when I see someone scrolling through one of their social media apps during a worship service. Perhaps they are bored with all of the goings-on. Some individuals would rather rush home to their football games, television shows, afternoon naps, and who knows what else instead of running to the throne of God. Others dislike the music and the message at church, only coming for the coffee hour, in search of social connections. While fellowship is important and time spent at home is pleasant, is it too much to ask people to spend an hour or two of their day in the presence of God Almighty?

Some of these same people would not even blink at the

thought of a sporting event going into overtime. In fact, they may be happy, especially if the extra time would benefit their favorite team. Some of them would actually choose a ball game over a church service. I recently saw a photo shared on social media that showed a stadium full of people with several inches of snow piled on top of them. The caption alluded to the fact that the weather was too severe to go to church, yet people were willing to sit outside in a blizzard to attend a sporting event.

Other individuals would not hesitate to purchase expensive tickets to attend a secular concert. Then they would have no complaints if the show extended beyond the advertised ending time, due to an encore performance. So why should they become angry when an extra song of praise is lifted to the very One who created them? Surely, God is more important than hearing someone sing songs about violence, drugs, or promiscuous activity.

When I think about the secular world of music, it saddens me to think that such talented musicians and vocalists could be sharing the Gospel through song, yet they choose to deliver explicit lyrics and mind-numbing noise as an alternative. The beat often becomes more important than the melody and some people may consider the person's appearance to be more important than the meaning behind the lyrics. Audience members even go so far as to raise their hands in honor of these artists who garner fame and fortune due to their widespread popularity. In essence, fans ultimately worship these celebrities as if they were gods. They are willing to worship other people, yet reluctant to worship the one true living God.

Jesus said we should only worship the Lord God Almighty (Luke 4:8). We are not to worship any other person or thing on this earth. God shares His glory with no one (Isa. 42:8). God is the only One whom we are to worship and adore! He alone is worthy of our praise.

Music used for anything other than glorifying God

disappoints my heart greatly. I wonder how God feels when He hears such disparaging sounds coming from the very men and women for which He gave His only Son. Since when did music become a means to mock God, rather than a way to magnify His holy name?

God is the only One whom we are to worship and adore! He alone is worthy of our praise.

Still others believe music is a vehicle with which to make a profit. To this day, people question why we stopped having our annual Old Tyme Gospel Sing. It was because the venue wanted to charge admission and sell alcohol during the concert. Why did they desire to contaminate this Christian, family-friendly event? Simply because the event was unprofitable, being that we acquired sponsors only to cover operational costs, often making ends meet with money out of our own pockets. Yet the unseen profits were plentiful, considering the fact that God changed lives through the message of the Gospel delivered through every song sung and every word spoken. Mark 8:36 says, "'What good is it for someone to gain the whole world, yet forfeit their soul?'" Even so, the people in charge of this concert venue preferred a secular event where they could cash in on alcoholic beverage purchases.

Although there are countless individuals whose priority in life is to make money, our primary focus should not be on reaching profitability. As Mark 8:36 states, you could own the entire world, yet lose your soul. Money cannot buy salvation. Only God can change someone's heart. Only God can rescue someone from his or her sinful nature. Only God can provide a road to redemption. Therefore, it troubles me when I see someone choose profits over people. The purpose of music is not to make money or to entertain.

Leonard Ravenhill, a highly regarded Christian evangelist and author, said, "Entertainment is the devil's substitute for joy."[2] He believed Christians needed more of the joy of the Lord instead of lackluster entertainment. How true! I believe the reason we have the gift of music is not to entertain, but to glorify Jesus Christ. When we glorify Jesus Christ, our Lord and Savior, we can experience true joy. Through our worship, we can experience the sweet presence of the Lord, which has the power to change lives. Only music that praises the name of Jesus has such a tremendous impact on individuals. No other music leads people to the infinite grace of God.

Music that exalts the name of Jesus is different from other types of music. The incomparable music arranger, orchestrator, and pianist, Lari Goss, once said that he loved gospel music because you could hear it at a distance and still recognize that it was music used to present the Gospel through song. Gospel music, if offered to honor God, has a completely different sound than secular music, one that is deeply evident, even to the most discerning ear.

Once when my dad and I were in New York City, we visited Steinway Hall. We both played a few songs on one of the pianos in the showroom. As we were leaving, one of the sales associates said she hears people from all over the world playing the piano all day, every day. Yet she said the music my dad played was different because she could *feel* something. We prayed that evening that God would use this encounter to speak to her heart and draw her close to Him. How profound that even someone in a secular industry could sense a difference about music written to worship the Lord.

Whether I am relaxing in my own home or walking down the sidewalk in a large city, there are many times throughout the day when a song pops into my head. Seemingly, out of nowhere, I begin to hum or even sing the song. Whether I am walking through the grocery store or strolling through a city park, I am sure people often wonder why I am softly singing the melody in my heart to the Lord. The music plays inside my head. The lyrics resonate in a special place within my heart. The message of the song is rooted deep within my soul. That is why I sing.

Psalm 34:1 says, "I will extol the LORD at all times; his praise will always be on my lips." The joy I feel when worshiping Jesus Christ while playing and singing songs is unmatched. I want to worship the Lord at all times. I want to praise Him forevermore. Music is one of the primary ways I can exalt the marvelous name of Jesus Christ. I am so grateful the music in me is the kind of music that glorifies the Lord.

Chapter Four

All for Jesus

"I do all this for the sake of the gospel,
that I may share in its blessings." (1 Cor. 9:23)

Every day, my heart yearns to tell others about Jesus Christ and His unconditional love. Anything else is secondary. I pray the light of Christ will shine forth to everyone I meet. My desire is to proclaim the name of Jesus Christ to all nations. This is God's calling upon my life.

There has never been a time in my life when I can remember purposefully trying to hide the light of Christ within me. It has not mattered if I was competing at the state fair in a youth agricultural contest, speaking at a state or national education conference, or serving on the professional development council for the school district where I teach. I strive to follow this principle in the Bible: "Whatever you do, do it all for the glory of God" (1 Cor. 10:31). God is a part of who I am and all that I do.

Although I will never stop sharing the Gospel, I have not always encountered full acceptance when entering into conversations of faith in the Lord Jesus Christ. Despite the negative reaction I may receive, my faith in Jesus Christ never wavers. I do not seek to please men, but to please God, for He deserves all of my adoration and praise.

Some people may be apprehensive when it comes to sharing Jesus with their coworkers, their neighbors, or even their own family. In lieu of being outspoken concerning their faith, they inevitably become what I regard as a "closet Christian." A few years ago, I discovered that Christianity is not the only religion where people keep their beliefs under lock and key.

On one of our visits to Europe, my dad and I had the opportunity to sing and minister in Budapest, Hungary. During our time in this historic city, we had the opportunity to witness to many people by giving them Gospel tracts we translated into Hungarian, their native language. One woman I encountered at a local business promptly handed the tract back to me, stating that religion was a very private thing for Hungarians. She said she wished not to discuss religion in any manner. Having met numerous Hungarians along our journey, I can tell you that this "private religion" philosophy is not one shared by all Hungarians. Ever since that night, I have continued to pray that God would speak to her heart and that she would come to know the truth, for the truth will set her free (John 8:32).

Just as a baker cannot afford to bake decadent cakes without sharing them with customers, we cannot afford to keep the wondrous Good News of the Gospel to ourselves.

Inevitably, no single nation has a monopoly on "closet" religions. Even in America, there are individuals who are hesitant to say anything, for fear of rejection or persecution. Certainly, there are parts of the world where professing one's faith could result in permanent injury or even death. While dangers loom all around us, we cannot keep our faith hidden under a bushel. We must trust God for His protection, carrying out the Great Commission, for all of the days God gives us on this earth.

If you were experiencing a power outage during the night, you would certainly place a lantern or candle on a table in the center of the room, which would create the maximum light possible. You would not put the light source under a bed or behind a cabinet door. Jesus said, "'In the same way, let your light shine before others, that they may see your good deeds and glorify your Father in heaven'" (Matt. 5:16). Do not hide your light. Shine forth the light of Christ everywhere you go.

Think about this. If you opened a bakery, you would not keep the fact you made cakes and cookies a secret, nor would you keep your location hidden from the public. On the contrary, you would advertise via social media, local newspapers, and other outlets to let everyone know what baked goods you were offering and where they could purchase them. Likewise, our faith is something we should share everywhere we go. Just as a baker cannot afford to bake decadent cakes without sharing them with customers, we cannot afford to keep the wondrous Good News of the Gospel to ourselves.

Instead of worrying about what people think of us when we tell them about Jesus, our hearts should be troubled over whether or not they know Jesus Christ as their personal Lord and Savior. He is the only source of salvation: "'Salvation is found in no one else, for there is no other name under heaven given to mankind by which we must be saved'" (Acts 4:12). Unfortunately, you and I both know people who are not followers of Jesus Christ. We all know individuals who will sadly hear Jesus say, "I never knew you" (Matt. 7:23 KJV), unless they receive the gift of salvation before it is too late. This fact alone should keep us up at night, praying for the souls of the lost.

The Important Thing

Pastor David Jeremiah said, "The important thing is to make the important thing the important thing." What is the most important thing in your life? Is it your family, your career, or your wealth? Above all else, is your primary focus on eternal things? Personally, I know there are moments in my life when Jesus is my central focus. Yet other times, stressful situations or even joyful occasions, such as getting ready for a trip, distract me. Whether it is technology or television, friends or family, we can all find ourselves sidetracked from what truly matters most. This world offers many things to take our attention away from Christ. Let us strive to set our minds on Jesus, rather than things of this earth.

Colossians 3:1–2 says, "Set your hearts on things above, where Christ is, seated at the right hand of God. Set your minds on things above, not on earthly things." When we focus on Jesus Christ, this does not mean we will never pay attention to our parents, spouses, or children. By placing the center of our attention on the One who matters most, everything else will fall into place.

One passage in the Bible that has been a great encouragement to me says, "All things work together for good to them that love God, to them who are the called according to his purpose" (Rom. 8:28 KJV). The take action words here are "them that love God." God will work all things together, if we love Him. What does it mean to love? First John 3:16 says, "This is how we know what love is: Jesus Christ laid down his life for us." If we devote our lives to God and give all of ourselves to Him, then everything will work out for His glory. By giving our lives to the cause of Christ, we can rest assured that His master plan will be at work in our lives.

You may be wondering how you can devote your entire life to the work of the Lord. The answer is in the Bible: "Whatever you do, work at it with all your heart, as working for the Lord, not for human masters" (Col. 3:23). When you buy groceries for your family, select the freshest quality items, as if you were buying them for the Lord Himself. When you go to work, let the joy of the Lord radiate from within you. When you talk to your friends and family, follow these words of wisdom: "Let your conversation be always full of grace, seasoned with salt, so that you may know how to answer everyone" (Col. 4:6).

As a public school teacher, I cannot openly share my faith with students, as the courts only permit limited freedom of religious expression. Our founding fathers promoted the free exercise of religion in America, as documented in the first amendment of the United States Constitution: "Congress shall make no law respecting an establishment of religion, or prohibiting the free exercise thereof."[1] Yet in today's society, many people consider a teacher expressing his or her personal religious beliefs the same as Congress establishing a religion. There are judges and lawyers in America, who consider the wearing of a Christian emblem, the presence of a Bible on a desk, or a short prayer at an athletic event as the act of the Congress of the United States of America establishing a national religion. Sadly, their interpretation of the first amendment is inconsistent with the original meaning. News articles frequently describe the removal of public officials from their positions for expressing agreement with the Word of God, in many cases where the individual expressed their beliefs outside the work environment. Never in the history of our country have we seen the kind of hostility toward Judeo-Christian principles as we are seeing today.

Even within the confines of these illogical limitations, I take every opportunity to treat each student as I believe Jesus would. I am joyful, even in the midst of moments that attempt to steal my joy. I strive to find the positive aspects of a negative situation. People often say that actions speak louder than words. I pray my actions speak volumes about my faith in Jesus Christ, so my students and colleagues will see something different about Miss Campbell. I want them to wonder what makes me different from other people they may know. In doing so, I want them to discover the eternal hope of Christ working within me.

Not too long ago, one of my students gave me a green glass marble imprinted with the words from James 4:8 (ESV): "Draw near to God and he will draw near to you." Imagine my surprise, considering the fact the student had only been in my classroom for a total of seven days. In this short span of time, they had come to the realization that I loved Jesus Christ and shared their faith in God. I was humbled, having received tangible proof that my life was a testimony of the love of Jesus Christ to this particular student. The Lord revealed to this student that Jesus lives within my heart, not through my words but through my actions.

The apostle Paul wrote to the Christians in Galatia, "I have been crucified with Christ and I no longer live, but Christ lives in me" (Gal. 2:20). As Christians, we need to live our lives as a testimony of God's grace. While it is fine for someone to learn about our favorite meal, best vacation, or most memorable milestone through a delightful conversation, the most important thing is whether people we meet will recognize that Christ lives within us. As soon as people see us, they should sense a difference about us, just as my student realized that Jesus is the difference within me.

We all have a mission field, whether it be encouraging someone on the subway or witnessing in our neighborhood. Our lives need to be a testimony of God's grace and mercy. Let us not just talk about the weather or the latest news. Instead, we ought to take the opportunity to tell them how Jesus has changed our lives. We need to extend the amazing love of Jesus Christ to every single person we meet. From personal experience, I can tell you that the opportunity to share Jesus Christ with another individual often comes along when we least expect it.

Unexpected Delays

On one of our flights out of New York City, we experienced a cancellation and numerous delays. We came very close to spending the night in the airport. We waited and waited, hoping to get a seat on a different flight as one of many on a standby list. Several flights left the airport without us. There was only one option remaining that would get us home in the wee hours of the night, as opposed to waiting until the next day.

When I spoke to the airline representative who said we would have a seat on the flight, I felt as if God had answered our prayers. Although my dad and I would not have seats together, we had found a way home! What a joy to walk down the jet bridge, able to exit an overcrowded airport that was unusually warm on a sweltering summer day in July. As we made ourselves comfortable in our newly assigned seats, a woman sat down beside me. We made small talk, comparing notes as to how many delays we had experienced and what our final destinations were.

On this particular flight, I knew that everyone was weary, having spent too much time in the airport that evening. Fearing I would be "that" person who talks incessantly throughout the entire flight, I briefly hesitated in striking up a conversation with this lady

We all have a mission field, whether it be encouraging someone on the subway or witnessing in our neighborhood. Our lives need to be a testimony of God's grace and mercy.

beyond the initial customary small talk. Yet in my heart, I knew I was supposed to speak to my seatmate, despite the negative reaction I might receive. I also knew we had a relatively short flight from New York to Atlanta, so if a conversation was to begin, it needed to begin almost immediately.

Thankfully, I listened intently to her introduction, recalling that she was heading to North Carolina. My parents and I spent nearly two decades vacationing at River Valley Campground in Cherokee, North Carolina. It was a tremendous blessing to have a permanent campsite across from a beautiful waterfall, which my mom affectionately referred to as "our waterfall." Since my seatmate was heading home to another town in Western North Carolina, I decided this common ground would be the perfect basis for a conversation starter. It was not too long before I recognized that this so-called "idea" was not mine at all, but the fulfillment of God's divine inspiration.

After an enjoyable conversation about notable locations in both North Carolina and New York (her work schedule allowed her to split her time between the two), I soon realized the plane had begun its descent. I felt led to give her one of my Gospel tracts on which I have written my testimony of how I was born dead and raised to life.

Words cannot adequately describe the rest of our time sitting beside each other, but as she read my story, tears fell from her eyes. What a humbling experience to know God used my testimony to minister to her heart in such a special way. While I may never see her again on this earth, I pray God sends someone to water the seed I planted that evening while cruising at an altitude of thirty thousand feet. I would count it a joy to meet her again in Heaven one glorious day.

Encounters such as this one teach me how important it is to listen to the still, small voice of God Himself. There are times in our lives when we become too busy, too overwhelmed, or too stressed even to pay attention to the Lord's leading. Even amid countless delays, we can rest assured that God will help us see the reason for the temporary disruptions. If we ignore His voice, we could miss unexpected blessings, and others around us may miss the opportunity to meet Jesus Christ, the Savior of the world.

If we do not tell them, who will? We cannot expect our pastor or local missionary to speak to every single person on earth. That notion is essentially preposterous. Nor can we place this monumental task in the hands of our fellow congregants. Some of them may never encounter the people we see at our workplaces, our neighborhoods, or our local supermarkets. It is up to you and me to share the Gospel of Jesus Christ with everyone we meet. God places people in our path for a reason. We cannot afford to disregard His gentle leading. We need to speak words of life everywhere we go. Let us hold nothing back as we give our all for Jesus Christ!

Chapter Five

Expanding Borders

"'And the gospel must first be preached to all nations.'" (Mark 13:10)

When I graduated from college with my Associate in Arts degree, my parents gave me a special graduation gift. They said I could choose to fly or cruise to any destination I desired, within the confines of the budget they provided. Having never flown in a plane or taken a cruise, the possibilities seemed endless! Since my parents had never sailed on a cruise ship before, I decided this would be the most enjoyable option, so we could all experience something new together. None of us knew then what a profound impact my first trip outside the United States would have on my life.

Since our first cruise to the Bahamas, I have had the opportunity to set sail many more times to locations all over the globe. One of the most memorable cruises I took with my mom and dad was a cruise to the Western Caribbean. Along with ports of call in the Cayman Islands, Mexico, and Belize, this cruise also visited Roatán, Honduras. However, the one thing that made this trip extra special was not a snorkeling excursion or a tour of Mayan ruins. It was a visit to the Sandy Bay Orphanage in Honduras.

Along with our suitcases filled with clothes and other necessities for our trip, we brought over five hundred pounds of school supplies, clothing, toys, personal hygiene items, and food. My mom gathered most of the donations, a ministry in and of itself. She was the first one to gather items for the poor, the orphaned, and anyone in need. The children at this orphanage became her children, but for a moment, as she made hand-sewn cloth bags for each child, which would hold handpicked items personalized for each one of them. Boxes were stacked in our cruise ship stateroom from the floor to the ceiling. In addition to the tangible items placed inside, those boxes overflowed with love.

New pairs of socks and shoes, stuffed animals, children's books, shampoo, bars of soap, and so much more, but the children's home residents were most excited about the canisters of peanut butter and the case of cheese. On the island of Roatán, the market shelves are often sparse and items like these are either unavailable or quite costly. I will never forget how some of the older children immediately made grilled cheese sandwiches for all of the children using the cheese we brought them. One could only guess the last time they had experienced the delightful taste of gooey cheesy goodness as we watched them savor this rare treat. The smiles on their faces were contagious. How incredible that a simple box of cheese, which many people take for granted, could bring such joy to these precious boys and girls.

As the children began to open their personalized bags, I knew these items meant more than we realized. Upon touring their bedrooms, it was evident they were content with very little. One little boy danced around with his new tennis shoes in his hands. Another young boy put on his new baseball cap and never took it off the whole time we were there. One precious girl cradled her new baby doll as if it was a real child. They were very grateful, even for these small gestures of love we brought to them. They especially enjoyed watching my mom put on a puppet show for them. The vivid image of my mom sharing Jesus with the children will be in my storehouse of memories forever, right along with the sweet picture of my dad helping feed one of the younger girls, who was having trouble operating the spoon with her tiny little hands.

Yet the moment goose bumps covered my arms was when I

stood inside the living room of this Christian refuge for children. Looking through the window, across their makeshift baseball field, with the Caribbean Sea in the distance, I was overwhelmed with gratefulness to God. As I sang the song, "Consider the Lilies," with my dad accompanying me on the keyboard, my eyes welled up with joy-filled tears as I did my best to take it all in and savor this precious moment. The opportunity to visit with these amazing children and to minister to them flamed the burning desire in my heart to tell children and adults alike about my best friend, Jesus.

While I had been out of the country before, this was my first time singing in a foreign land. I do not know if it was the enormity of the event or the fact I was uncertain as to when I would have this opportunity again, but I remember praying that God would allow me to minister to people in other countries. I could have never imagined the ways in which He would answer this humble, silent prayer.

For many years now, we have traveled to various parts of the Caribbean and Central America, including Costa Rica, Panama, Aruba, Saint Lucia, Barbados, and other regions. On our trips there, I give small bags to children, filled with candy, toys, school supplies, and most importantly, a Gospel tract in their native language. Some of the most cherished experiences have come quite unexpectedly, such as the time a young couple invited me to step over the threshold of their home in Mahahual, a small fishing village near the town of Costa Maya, Mexico. While I only spoke a tiny amount of Spanish, I was able to communicate to the parents that the bags were for their children. By their reaction, you would have thought the bags contained a few nuggets of genuine gold. While the contents held little value, the message inside was priceless.

On another trip, a woman in Mexico insisted on giving me a beautiful handmade shell necklace, as a thank you for the children's gifts. I will cherish the necklace always, as it is a tangible reminder of the words spoken by the Lord. Jesus said, "It is more blessed to give than to receive" (Acts 20:35 KJV). I can tell you firsthand that this is entirely true. The heartfelt joy I experience when I share something with another individual is very special.

Every November, I pray over each Operation Christmas Child shoebox that I pack for Samaritan's Purse. I am not so concerned with the brand new washcloth, colorful pencils, cuddly teddy bear, or other items enclosed inside. Instead, I have a burden on my heart for the child who will receive the box: the child who may feel hopeless, the child who may feel alone, or the child who may feel unloved. One such child left an enduring impression on my heart.

One ordinary day, I received an extraordinary email. It was from a little girl in Uganda who received a shoebox from my dad and me. She told me that she and several members of her immediate family suffered from HIV/AIDS. My eyes filled with tears when I read the words she conveyed to me. She wrote, "Most people hate me when they get to know that I have AIDS, but I hate it. Let me hope that you Jennifer and your family will not hate me because of my illness."[1] As I struggled to read the rest of her message with teardrops rolling down my face and falling onto my keyboard, I prayed Jesus would wrap His loving arms around this little girl, giving her strength and health. I promptly replied to tell her that we love her and Jesus loves her, too. In a later email, she asked to know more of Jesus. More than seven years later, we still keep in touch. I pray God will allow me

It was not about how many souvenir postcards we could bring home, but how many Gospel tracts we could leave behind.

to meet this precious young lady and her family one day, so I can share the love of Jesus with her in person.

When I pack a shoebox, I am not just putting mere things in a box. I pack the love of Jesus inside. Likewise, when I give someone a Gospel tract I have written, I am not promoting myself. I do not care if they even remember my name. My concern is whether they call on the name above all names, Jesus Christ. Everything I do is for the glory of the Lord. I am actively following the disciples' lead and fishing for souls.

Europe Shall Be Saved

I have a burden on my heart to see Europe come to know Jesus Christ. In 2011, I traveled to the continent of Europe for the very first time. My dad and I toured France, England, Norway, Scotland, and the Netherlands. This trip was extra special, since I had the opportunity to see two of my ancestral homelands, Scotland and Norway. One year later, we had the opportunity to visit many places in the Mediterranean, including Spain, Italy, Greece, Turkey, Croatia, Monaco, and Tunisia. Even now, I am amazed at the places God has taken us. Having traveled to Europe two consecutive years, I wondered when I would ever have the privilege of returning to this special continent. As I pondered this thought in my mind, the answer came much sooner than expected. Only God knew then that we would travel to the Baltic in 2015, just three years later.

Though the previous trips to Europe were exceptional, the third time was different. Our focus was not on ornate castles and historic monuments, but instead, our focus was on ministry. Armed with hundreds of Gospel tracts in nearly every language spoken in the countries we would visit, we began this trip with a different mindset. It was not about how many souvenir postcards we could bring home, but how many Gospel tracts we could leave behind.

God allowed us to hand out tracts in Sweden, Denmark, Finland, Estonia, Germany, and Russia. What an extraordinary opportunity to bring some encouragement and hope to this part of the world. Along our journey, God opened the door for us to witness to many individuals, including one kind man we met in Germany, who ran a delightful fruit stand in the middle of the town square. God even opened the door for us to minister at the First International Baptist Church of Copenhagen. While we were amazed at the way God expanded our borders of ministry, He had only begun working in our midst.

In 2016, God granted us an incredible opportunity to return to Europe for the fourth time. We began our journey in Budapest, Hungary, a beautiful city filled with rich history. The highlight of the whole tour was singing at the International Church of Budapest. The congregation was so welcoming. The main thing I noticed about them is the importance they placed upon prayer. They took the words, "Pray continually" (1 Thess. 5:17), to heart. As I walked away from the conservatory building where they held their church services, I had tears in my eyes after saying goodbye to the precious pastor's wife. I silently prayed God would open the door for us to return there one day. God answered my prayer just two years later when God gave us the opportunity to travel to Europe once again.

Welcome to the Mission Field

Traveling can broaden your horizons, make you more creative, and even give you a different perspective on the world. I have been to more than fifty countries and territories. Yet the greatest thing about traveling is not the location itself. Nor is it the idyllic landscapes, fairy-tale castles, or enchanting waterways. Even the mouth-watering cuisine and shimmering shorelines will never compare to my personal love of travel.

As a little girl, my grandmother had a plaque hanging on her wall that featured a poem by Helen Steiner Rice titled, "Strangers Are Friends We Haven't Met Yet." My Grandma Ethel's plaque now hangs on a wall in our home. Each time I travel, whether at home or abroad, the friends I make along the way are the ones who make the trip special. As we pull out of one city and travel on to the next, the mistiness in my eyes stems from a deep desire in my heart to have the opportunity to see the precious friends we meet again in the future.

On our fifth journey to Europe, we traveled via a transatlantic flight from Jacksonville, Florida, to Bucharest, Romania, with brief layovers in New York City and Amsterdam. Soon after our arrival in Romania, Pastor Peter, a Sudanese refugee who has been ministering in Bucharest for more than twenty years, greeted us at our hotel. Although we had only become acquainted via LinkedIn, the moment he stepped out of his car, it seemed as if we had known him for years. After spending three days with them, he and his family have become an extension of our own family. I think of them, and pray for them daily, that God will be with them and use them for His glory.

Prior to our arrival, I never realized just how much this brief stay in this former Soviet country would influence my life in such a positive way. On Friday evening, women from two churches came together to hear my testimony and listen to my dad and me minister in song. But some of the most precious moments were when the ladies shared their hearts and lived out the verse that says where two or three gather together in the name of Jesus, He will be in their midst (Matt. 18:20). To close out the service, the pastor invited two dear sisters to share a song sung in their native language, as a way to bless us for our service to the Lord. What gorgeous harmony they created as they worshiped the Lord in song! The sweet spirit in the sanctuary was something I will always remember.

Someone once said the best is yet to come. In the case of our time in Romania, they were absolutely right. Saturday afternoon, we joined the pastor and another brother in Christ for a day of evangelism. After a word of prayer, we went out into the gypsy neighborhood surrounding the church. I had no idea what to expect. Would the people be receptive to the Gospel or be adamantly against our message? As we walked away from the church doors and out into the world, I must say that I felt a little like the apostle Paul ministering to the Ephesians. We were fulfilling the Great Commission of going to all creation to share the Gospel.

One of the first people we encountered was Stephen. He allowed us the honor of praying for him and his physical needs right there on the sidewalk. So many times, we tell people we will pray for them, but how often do we have time to stop what we are doing, lay hands on them, and pray that instant? This was not the only instance where God would give us this special opportunity to go to the throne of grace. One family had a son who was unable to return to school due to health concerns. They acted as if we had given them something of great value. We listened to them, and we prayed with them. This moment served as a reminder that the greatest gift we can ever give someone does not come wrapped in a box, but instead, prayer is a gift we can freely give when we take time to show concern for one another.

Our day of evangelism ended in a local park, where we talked to young and old alike. One young woman was sitting on a park bench. As we approached her, I noticed she had been crying. After speaking to her, I asked if I could pray for her. I placed my hand on her shoulder and prayed for God to comfort her and help her. When I opened my eyes, I could see more tears streaming down her face. I stand amazed at the way God orchestrated such a long line of divine appointments for us that day. What an honor to be about God's business!

We talked, we prayed, and we sang our way through busy streets and a city park. Our message was simple. We shared

God's love and the message of the Gospel with them. We also invited them to church. Many said they would come. What a delight to see their smiling faces as they walked through the sanctuary doors on Sunday! Still, the greatest joy was the fact that some of them dedicated their lives to Christ that very day.

Late Saturday evening, we fellowshipped over a delicious meal of chicken curry and rice, along with brownies and gelato for dessert, all prepared by the precious pastor's wife and her daughters while we were out working in the field. I was humbled to sit at the dining room table of this special family who welcomed us into their home. Our enjoyable conversations took us through the midnight hour, yet there would be much more fellowship to be enjoyed the following day.

Sunday morning brought us to Hope Baptist Church of Bucharest, where the pastor graciously opened the door for us to sing and share our testimonies. At this service, they were also serving communion, my first time receiving communion while abroad. This was a weekend of many firsts, as it was also my first time attending a service spoken solely in a language foreign to my own. How special it was, especially since I had my new friend Mari by my side, whispering the English translation to me throughout the service. She interpreted for me on Friday and on Sunday as well. Now my interpreter has become a treasured friend. Although I know my pronunciation must have been less than desirable, I cheerfully sang the words to the hymns in Romanian, with assistance from the words on the screen and the beautiful voices of those around me.

Afterward, a sweet sister in Christ gave me a gorgeous bouquet of some of the largest red and white roses I have ever seen. The sweet aroma from these amazing flowers was just as sweet as the gesture itself. Another precious lady gave me an angel votive. They both told me they wanted to thank me for being a blessing. What a blessing it was to me personally to find such loving, compassionate members of the body of Christ. I am forever grateful to have had the priceless opportunity to share the Gospel through word and song with these precious people. There is no greater honor than telling someone about my best friend, Jesus Christ.

Soon we made our way down to the second church of the day, Spiritual Revival Baptist Church, where we ministered that afternoon. As soon as we walked through the doors of the church, we were quickly ushered into the kitchen where they had placed two chairs in front of a prep table. Filling the table was a bounty of homemade food showcasing the culture of Myanmar, including bamboo chicken, rice with vegetables, fresh tomatoes and cucumbers, and butter lettuce; what a special honor to be fed lunch as the honored guests. The food was very delicious, but the most memorable moment sitting in the kitchen that day was when my dad leaned over to me and said, "Welcome to the mission field."

The food was very delicious, but the most memorable moment sitting in the kitchen that day was when my dad leaned over to me and said, "Welcome to the mission field."

The mission field: the place I have always wanted to be, the place I have dreamed about, the place I have longed for. Although I had experienced other mission outreaches in Europe, the Caribbean, Central America, the United States, and Canada, this time was different. As I sat in the kitchen, tasting scrumptious food prepared by members of the church congregation, I knew this would not be the last time we would be on the mission field together. Something deep within my spirit said this is what I was born to do. I also felt we would return one day to Bucharest, Romania, the city that made a lasting impression on my heart. Not because of the palaces and villages, but because of the special people who live there. The people we shared meals with, the people we prayed for, and the people we grew to love. Most importantly, the people we told about Jesus.

My heartbeat is sharing the love of Jesus Christ. The longing in my heart to share the Gospel is so very great. When I wake up in the morning, I want my first thought to be, "Who can I tell about Jesus today?" We need to all strive to put Jesus first in our lives. Life is not about living for ourselves; life is about living for the One who gave His life for us. Every day, we will encounter people who need a word of encouragement. Let us go forth and treat every day as if we are on the mission field, whether we are traveling in a foreign land or passing through a familiar neighborhood. I can tell you from personal experience that God will set up divine appointments along our way. Sometimes, we may even encounter a stranger who becomes a friend.

Along our journey through Eastern Europe, we met some endearing, precious people, not only in Romania, but in Bulgaria, Serbia, Croatia, and Hungary as well. There are several whom I still pray for daily. We encountered individuals who needed encouragement as Christians, those who practiced other religions, and some who were adamantly against all religion. I pray God will send someone to water the seeds we have sown. These people are so very important, not only to my dad and to me, but especially to God.

God does not wish that anyone would perish, "but everyone to come to repentance" (2 Pet. 3:9). I feel the same way. There is a burden on my heart to see the lost come to know Jesus Christ as their Lord and Savior. If you were a doctor seeing a patient, you would prescribe a treatment to help them get well. In the same way, a chef would prepare food that would be nutritious and delicious for hungry customers. So why would we not want to share the only anecdote for sin with every single person we meet? God's Word says, "All have sinned and fall short of the glory of God" (Rom. 3:23). If we are all sinners, then every single person on earth needs redemption. The only road to redemption is through Jesus Christ, the Savior of our souls.

Jesus Christ died for the salvation of all who believe. John 3:16 says, "For God so loved the world that he gave his one and only Son, that whoever believes in him shall not perish but have eternal life." Sadly, though, many people do not know about the gift of eternal life. Some people are living in such despair. I recall the faces of some of the people I have met in Europe. They look so downcast. They need to know about the only eternal hope. How can they hear unless someone tells them? Romans 10:14 asks the question, "And how can they hear without someone preaching to them?" It should be our daily mission to share the Good News of the Gospel with the world while we still can. It is up to you and me to tell them about the hope we have in Jesus Christ. Join me in sharing the Gospel as we strive to see the lost come to know the wondrous grace and eternal redemption found through Christ alone.

Harvest Time

In all of my travels, I have seen firsthand the indelible truth of the Scriptures revealed within our modern-day society. Just as it was in the days of Noah, the world is filled with abundant evil (see Matt. 24:38–39). Since abortion became legal in 1973, between one and two billion babies have been brutally murdered.[2] Millions of people engage in promiscuous sexual behavior; sadly, this type of immoral activity has become the acceptable norm. Innumerable people profusely blaspheme the name of the Lord. There are false prophets, famines, earthquakes, and wars (see Matt. 24:6–11). Nations are rising against one another (Matt. 24:7). The persecution of Christians is an everyday occurrence around the world (Matt. 24:9). Hatred is prevalent throughout the land. The Golden Rule of "Do unto others as you would have them do unto you" has widely been thrown out with yesterday's newspaper. The world needs Jesus Christ more than ever before, but the number of people telling others about His amazing grace has sadly decreased.

Jesus said, "'The harvest is plentiful but the workers are few'" (Matt. 9:37). How true this is in the twenty-first century! I recall a time when my dad planted a massive garden, filled with fresh corn, green beans, and so much more. When the time came to harvest the vegetables, we had copious amounts, more than we could possibly consume or preserve. As such, we invited friends and neighbors to come over and help themselves. While a few people did take advantage of this delightful bounty of vegetables, the majority of people were more interested in having us pick, clean, and deliver the items to them. Because of their unwillingness to partake in the bountiful

When I look at a smartphone, computer, or tablet, I do not see an electronic device. I see a transmitter for spreading the love of Jesus Christ to the furthermost reaches of the earth.

blessings God had given us, they missed some delicious fresh produce and some vegetables went to waste. All because the harvest was plentiful, but the workers were few.

Unfortunately, many people feel the same way about the harvest Jesus is referring to in the Gospel of Matthew. We are called to share the Gospel of Jesus Christ around the world (Mark 16:15). While you may not be able to travel, you can still do your part in sharing the Good News of the Gospel. When I look at a smartphone, computer, or tablet, I do not see an electronic device. I see a transmitter for spreading the love of Jesus Christ to the furthermost reaches of the earth. Instead of complaining about the lack of a promotion at work, or venting about the latest outcome of a popular sporting event, social media and other online entities should be methods of uplifting and building the Kingdom of God. Even if you do not have the Internet, you can still share the love of Jesus with the cashier in the checkout lane, your neighbor next door, or the wait staff at your local diner.

Unlike those vegetables that decayed on our family farm, we cannot afford for a person's soul to go by the wayside. When I approach the judgment seat of Christ, I want to know I did all I could to spread the Gospel. The Bible says, "For we must all appear before the judgment seat of Christ, so that each of us may receive what is due us for the things done while in the body, whether good or bad" (2 Cor. 5:10). I want to know I spent every moment engaged in harvesting souls for Christ.

We need to do all we can for Jesus, "so that when he appears we may be confident and unashamed before him at his coming" (1 John 2:28). It is troubling to think about an individual who stands before Jesus, ashamed at the way they lived their life. I pray I will stand before Him unashamed, confident, and worthy in His eyes. I want to make my Heavenly Father proud, even in the midst of a world filled with turmoil. Before long, the harvest will be complete and a new day will break forth like the dawn.

We have the promise of eternal hope through Christ. One day soon, Jesus Christ will return to this earth. No one knows when He will return. The only One who knows is God Himself. Jesus said, "'But about that day or hour no one knows, not even the angels in heaven, nor the Son, but only the Father'" (Matt. 24:36). Many people today say we have waited for the coming of the Lord for years and it will likely never happen. Would you avoid purchasing a security system for your home or business, with the notion that a burglary is "not likely to happen?" Certainly not! We want to guarantee our valuables are safe.

Likewise, we need to ensure the one priceless possession we

have on this earth, our soul, is not lost. Jesus said, "'If the owner of the house had known at what time of night the thief was coming, he would have kept watch and would not have let his house be broken into. So you also must be ready, because the Son of Man will come at an hour when you do not expect him'" (Matt. 24:43–44). Make sure your heart is ready. Do not wait to see what happens. Secure your future in Jesus Christ today.

If you have already put your trust in Jesus Christ, consider the following question. How many of your coworkers, friends, relatives, or neighbors need to hear of the Lord's return? Are you leaving them in the dark, so to speak, not sharing with them the most glorious news ever declared upon this earth? We need to introduce everyone we know to Jesus Christ, our Lord and Savior. For those who put their trust in Jesus will "meet the Lord in the air. And so we will be with the Lord forever" (1 Thess. 4:17). Those who do not know Jesus Christ will hear the words, "Depart from me," and will be condemned to an "everlasting fire" (Matt. 25:41 KJV). Let us take time to share Christ with them before it is too late.

I want to devote my life to the work of the Lord. That is why Jesus raised me from the dead as a premature little baby girl. He wanted me here on this earth to share the resurrecting power of Jesus Christ. I will always give one hundred percent to the cause of Christ. Yet I cannot accomplish the work alone. God needs more workers in the field. Do you know what the best part is? Working for the Lord does not necessarily take any special training or prior experience.

The first two men Jesus called to be His disciples were fishermen by trade. Although I have never worked as a professional fisherwoman, I have dabbled in recreational fishing ever since I was a little girl. When I was younger, my parents and I would go out on our fishing boat on a mission to catch bass, brim, or some other type of fish found in our local lakes and rivers. Sometimes we were successful and other times, we simply enjoyed a nice day on the water. One time, though, we went to a trout farm in North Carolina. We literally could not catch them fast enough, since the fish would take the bait as soon as it hit the water's surface. This experience definitely boosted my confidence in my fishing ability, even though I realize the controlled environment made it nearly impossible *not* to catch a fish!

While I have many fond memories of fishing with my parents, there were also times when the situation was not so enjoyable. I remember the time when there was a cloudburst and we were in our small aluminum boat with lightning striking all around. My dad took us up to the shoreline where we jumped out of the boat and waded into the brush amongst the trees to find shelter. Of course, my favorite baby doll, Kristi, was under my arm, out of harm's way as well. I also recall a time when we saw an alligator in Suwannee Lake, and we warned a fisherwoman who was on shore, since it was heading her direction. Thankfully, no one sustained injuries during this ordeal. Finally, I must make mention of the time I caught a large stingray in the Tampa-St. Petersburg area. Now that was an unusual experience!

Yet with all of these fishing memories, only one type of fishing keeps tugging at my heartstrings. My greatest passion in life is fishing for souls. There is no greater privilege than sharing the love of Jesus Christ with someone. It is the most important message we could ever share. Jesus' disciples knew the importance of fishing for men and women, which is why they did not let anything or anyone stop them from proclaiming the Good News as they followed Jesus Christ.

Jesus said to His disciples, "'Follow me, and I will make you fishers of men'" (Matt. 4:19 ESV). Jesus was speaking to two brothers who were fishermen by trade. They did not attend seminary or go through a rigorous evangelistic training. These two men may have lacked a degree in theology, but they had the skills they needed in order to catch fish, or in the case of being two of Jesus' disciples, how to catch people.

Jesus chose them because they were willing to be God's servants. He knew everything else would fall into place, as long as their hearts were fully committed to the cause of Christ. Simon Peter and Andrew did not debate the issue either. They did not tell Jesus they were unqualified. Nor did they make excuses about having to put things in order at home before going into full-time ministry. These two men did not even pack up their fishing gear. This was their response: "At once they left their nets and followed him" (Matt. 4:20). They knew Jesus had called them to a greater task than any they could have ever dreamed. Instead of fishing for seafood, they would be fishing for souls!

What are you doing for the Lord? No matter where you live, there is work for each of us to do. God has called us to share the Gospel with all creation. Within your own community, God's work is all around you. Volunteer at the local hospital, collect items for a food bank, or visit the homebound. Jesus said, "Inasmuch as ye have done it unto one of the least of these my brethren, ye have done it unto me" (Matt. 25:40 KJV). Every nourishing meal, every stitch of clothing, and every kind word or deed shared out of love for Jesus Christ is just as if we have done it unto Him. No task is too small in the eyes of the Lord.

Every single soul is important. The Lord desires for everyone to receive the gift of salvation. The Bible tells us, "He is patient with you, not wanting anyone to perish, but everyone to come to repentance" (2 Pet. 3:9). We need to share this gift with others. Perhaps someone you know is lonely after losing a loved one. Encourage them with the scripture that says Jesus is "closer than a brother" (Prov. 18:24). Spend time with the individual whose family has forgotten them in the nursing home. Talk to your colleague who is struggling with depression. Let them know you care. Every person has a story. Every person is lost until he or she finds salvation. People need someone to introduce them to the redeeming grace of Jesus Christ. Will you be the one to answer the call?

Chapter Six

Stuck in the Sunset

"Weeping may stay for the night, but rejoicing comes in the morning." (Ps. 30:5)

When I was a teenager, I wrote a song titled, "There's Sunshine Awaiting You." The moment I finished writing this song, I knew the Holy Spirit had given me the lyrics. How did I know? I was confident of this fact because this song held a message, which transcended the limits of my understanding at this point in my young life.

As a young person, I had never even been on a date, much less had a child. Yet the first verse talks about a mother who has lost her child. While I had known people who had gone through such a difficult trial, I thankfully had not personally experienced this sort of tragic loss firsthand. Still, God knew my mom was the one who needed to hear the lyrics of this song.

> Somewhere in the distance,
> A mother cries
> For her child who has gone on.
> I can feel her pain,
> And it's too much to bear.
> But God has promised victory,
> Even when there is none there.
>
> *Chorus:*
> There's sunshine awaiting you,
> Just wait and see.

'Cause in the lowest valley,
He sends you to your knees.
And when you just can't go on,
This is what God says.
When you're in the sunset,
There's sunshine awaiting you.

Have you ever seen a sunset
That seemed forever?
Have you ever faced grief and pain?
Have you ever seen someone
Who just couldn't stop crying?
Or was that someone you;
Do you need life anew?

Chorus:
There's sunshine awaiting you,
Just wait and see.
'Cause in the lowest valley,
He sends you to your knees.
And when you just can't go on,
This is what God says.
When you're in the sunset,
There's sunshine awaiting you.[1]

My mom was the first one who heard the song, and she was the first one who cried as she listened to the heaven-sent lyrics. She even paid me the highest compliment possible when she told me it was one of her favorite songs, sitting right up there with songs like "Blessed Assurance," "I Love to Tell the Story," and "Go, Tell It on the Mountain." Talk about a confidence booster! My mom was my perpetual cheerleader, always encouraging me and telling me I could do what I thought was outright impossible. Of course, I knew my mom's love for the song went beyond her desire to help build my self-confidence.

When I was a little girl, my two premature baby brothers passed away as infants. I am almost certain this is why the first verse of this song touched my mom's heart in such a special way. As I sang the song repeatedly over the years, and even recorded it on my first album, I was humbled to see how God used it to minister to people on so many levels.

When you're in the sunset, there's sunshine awaiting you.

Unquestionably, I enjoyed singing this song. I thought the soundtrack my dad produced was beautiful. I knew in my heart that the Holy Spirit had anointed the lyrics. Still, I could not personally identify with the lyrics of the song, having never been through such a dark time in my life. I had always been the one to smile, no matter what circumstances surrounded me. I could always see a glimpse of sunshine, even behind the darkest storm cloud.

I had witnessed the death of more close friends and loved ones than many people I knew had even been to funerals. I had lost two infant brothers, both of my grandfathers, one of my grandmothers, and numerous aunts, uncles, cousins, and friends—so many loved ones going on to be with Jesus. Yet even in the midst of the sorrow, my mom, dad, and I remained a close-knit Christian family. No matter what happened around us, we knew the three of us would love and support each other through sunshine and rain. We were like the Three Musketeers. I had faith God would always keep us together, no matter what storms were brewing overhead.

The first time I sat down at the piano to sing, "There's Sunshine Awaiting You," I immediately knew God had given me this song, as I could not have penned the lyrics on my own. This song held a maturity beyond my years. I never realized then how this song would one day hold a much more significant meaning to me on a very personal level. More than a decade later, I would be the one who was stuck in the sunset.

When Life Changes

On August 2, 2008, the darkest storm of my life came upon me as suddenly as a tornado can flatten an entire town. There was no warning. Neither my dad nor I could silence the violent storm.

My parents and I were vacationing in the Great Smoky Mountains in Western North Carolina. For nearly two decades, we camped beside a beautiful waterfall that cascades down into Raven's Fork Branch. I did a lot of growing up there, so it felt like a second home at the time. This particular summer, we were enjoying our new fifth wheel camper. Life seemed grand. Then, life changed forever.

One evening, we were sitting in the living room watching an episode of *The Waltons*. One moment, all was well. The next moment, life spiraled into a living nightmare. In a split second, my mom sat up, stared straight ahead, and despite our pleas to God to allow her to stay with us, my mom went home to be with Jesus.

We did not have a chance to say our goodbyes. I do not even know what our last words were. We could do nothing to change the circumstances. Life just changed in a matter of seconds.

During the weeks and months following that heartbreaking night, I continuously pondered the question, "What if?" *What if the paramedics had arrived more quickly? What if I had dialed 911 a millisecond faster? What if we had not been on vacation? What if . . .*

My dad and I called out to the Lord, pleading for Him to spare her life. I needed my mama to be with me. I wondered for a moment if God had stopped loving me. I thought that maybe I had done something wrong. Why else would our loving God not save my one and only mama? I hoped He was waiting to perform a miracle.

Sure, the EMTs said it was too late. They said my mom had suffered a heart attack. Still, I waited silently, at first, assured in my heart and soul that God was going to perform a miracle. I knew nothing was impossible with God. I knew He would not let me down. I knew He would intervene.

Jesus said, "What is impossible with man is possible with God"' (Luke 18:27). I believe God's Word with my whole heart. Even in the dark place in which I found myself, I clung to the words of this verse, knowing it was not too late. What the EMTs could not do was entirely possibly with God! I knew a miracle was possible. I knew God could raise my mom up, just as He rose up Lazarus in the Bible.

Yet time passed by, a blur of men and women in uniform and fellow campers offering their condolences. My dad and I found ourselves in the lowest valley we had ever walked through. God could have intervened, yet there was no divine intervention.

Do I understand His purpose? No, I do not always understand God's decisions. Still, I know He has a master plan for us and He is working everything out for our good. Romans 8:28 says, "And we know that in all things God works for the good of those who love him, who have been called according to his purpose." Notice this scripture does not say all things work together the way we choose. It does not say God answers our prayers exactly the way we want; it says God works in all things. God works in our lives the way He knows is best. Instead of seeing the next day, week, month, or year, He sees the big picture. God is not just looking at the next ten, twenty, or even fifty years. He is looking at your entire life, from the very beginning in your mother's womb to the moment you enter into eternity in either Heaven or hell.

Of course, it is often hard for us to consider the "big picture." It is easier to focus on the present. In my human mind, I wondered why God did not perform a miracle in our camper that night. I did not understand how this could possibly work together for good. I repeatedly questioned why God did not intervene when He heard my heart's deepest, most desperate cries for help.

I knew God was a miracle-working God. I had seen evidence of this through my own journey into this world, even to the point of God raising me from the dead. Why was He not working now on our behalf?

I could not comprehend how God would take this tragic loss and use it for my good. Gradually, I began to sink into a depressed state of mind. Although I pasted a smile on my face, it was not always genuine. Even though I exhibited joy around friends and family, my pillow became tear-stained nearly every night. Every day, it became more and more difficult to see the sunshine through my tears.

Our Heavenly Father walks with us in the brilliant light of the sunshine and in the dimming glow of the sunset.

After three years of holding on to the heartache, I finally learned to let go. I did not let go of the cherished memories or the unconditional love I have for my mom. I let go of the "stuff" that was holding me back from truly enjoying life: the grief, the sorrow, the heartbreak.

Specifically, a significant change came when God helped me stop reliving the night my mom stepped into the presence of Jesus. This night haunted me for three years. The distressing scenes flashed by my eyes like a newsreel, playing repeatedly in my mind. The scene of my dad administering CPR while I was on the phone to 911 was still extremely vivid in my mind. The face of the EMT as he said, "I'm sorry." The moment my dad and I sang the most difficult song of our lives, "Living by Faith," sitting beside my mom as we said our final goodbyes, with the knowledge that her soul was already in Heaven.

Other scenes would not leave my thoughts, such as the raspberries I ate in the wee hours of the night to keep them from spoiling. They were my mom's favorite fruit. The tears streaming down my face as we called loved ones to tell them the heartbreaking news. The moment we had to step out of our camper, so the funeral directors could carry out their duties. The minute we had to reenter our camper without my mom. The sleepless night I lay down, only to place my head on a pillow saturated with tears. The mindless days that followed, a constant blur, with an overwhelming void in my life. Words cannot describe the turmoil, which resided deep within my heart.

Since that tragic night, God has spoken to my heart on several occasions. He has filled my mind with peace that passes all human understanding, just as God's Word promises in Philippians 4:7. Still, I do not have all of the answers. I do not understand why my mom is not here, eagerly waiting to read this book, my very first book, something for which she would have been so proud. Nor can I explain why my dad and I are not living in our home as a family of six, my mom and my three siblings still with us.

Nonetheless, I know beyond any doubt that God has a master plan for our lives. Our Heavenly Father walks with us in the brilliant light of the sunshine and in the dimming glow of the sunset. He will hold our hand, whether we are climbing mountains, traversing a rocky terrain, or wading through a raging river. Psalm 23:4 says, "Even though I walk through the darkest valley, I will fear no evil, for you are with me; your rod and your staff, they comfort me." Through every heartrending moment we face in life, we do not have to be afraid. We can rest in the knowledge that the Lord will be with us amid all of our sorrows.

If you are walking through a dark valley right now, be encouraged and know God will be with you. He will guide you through whatever trial you face. Even in the fiercest storms, when the clouds enshroud you, God will comfort you in all of your tomorrows.

I'm Fine, *Really*

During the months after my mom went to be with Jesus, people would constantly ask me how I was doing. I typically answered with one of two well-rehearsed responses: "I'm fine" or "It depends on when you ask me." In reality, these two responses were only to avoid telling people how I really felt. I gave my dad a genuine answer every single time, but everyone else received my generic, lackluster response, regardless of what was really going on in my head or in the depths of my heart. It was not that I did not want to be completely honest with them. Instead, I wanted to avoid reliving the night my mom passed away. By giving a short answer, I could change the conversation to a different topic, one I could discuss more easily.

As human beings, we want people around us to perceive us as strong men and women, even during the times when we are weak inside. In order to maintain this so-called "strength," we put up a façade, parading around as if everything is okay. It is almost as if we attempt to place a bandage over our emotions. We want the world to believe we have it all together, so to speak, when in reality, we may feel like the world around us is crumbling into a million pieces.

If you are going through a similar situation, I pray you have friends and family like the ones God has placed in my life. What a blessing they are to me still today, and what a godsend they were to me during the weeks and months following the loss of my mom. My dad was my rock when the absence of my mom seemed too great to bear. He always knows how I feel, even if I cannot find the words to express myself. What a blessing to have a father who is not only my dad, but also my trustworthy confidante and loyal friend.

The night my mom went home to be with Jesus, we called several family members to share the heartbreaking news. In addition to relatives, I only spoke to one other person on the telephone that night. I called my dear friend, Angie, who is like a mothering big sister to me. I needed someone else to remind me that Jesus would walk with me through this valley, just as God's Word promises in Psalm 23:4. Although I do not recall the words Angie shared with me that night, I know she spoke words of life. Hearing the voice of a dear and treasured friend was a comforting, priceless gift. Since I was a young girl, we have always remained close, and even more so in adulthood. She is constantly serving as my cheerleader, encouraging me and inspiring me to give all I can to the work of the Lord.

Another friend of mine, Goldie, can read me like a book. On the way to my classroom one morning, shortly after I lost my mom, I saw her in the office of the school where I teach. Instead of saying, "Good morning," I stated emphatically, "This is *not* a good day." I can still recall the look on Goldie's face as I walked away. She was probably wondering, *Who was that and where is Jennifer?* With the bell ringing in a matter of minutes, there was no time to apologize. Therefore, I covered up how I really felt and continued on my merry way.

During this difficult time in my life, most people likely had no clue about the internal battle I was fighting. I did what I had to do. I smiled and carried on, week by week, day by day, moment by moment. They saw my smile and thought I was okay.

Everyone knew I was a positive person. I have smiled beside the bedside of loved ones who were tottering between here and eternity, not because I was happy about the circumstances, but because I had peace and assurance that God was in control. This time, it was different. The smile on my face was sometimes genuine; other times, it served as a shield to cover up how I really felt on the inside.

I just wanted to know *why*. Why did God not choose to spare my mama's life? Why did we have to walk through such a dark valley? No answers came. I could not comprehend why God would allow this to happen. This was not supposed to happen, not now, not ever, at least not in *my* plans. What I failed to realize fully then was that God has a master plan.

God's plans are often different from our own. Even when we feel helpless, He is our help in our time of need. All we have to do is go to the throne of the Almighty and ask Him to help us. God's Word tells us how to receive His help: "Let us therefore come boldly unto the throne of grace, that we may obtain mercy, and find grace to help in time of need" (Heb. 4:16 KJV). If we come to Him boldly, God will always send us a lifeline to deliver us from the depths of our despair.

After school that day, my friend embraced me with open arms. She imparted words of wisdom that I now share with others who are struggling with difficulties. Goldie said, "There is no such thing as having a bad *day*. There are twenty-four hours in a day. You may have a difficult morning, afternoon, or evening, but you can always choose to have a good *day*." Such simple words, yet they made a profound impact on the way I look at life.

When a tragedy occurs in our lives, it is easy for us to choose to have a bad day. We may even throw a pity party for ourselves. However, this will only make us feel better for a fleeting moment. God desires for us not to live a life of defeat, but a life of victory. Jesus said, "'The thief comes only to steal and kill and destroy; I have come that they may have life, and have it to the full'" (John 10:10). He came so we could live a life of abundance.

Jesus wants us to live a life of freedom, a life of joy, and a life of hope. He wants His children to have 365 good days per year. On the contrary, Satan wants every day to be a bad one. The devil wants to be the guest of honor at our pity parties, bringing us the "gifts" of discouragement, anger, hatred, despair, sorrow— all of the things that vacuum the life right out of us.

As my friend wisely told me, though, we are the ones who can choose to be grateful our Heavenly Father gives us a brand new day, every twenty-four hours. We choose whether to thank Him for the first breath we take each morning when we awaken. Whether our world is like a stunning sunrise or a stormy sunset, we should rest in the joy of knowing Jesus will walk beside us, in the good moments and the not-so-good ones as well.

God desires for us not to live a life of defeat, but a life of victory.

The Twenty-third Psalm tells us the Lord will not only lead us beside peaceful waters, but He will also guide us down the path of righteousness. He will comfort us and be with us, even in the valley of the shadow of death (Ps. 23:4). No matter where you are right this moment, Jesus Christ is with you. Inside your home, on vacation, at your workplace, in a hospital bed or nursing home, on the battlefield, inside a prison—He will meet you wherever you are. He will never abandon you (Heb. 13:5).

Since the moment I told my friend I was not having a good day, I have had thousands of good days. In fact, I now realize more than ever that every day is a good day. Sure, there have been disappointments along the way. Tearstains have graced my pillow on more than one occasion. Regardless of the curveballs thrown my way, my faith in God has never wavered. He is the One I can lean on when I am too weak to stand.

A Secret Place

As a little girl, my mom and I would always go to our "Secret Place." Our Secret Place consisted of a lower piece of ground in my Papa Joe and Grandma Ethel's woods. I would often pull my little red wagon out there, full of baby dolls and stuffed animals. Which toys I brought varied slightly, but my favorite doll, Kristi, was always a part of the action. My mom and I would spread a blanket on the ground and have a picnic together in this peaceful spot covered by a canopy of giant oak trees.

Other times, we enjoyed playing dress-up, playing with dolls, and baking cookies at home. Even as I grew older, we still did many things together, like making jewelry, scrapbooking, and of course, we still baked sweet treats together. She even helped prepare activities for my students during my first two years of teaching. For twenty-six years, my mom and I were very close friends who did everything together.

While my heart was broken the night my mom went home to be with the Lord, my heart also rejoiced. Although tears ran down my face as rapidly as the river beside our camper that night, I know in my heart that August 2, 2008, was the happiest day of my mom's life. She was a Christian who loved Jesus Christ with all of her heart. Second Corinthians 5:8 (KJV) says to be absent from the body is to be present with the Lord. While the absence of my mom is extraordinarily difficult, I know the moment she entered the presence of the Lord, she began worshiping and praising our Lord and Savior, Jesus Christ. My mom has not gone to a "Secret Place." I know where she is, and I am pleased to say that her new home is not a secret location, nor is the method of getting there a secret.

For Christians, this world is a temporary home, similar to a waiting room at a doctor's office. We are waiting for God to call us to our true home in Heaven. Still, this wait may seem never-ending, or it may seem to end abruptly, especially for loved ones left behind. It is in these difficult moments when you find out who you really are as a Christian. This is when your faith in Christ is truly tested.

Whether we are celebrating a victory or recovering from defeat, our faith should be an ever-present part of our daily lives.

The Bible says, "For we walk by faith, not by sight" (2 Cor. 5:7 KJV). We need to walk as if our eyes were closed, allowing God to guide our steps according to His perfect will.

Psalm 18:30 says, "As for God, his way is perfect; The LORD's word is flawless; he shields all who take refuge in him." Satan may try to convince us otherwise, but God is a sovereign God. His ways are perfect. He has a plan for our lives that far exceeds all of our expectations. We must have faith that God will guide us safely through the storms of life.

God will never lead us through a sunset without providing a sunrise. He will never take us into a storm without providing a rainbow. God's Word says, "Trust in the LORD with all your heart and lean not on your own understanding" (Prov. 3:5). This means we may not always comprehend the way God is working in our lives. Instead, we need to lean on the Lord and trust that He will give us strength to weather every storm.

The journey of life is full of uncertainties and frequently seems like a frightening place to be. Even so, we will never find ourselves trapped in a tunnel of darkness. In every situation, Jesus is the eternal light at the end of every tunnel. He is the light of the entire world.

God will never lead us through a sunset without providing a sunrise.

Jesus extends an open invitation to all who believe. I know in my heart that my mom would not want me to write this book without extending the same invitation to you. Accept Jesus Christ as your personal Lord and Savior today before it is too late. I can assure you, the valley I have walked through would have been too great to bear, if it was not for my relationship with Jesus Christ.

Jesus gives us eternal hope, even in the midst of seemingly

hopeless circumstances. Jesus offers everlasting life to every single person on this earth, but we must repent of our sins and call on the name of Jesus Christ. The Bible says, "'Everyone who calls on the name of the Lord will be saved'" (Rom. 10:13).

My mom, dad, and I accepted this invitation many years ago. Because of this, my dad and I will see my mom again when God calls His children home. While we miss my mom greatly here on earth, we know she is in Heaven. Although our hearts hurt, we have everlasting hope through Jesus Christ. My dad has not lost his wife. I have not lost my mom. Pamela Suzanne Campbell is not lost because we know exactly where she is, for her new home is not a secret place.

One glorious day, we will see her again in Heaven, where there will be no sorrow or tears, sickness or pain. Until that happy reunion, we can rejoice concerning the promise found in Isaiah 25:8 (NLT): "He will swallow up death forever! The Sovereign LORD will wipe away all tears." Everyone who puts their trust in Jesus Christ will one day be free from all of the grief on this earth. Heaven is not a secret; it is only a prayer away.

Chapter Seven

Mayday!

"In my distress I called to the LORD; I cried to my
God for help. From his temple he heard my voice; my cry
came before him, into his ears." (Ps. 18:6)

In 2011, the pastor asked me to sing at our home church on Mother's Day. For many singers, this would not be a problem. In the past, I would have jumped at the chance. This time, it was another story. The moment I heard the pastor's request, a red flag shot up. I thought, *No, I could not do that. I can happily sing any other Sunday, but not that one.*

I think the pastor must have seen the look in my eyes, resembling a deer caught in the headlights, and he quickly asked if it would be too difficult for me. I will be honest with you. I wanted to respond, telling him it would be virtually impossible for me to sing on Mother's Day. I am sure the pastor would have accepted this and asked me to sing at another time. However, something tugged at my heart. Immediately, I knew this was something I must do.

As I told the pastor I would sing, I pondered the song I would share on this special day on which we honor our mothers. I considered what I would sing if my mom could be in the congregation for this special occasion. Of course, the answer was simple. I would sing my original song, "There's Sunshine Awaiting You."

There was one small glitch in this plan though. I had not sung this song since I sang it at my mom's funeral. As such, I quickly began seeking God for a different answer other than the one I knew He had given. I already felt as if I could not sing on Mother's Day much less sing this song. Have you ever had one of those moments when you thought God had more confidence in you than you had in yourself? Well, this was most definitely one of those times.

God does not require perfect vessels but willing vessels.

Since I had not sung this song in quite some time, I decided to practice at home a few times first. The first time I ran through the song, I heard the lyrics in a new light. My own original song was ministering to me. I realized I had been stuck in the sunset. That is why I needed to sing this song. God knew all along that these words would encourage me, just as He would use it to encourage the congregation.

When I stood on the platform on Mother's Day, I may have stumbled over my words some as I introduced the song, and I am sure that pitch took on a completely new meaning by the time I reached the song's end. Thankfully, serving the Lord is not all about eloquent speech or perfect pitch. Sometimes it is about answering His call, even if we falter a bit along the way. God does not require perfect vessels but willing vessels.

The lyrics of my song speak about a sunset that seems to last forever and about how it is difficult to face grief and pain. The sunset you find yourself in may seem as if it will never end, but it is not forever. When you reach the lowest, darkest valley, God will bring you to your knees. When you cannot go on one more mile, God will carry you through every storm. When you find yourself stuck in the sunset, there is sunshine awaiting you.

As I sang the lyrics of this song, I was reminded that the sun will shine forth again with splendor, as beautiful as a gorgeous spring day. When I was growing up, spring activities included flying kites, planting flowers, and of course, picking wildflowers.

Even though some people might consider them weeds, my mom was always delighted when I handed her a colorful bouquet of phlox, dandelions, and black-eyed Susans. To this day, I still enjoy photographing these special blooms of springtime.

While the first day of spring will always bring to mind fond memories from my childhood, life has not always been full of sunshine and blue skies. There have also been times when I was venturing through a dark storm. At times, I have felt I would drown in a sea of sorrow, due to the figurative torrential rain pouring down upon me. You could liken my distress to the captain of a ship who has suffered a major breach in the hull of their ship, striving to remain focused on getting the lifeboats launched and other emergency operations under way. Other times, I felt like a pilot who is flying in the darkest of night, with zero visibility, struggling to control the plane due to the wind, rain, and hail falling down from the heavens above. Certainly, in a dire circumstance such as this, the pilot would call out, without hesitation, "Mayday! Mayday!"

While mariners and aviators are the ones who primarily use the distress signal, "Mayday," the term would likely be appropriate for any sort of emergency. The term *Mayday* comes from the French *m'aider*, meaning, "Help me."[1] Even though we may not have a radio on which to call for help, there is never a time when we cannot call on the name of Jesus Christ to help us. He is always waiting to hear our voice. Even amid the storms of life, Jesus will be our shelter in the storm.

When Storms Come

During the summer of 2012, an unprecedented storm ravaged my local community. Tropical Storm Debby dropped over twenty inches of rain in a matter of hours, causing massive flooding and destruction. The storm destroyed hundreds of homes and vehicles. Many people lost everything they owned. To complicate matters further, over one hundred sinkholes opened up in Suwannee County alone. Gratefully, no lives were lost in our county, with the exception of the many livestock and pets swept away in the storm. Even so, this disaster rattled many Floridians to their innermost core.

My longhaired miniature Dachshund, Lucy, along with my two pygmy goats, Charlotte and Savannah, were lost in the flood. Our backyard became a huge lake, something we do not have on our property. The water came within a few feet of flooding my dad's workshop and our home as well. Looking at the photographs, I cannot quite comprehend how the water was between five to six feet high toward the back of our property, yet did not make its way into the house. If the water had flowed level, I am almost certain this would have been the case. Still, several friends of mine were not so fortunate and woke up to several feet of water in their homes.

Truthfully, we faired very well when you compare the gentleness of Tropical Storm Debby to the wrath of other disastrous storms. In August 2017, Hurricane Harvey ravaged the eastern coast of Texas and other parts of the United States as it continued to unleash its fury over a period of almost two weeks. This storm system made landfall as a category four storm, with winds gusting around 130 miles per hour. The most significant damage came from the unprecedented rainfall, totaling more than fifty inches of rain in some areas. I know Texans will be resilient, continually working to rebuild their homes and their lives, even though life may never be quite the same again.

Eighty-eight people lost their lives because of this horrific storm.[2] The billions of dollars of damage will never compare to the value of human life. Families will have Thanksgiving and Christmas with empty chairs at the table. Children will spend sleepless nights during the next rainstorm, wondering if it could initiate another tragic flood that will sweep away what little they have left. Parents will question what they could have done differently as they try to understand what happened and attempt to determine where to go from here.

Although this hurricane produced catastrophic damage, it did not even compare to Hurricane Katrina in 2005, which generated the highest storm surge ever recorded in the United States. A storm surge of nearly twenty-eight feet rapidly came ashore at Pass Christian, Mississippi.[3] This storm produced mass destruction in the city of New Orleans, Louisiana. Sadly, Hurricane Katrina claimed more than fifteen hundred lives, making it one of the most deadly hurricanes in United States history.

Natural disasters are one of the many things in life beyond our control. We cannot reposition a hurricane, no more than we can tell a tornado to stop spinning. Nor can we cancel earthquakes, tsunamis, or landslides. Even though we cannot stretch out our hand to stop these cataclysmic disasters from happening, we can do something. We can call on God to be with us through every single storm. He will watch over us and be our refuge in the midst of the storm.

Our Protector

The Ninety-first Psalm is the Psalm of Protection. This psalm reminds us that God will always protect us, if we put our trust in Him. The Bible says, "'Because he loves me,' says the LORD, 'I will rescue him; I will protect him, for he acknowledges my name. He will call on me, and I will answer him; I will be with him in trouble, I will deliver him and honor him'" (Ps. 91:14–15). Notice the very first thing the Lord said in this passage. Because we love Him, He will rescue us. There is no registration form to get on the list for God's protection. No letters of recommendation are required. The only prerequisite is to love God. Loving God should be an easy task, considering the fact that "he first loved us" (1 John 4:19).

Yet there is one more thing we should do. The Lord said, "'He will call on me, and I will answer him.'" If we want the Lord to answer us, we must first call on Him. Consider the last time you made a phone call. Did you wait for the person you were calling to answer before you even picked up the phone to dial their number? Unquestionably, this would make no sense at all. In order to make a call, you must first pick up the phone and dial the number. Likewise, we must take the initiative and call on God for His help. No telephone is necessary. We can call on Him twenty-four hours a day, seven days a week. He is always listening, waiting to hear from us.

Regrettably, some people do not understand the concept of God's protection. They become angry with God because He does not answer their prayers within their timeframe, or they turn their back on God, blaming Him for some catastrophe that occurs in their life. In these moments when we find ourselves at our lowest point, we should draw closer to God, rather than pull ourselves away from Him. When we refuse the Lord's help, our intrinsic need for His almighty strength becomes crystal clear. Life will have its share of difficult valleys, but a life without God is like a calamitous train wreck.

After years of following the Lord, even the Israelites turned away from God. They became impatient with the Lord, taking matters into their own hands. The Lord knew they would direct their anger toward Him, as we read in Deuteronomy 31:17 (KJV), when He said, "Then my anger shall be kindled against them in that day, and I will forsake them, and I will hide my face from them, and they shall be devoured, and many evils and troubles shall befall them; so that they will say in that day, Are not these evils come upon us, because our God is not among us?"

The Israelites accused God of not being there to protect them, yet they were the ones who had broken the Lord's covenant. Because of their rebelliousness, they endured much suffering, since God allowed them to experience life without Him in order to show them how much they needed Him in their lives. We have the freedom to choose whom we will serve (Josh. 24:15). The only living God does not impose Himself on people. He is there for us, 365 days per year, but He allows us to decide whether we will invite Him into our lives.

Consider your family dinner table. If you invite a family member or friend to join you for dinner, they would surely accept your invitation to share a meal with you. On the other hand, if you do not first extend an invitation, how would they know what day and time to come to your home? Similarly, we must invite God to be a part of our daily existence. He wants to be a part of every aspect of our lives, guiding us through the rough spots and rejoicing with us in the cheerful moments.

What we do not always understand is that our lives form a much larger picture than we could ever comprehend. While we are concerned about the next week, month, or year, God may be examining the next fifty years, or even the next thousand years. He knows every intricate detail of our future, not only pertaining to this world but also for eternity. Why would we depend on anyone else but Him to guide and direct our comings and goings?

We cannot be like the Israelites, only turning to God when we are desperate or when life seems perfect. We need to be like the apostle Paul, who said "to live is Christ, and to die is gain" (Phil. 1:21 ESV). He knew there was nothing greater than serving Jesus Christ, our Lord and Savior. Even during imprisonment, Paul said, "What has happened to me has actually served to advance the gospel. As a result, it has become clear throughout the whole palace guard and to everyone else that I am in chains for Christ. And because of my chains, most of the brothers and sisters have become confident in the Lord and dare all the more to proclaim the gospel without fear" (Phil. 1:12–14). Paul knew leading the lost to Christ was more important than anything else was in the world. No matter how hard life became, he put his trust in Christ. He proclaimed the Gospel through faith, whether he was sad, tired, or even in chains. He knew God would be with him, regardless of his dire circumstances.

In life, we will experience things we may never be able to comprehend completely. These events may cause us to question our family and friends, question our beliefs, and even question God. Yet it is also in these moments when we can find a rainbow amid the clouds: the pets we rescue, the belongings we salvage, and the loved ones we cherish. On a deeper level, we may recognize that we have hope, even in the most desperate conditions. No matter what happens, God will always be there for us. He is always faithful. He will bring us through every storm.

No matter what happens, God will always be there for us. He is always faithful. He will bring us through every storm.

Are you facing a storm in your own life? Maybe it is not a natural disaster. Perhaps it is an emotional, a physical, or a financial storm. You may be going through a demoralizing divorce or struggling with irrefutable depression. There may be someone in your family fighting for their life in the hospital. Someone you know could be suffering from the effects of Alzheimer's, Parkinson's, cancer, or some other disease. Whatever you are facing, I want to encourage you right this very moment. Do not be afraid. Call on the name that is above every other name, Jesus Christ. He loves you more than you could ever imagine. Jesus will silence the tumult in your heart and mind. He will calm your fears. Jesus will be your shelter in the storm.

God's Word says, "'The Lord is my helper; I will not fear'" (Heb. 13:6 ESV). If you find yourself drowning in despair, call out to Him. If you are struggling to find a reason to get out of bed in the morning, ask Him to give you strength and purpose. If you feel as if your life is falling apart, send out a Mayday call to Jesus. He will answer your call and help you in your time of need.

On that particular Mother's Day a few years ago, I felt like calling out, "Mayday," as I sang one of my mom's favorite songs that I have written. My emotions pulled my heartstrings in every direction. My mind was racing with nerve-racking thoughts. *Will I be able to sing on key? Will I forget the words? Will I cry in front of everyone?* I called on the name of Jesus to help me. When I called out to my Heavenly Father, the doubts in my mind vanished. I sensed a sudden calm. It was as if Jesus said to me, "I heard your distress call, my child. I am here to help you. You can do it. I will be standing right beside you, so do not fear."

Jesus Christ does not desire for any of His children to experience fear, hopelessness, or despair. He does not want us to feel as though we are in a dark tunnel from which we will never escape. He wants us to see the light, not the proverbial light at the end of the tunnel, but the eternal light of hope, Jesus Christ.

Jesus said, "'I am the light of the world. Whoever follows me will never walk in darkness, but will have the light of life'" (John 8:12). Jesus is the light of the entire world. He can take away the darkness that surrounds you. He can make the sun shine again. With Jesus on your side, the metaphorical shipwrecks and plane crashes of life will seem less treacherous. The hurdles you are required to jump over will seem less strenuous, and when you feel the walls closing in around you, Jesus will be there to help you. He will take your cloud-enshrouded nightmare and turn it into a sunshine-filled dream.

Chapter Eight

Life in the Balance

"And God is faithful; he will not let you be tempted beyond what you can bear. But when you are tempted, he will also provide a way out so that you can endure it." (1 Cor. 10:13)

While my sweet sixteenth year on this earth began with an All-Day Singing and Dinner on the Ground in January; it ended in a much different realm. My mom was in the hospital in a nearby city, about an hour from our home. I walked into my closet to change clothes, so my dad and I could go visit her that evening. All of the sudden, I felt as if I had been stabbed in the side. It was the most excruciating pain I had ever felt in my life. I began experiencing incredible nausea and knew something was terribly wrong. I immediately told my dad, who quickly ushered me out the door. We went directly to the hospital emergency room. I was evaluated, and it was determined that my colon had perforated and my heart rate was dangerously high. My condition was life-threatening.

As they prepared me for emergency surgery, my dad obtained permission to bring my mom down to see me before I went into the operating room. My mom and dad later told me they wanted to see me one last time, in case I did not make it. While I knew the circumstances were critical, I had complete assurance that Jesus would be with me in the operating room, guiding the surgeon's hands. Although I realized peritonitis and all of the medical terms spouted off by the medical staff added up to a very serious situation, I did not worry one bit. I even recall telling my parents that everything would be fine, and that Jesus would take care of me. Even in the midst of what looked like a life or death situation, I had complete faith He would see me through. I believed without a doubt that God would heal my body and restore my health.

I came through surgery with a few complications, stayed in the Intensive Care Unit before transferring to a regular room, and was finally able to come home several weeks later. During the time I was in the hospital, my mom was discharged from the hospital, and my parents both stayed by my side every day and night, except for the times when my dad had to briefly return to work. I know it was a very trying time for them, worrying about their little girl. Still, my faith never wavered. I knew God would keep His promise.

All my life, I had read, "By his wounds we are healed" (Isa. 53:5). I claimed this promise and I knew God would bring healing to my body. How could I have had such strong faith at the young age of sixteen? Because I was confident that God, who created the heavens and the earth and who raised me from the dead as a newborn, would not let me down. I had confidence then and have confidence now that God will never fail. Even though I lay there in excruciating pain, I had reassurance God would heal my body. Hebrews 11:1 says, "Now faith is confidence in what we hope for and assurance about what we do not see." My faith allowed me to see something I could not see with my physical eyes: the healing touch of the hand of Jesus. Weeks later, God restored my health. God performed a miracle in my life once again, just as I knew He would.

James 1:2–3 says, "Consider it pure joy, my brothers and sisters, whenever you face trials of many kinds, because you know that the testing of your faith produces perseverance." When trials test our faith, we will develop a stronger faith in God. Although we should not rejoice for the trials, we can be joyful during the trials, knowing we will come out on the other side with a steadfastness that cannot be broken.

Through the years, I have had my faith tested many times, including the times when my mom was in the hospital for various illnesses. There were nights I stayed at my grandparent's house as a very young child, simply saying to them, "Go home." As I grew older, I began staying at the hospital with my mom, to ensure she had everything she needed and to make sure she was getting excellent care. There were nights I slept in a straight back chair, leaning on the rail of her hospital bed, wondering if I would awaken to a jolting code blue alert.

My family and I have endured many sleepless nights, close calls, and tearful prayers, yet through all of the moments of uncertainty, one thing has always remained sure. God has never failed us. We put our complete trust in Him. I trust the Lord in every aspect of my life. Even in my times of distress, I have complete assurance that God will be faithful to me.

When Life Does Not Make Sense

As a young girl, I faced circumstances most people do not have to face until they are much older. My two baby brothers were both born prematurely, a few years apart. Standing beneath the giant oak trees on our family farm, I sang at each of their funerals. While I do not recall the thoughts that ran through my young mind, I am sure I wondered why God was allowing us to endure such grief, not once but twice. Three times for my parents, as my mom suffered a miscarriage before I was even born. I have three siblings in Heaven, yet none here on this earth.

Christians and non-Christians alike constantly ask the question, "Why does God allow bad things to happen?" While we cannot fully understand the way God works in our lives, we can have confidence that He has everything under control. God's Word says, "And we know that all things work together for good to them that love God, to them who are the called according to his purpose" (Rom. 8:28 KJV). God will work all things out for our good. This does not mean life will be a bed of beautiful roses, for even roses bloom among thorns. Yet this verse does promise that God will take everything that happens to us and use it for our good. God will be at work in our lives, if we love Him with our entire soul and our entire mind (Matt. 22:37). When we love God wholeheartedly, He will work everything out according to His divine providence, even when figurative storm clouds are brewing overhead.

Even God's only Son, Jesus Christ, experienced great sorrow here on this earth. Isaiah 53:3 (KJV) says, He was "a man of sorrows, and acquainted with grief." Jesus endured His share of trials. Nearing the time of His Crucifixion, Jesus led the disciples to the Mount of Olives, where He asked them to pray. Jesus knelt down and prayed, "'Father, if you are willing, take this cup from me; yet not my will, but yours be done.' An angel from heaven appeared to him and strengthened him. And being in anguish, he prayed more earnestly, and his sweat was like drops of blood falling to the ground" (Luke 22:42–44). God's own Son became so troubled that He essentially began sweating blood.

Jesus knew His Father's will was perfect, yet He still experienced grief when He considered the coming days. He would be beaten, scorned, and rejected among men. Then He would suffer an agonizing death on a cross. Even though Jesus knew the pain He would have to bear, He never once tried to ignore His Father's will. He was obedient, trusting God's plan. Jesus knew God would never fail Him, even though He had to endure such torment. The trial Jesus faced did not last forever. Three days later, He rose up from the grave. Jesus was victorious, even over death, because of God's resurrection power.

When we face trials, we need to realize that trusting God is not always a walk in the park. In the Bible, we read of a man named Daniel who had to have faith that God would keep the mouths of the lions shut (Dan. 6:22). God's Word tells us the reason why the lions did not attack him: "And when Daniel was lifted from the den, no wound was found on him, because he had trusted in his God" (Dan. 6:23). He was able to avoid the wrath of the hungry lions because he put his trust in God. Furthermore, his reliance on God resulted in the entire kingdom being issued a decree to "'fear and reverence the God of Daniel'" (Dan. 6:26). God used Daniel's faith to change the entire territory. When we trust God completely, miracles happen.

In August 2009, God used my faith to change me. One morning when I got out of bed, my face was no longer normal. As I looked in the mirror, I immediately realized I could not blink my eyes, talk clearly, or even smile. Fear dominated my thoughts. Countless questions filled my mind, as I wondered why God would allow me to bear yet another trial, with all that my dad and I had already endured in the previous year. This ordeal put me in one of the lowest places I had ever been.

I went to my family physician, hoping to receive some good news. My physician suggested several possible diagnoses, a few quite severe, and referred me to see an optometrist. After a full examination, I found out that I had a severe case of bilateral Bell's palsy. I received several prescriptions to help with swelling and infection, along with instructions to go home and wait it out. Neither the optometrist nor the ophthalmologist could tell me how long it would last, but they said it could be anywhere from days to weeks to months, or it could be permanent.

They said one of the possible causes could be stress-related factors. When I look back on that time in my life, I realize this was most certainly the case. It was the one-year anniversary of the loss of my mom. The more I tried not to think about this anniversary, the more I thought about it. Every time I tried to miss my mom a little less, I missed my mom a whole lot more. School was starting, which meant the end to our summer travels, and my to-do list seemed longer than the Nile River. The absence of my mom made even the smallest minor setback seem like an international incident.

My close family, friends, and acquaintances know that I smile all of the time. For me, the inability to smile due to this condition was truly discouraging. Essentially all of my facial muscles became seemingly frozen in time, affecting my ability to blink my eyes, raise my eyebrows, speak clearly, or even chew properly. I prayed for divine healing, so I could continue to shine forth the love of Jesus Christ without hindrance.

Approximately four weeks later, God completely healed me of Bell's Palsy. It was a gradual pathway to healing, but it was a journey of hope and healing ordained by God. Every time I blink my eyes, each time I move any part of my face, and all of the times I smile, I remember when God fully restored my health. Each moment I express myself is a gift from God, which I will never take for granted. I may not understand God's purpose for my temporary misery, but I know He will always use everything for my good (Rom. 8:28).

Every single struggle I have experienced in life has had one thing in common. No matter how difficult the situation has been, God has always proven faithful. He always has a way of taking the broken pieces of life and putting them back together again. Only He does not just use superglue for a quick patch job. When He is finished restoring the brokenness, the newly created masterpiece is more beautiful than the first. God has a master plan for our lives; He will never fail us. When we put our trust in God, tribulations can lead to triumphant ends.

God Is Faithful

Carol Cymbala, director of the Brooklyn Tabernacle Choir, wrote a song titled, "He's Been Faithful." In this song, she reflects back over the constant faithfulness of God in her life. As I look back over the course of my life, I can tell you that God has always been faithful to me and continues to be faithful every single day. I can see how God's hand began working in my life from the very moment I was born. I know He has called me to live for His glory. First Thessalonians 5:24 says, "The one who calls you is faithful, and he will do it." When we believe with our whole heart that He is faithful, God will perform a miracle on our behalf.

In God's Word, we read about the centurion who had such great faith that he believed Jesus would heal his paralyzed servant, without even coming to him. Jesus took notice of this man's strong faith. Jesus said, "'Truly I tell you, I have not found anyone in Israel with such great faith'" (Matt. 8:10). Because the centurion believed, his servant was healed that very moment (Matt. 8:13). If we have faith, God will answer our prayers.

So what happens if a person does not have faith? Hebrews 11:6 says, "Without faith it is impossible to please God, because anyone who comes to him must believe that he exists and that he rewards those who earnestly seek him." If we do not have faith, we are disappointing God, our Heavenly Father. We cannot please God unless we believe that He is God and that He will take care of His children.

When we put our trust in God, tribulations can lead to triumphant ends.

There were many faithless people, even when Jesus walked upon this earth. Jesus found His own hometown did not even have much faith, according to Mark 6:5–6: "He could not do any miracles there, except lay his hands on a few sick people and heal them. He was amazed at their lack of faith." Could you imagine? Jesus Christ returned to Nazareth, yet many people there did not have faith that He could bring salvation and healing to all who believe. As a result, they missed divine blessings because of their lack of faith.

In contrast, people in other towns believed Jesus would heal them and they saw many miracles performed because of their faith. God's Word says, "The people brought to Jesus all who had various kinds of sickness, and laying his hands on each one, he healed them" (Luke 4:40). Jesus did not just heal a small number of them, as He did in His hometown. Instead, He healed them all because they had faith to believe He would heal them. Jesus said, "'You may ask me for anything in my name, and I will do it'" (John 14:14). All we have to do is ask in faith and believe He will answer when we pray.

God does not require a large quantity of faith. A mustard seed of faith can move mountains. Jesus said nothing will be impossible for us if we "have faith as a grain of mustard seed" (Matt. 17:20 KJV). A mustard seed is very small. It takes fifteen thousand mustard seeds to equal the weight of one single ounce. Yet it only takes one single mustard seed of faith to move a massive mountain.

Have you ever felt as if you were running low on faith? There are times in my own life when it seems I need greater faith to receive an answer from God. Other times, I have faith so great, that it appears it would be possible for me to move a gargantuan mountain like the Matterhorn in Switzerland. I have a genetic connective tissue disorder that requires me to walk with a crutch and a brace. Although I have had a clubfoot for more than two decades, it has never stopped me from literally climbing mountains and crisscrossing cities. My dad and I have gone hiking in the Great Smoky Mountains and we have trekked through dozens of cities all around the world. Our record-breaking days have been eight and a half miles in Vienna, Austria, and nine miles in Bucharest, Romania. No matter the physical challenges I face, I have always been one to forge ahead, no matter what literal or figurative obstacles I may encounter.

On July 25, 2018, I encountered what would become an enormous roadblock on the road of life when I began experiencing an unusual type of pain in my leg. Discounting it as overexertion from our summer vacation, I tried to ignore the severe pain in my leg and foot. However, as I hobbled through pre-planning week at the school where I teach, I could sense the pain was getting worse. By the time classes began, it was all I could do to stand at the bathroom counter in the mornings to brush my teeth. The pain was so great; it caused my blood pressure and heart rate to reach dangerous levels. Just putting my foot on the floor was often so agonizing that it nearly took my breath away. Other times, the muscle cramps in my leg caused tears to flow from my eyes as my hands shook from the intensity of the pain.

On my first trip to the doctor, I received a prescription to treat possible nerve damage. Unfortunately, this medication did not improve my condition at all. As my pain worsened and a small lump on my leg began to enlarge, my family physician referred me to an orthopedic specialist. The orthopedic surgeon ordered a magnetic resonance imaging (MRI) test to investigate the problem. As I lay in the futuristic-looking apparatus that took more than three hundred internal pictures of my leg, I prayed continually that God would deliver me from the trial in which I found myself. Although I had complete faith He was with me, even in this sterile, cold environment, I am afraid my human flesh was a bit concerned. Unfortunately, the rest of the day resembled a downward spiral, which did nothing to alleviate my apprehension.

This particular day began when the alarm clock awakened my dad and me at 3:30 a.m. My appointment time was 6:30 a.m., at Mayo Clinic in Jacksonville, which is approximately one hundred miles from our home. As we left the hospital, planning to return in the afternoon for the consultation with the doctors concerning the MRI results, I received a call on my cell phone. Imagine my dismay when they told me to return for an impromptu blood test and ultrasound biopsy straight away. My mind was racing, for the only thing I could equate with the word *biopsy* was the dreaded *C* word. I silently prayed God would take away these fears and give me peace about this whole ordeal.

The next few hours were a blur of appointments and tests, culminating with the previously scheduled consultation with the doctors. As my dad and I sat in the examination room, waiting for the doctors, I think we both felt as if a dump truck had run us over. The events of the day had drained us both physically and mentally. When three doctors came in, instead of two, my anxiety level increased drastically. Although I cannot tell you all that they said, due to my inner struggle to keep myself together emotionally, I particularly recall the picture on the computer screen, which the orthopedic surgeon described as a soft tissue mass. In that instant, the so-called mass looked enormous. He gave us several possible scenarios, but we would not have confirmation of a diagnosis until the biopsy results were available sometime within the following two weeks. There is something very unnerving when a doctor asks if you want him to call with the results, even if it is something serious. Due to the travel time and distance involved, we opted for a phone call, even though he said one of the possibilities could be a very large cancerous, malignant tumor.

For the next week, my heart skipped a couple of beats every time the phone rang. My dad and I prayed, studied God's Word, and sought the Lord's wisdom in all of this. Still, the enemy tried to defeat us, placing all sorts of notions in our vivid imaginations. There were countless sleepless nights for both of us. Even with all of my trepidation, I knew God would be with us. I knew He would give us the strength to make it to the other side of this valley. The following Friday, when the caller ID read Mayo Clinic, my hand visibly shook as I answered the phone. I could hardly find a breath to say hello.

The doctor said the biopsy results were inconclusive. Considering the alternatives, I praised the Lord for this report, even though the doctor continued by saying that a computerized tomography (CT) scan and possibly an open biopsy were necessary. Two weeks went by before the CT scan appointment. Following the CT scan, I received a diagnosis. I had a pseudo aneurysm in my lower right leg, caused by an aneurysm in one of the arteries in my leg. One night following this phone call, I remember purposely looking in the mirror and pulling several strands of hair toward my face and kissing them, relieved to know God had spared me from enduring something much worse.

It was determined that surgery was required, but they were able to offer an interventional radiology procedure as opposed to open vascular surgery. Unfortunately, the first opening for a consultation with the doctor's choice surgeon was December 3, 2018. As someone who had dealt with this excruciating pain for nearly three months, I could hardly fathom the idea of waiting another month and a half. My dad and I stressed to the doctor how the swelling and pain had increased, even over the course of the previous week. Thanks to my mathematician dad, we had actually been measuring the circumference of my leg and had objective evidence that it was increasing in size as well.

On the way home that afternoon, we received a call from the doctor's nurse, letting us know they found another surgeon who could perform the procedure exactly one week later. My dad later discovered that this new surgeon was internationally renowned in his field of practice. That is just like God. He always knows best. On October 26, 2018, I found myself sitting in a waiting room, before the nurse escorted me to the preoperative area. I must admit, I was nervous. I diligently read my Bible, I had gone to the throne of grace on more than one occasion, and everything seemed to have fallen in place as if God was the One who had put the puzzle together in the first place.

Yet there I sat, repeatedly reading Psalm 103:3 (NLT), which says, "He forgives all my sins and heals all my diseases." Although I knew God would heal me, I was worried. So what did I do? I called my daddy in the waiting room to ask him to pray with me over the phone. After he prayed with me, the nurse came to take me to the preoperative room, so I had to hang up the phone.

Soon I was lying on a hospital bed, complete with wires coming out of both arms, wearing one of those dreaded gowns that seem like a rookie tailor made a horrible mistake by forgoing a zipper in the back. The nurse asked me if I wanted my dad to wait in the preoperative area, which would double as the recovery room. Of course, I said, "Yes!" He walked right alongside me throughout this trial, helping me in so many ways, especially through prayer. I am so grateful to have such a loving father, who will seek the Lord on my behalf. As soon as my daddy sat down by my bedside, my anxiety slowly disappeared. Even at the age of thirty-seven, I still need my daddy.

Similar to the way my dad's presence calmed some of my fears, my Heavenly Father's presence is what brought about a complete change to my frame of mind. As I sat there, awaiting my procedure, I finally began directing my thoughts to my Savior instead of my surroundings. All of the sudden, I was completely calm as I began to live out the verse that says, "Do not be anxious about anything, but in every situation, by prayer and petition, with thanksgiving, present your requests to God. And the peace of God, which transcends all understanding, will guard your hearts and your minds in Christ Jesus" (Phil. 4:6–7). In the midst of this trying circumstance, knowing I was bound for the operating room, I had peace that passes all understanding. I knew the Great Physician was healing me, even from that very moment.

God placed six simple words in my mind to bring me consolation: Jesus is my refuge and strength.

As I lay flat on my back on the operating table for

approximately three hours, there were times when I experienced some discomfort and even acute pain. In those difficult moments, God placed six simple words in my mind to bring me consolation: Jesus is my refuge and strength. He was the source of my comfort even in the midst of a very uncomfortable situation. God used the hands of an experienced surgeon to repair the damaged artery in my leg using twenty-five miniature coils. Yet the true healing came from Jesus Christ, for God's Word says, "By his wounds we are healed" (Isa. 53:5). Divine healing can only come from our Heavenly Father, for He is our Healer. I praise Him for healing my body. God raised me to life when I was born. Once again, He has raised me up for His glory.

For nearly three months, I had mostly sat on our living room sofa, unable to do little more than walk to the kitchen or restroom. After much prayer and rest, there was some very slow, but gradual improvement. I returned to teaching school in early September, even before I was better, knowing my students needed a consistent teacher. The increased level of activity slowed my progress, causing several setbacks. Eventually, the pain, cramps, and swelling increased to the point where I had to stay home on medical leave. Nonetheless, God continued to work on my behalf. Following my surgery, I only experienced a small amount of discomfort. What a blessing not to be writhing in pain after such a long struggle with this battle. Although sitting on my living room sofa for two weeks following the surgery was quite monotonous, it was a joy to know I was on the road to recovery!

Reflecting back on this lengthy health battle, I can see how the enemy sought to harm me, both physically and spiritually. But I echo the words of Joseph, who said to his brothers, "'You intended to harm me, but God intended it for good to accomplish what is now being done'" (Gen. 50:20). Satan may have attempted to destroy me, but God will always work things together for my good (Rom. 8:28). Even in the darkest days of this trial, I knew no weapon formed against me would prosper

(Isa. 54:17). I had full confidence that God would complete the work He started and I would be victorious.

Inevitably, there were times I became discouraged, especially when I saw little progress in my recovery. I wondered if I would ever be able to get back to even doing simple things like sweeping the floor, much less setting out for mission trips with my dad. Still, I held on to the words of Psalm 40:1: "I waited patiently for the Lord; he turned to me and heard my cry." There are times in life when it will be difficult to wait on God. There will also be times when it will be hard even to have faith. Yet this is when our faith needs to be stronger than ever. We must cling to the hope we have in Jesus Christ, believing He will see us through. Even though my faith may have wavered, I knew God would bring me through this trial, so I could be more than a conqueror through Jesus Christ (Rom. 8:37). God has brought me out of the most violent valleys and helped me forge raging rivers. He will do the same for you. God will always remain faithful.

Chapter Nine

God Has a Master Plan

"'For I know the plans I have for you,' declares
the LORD, 'plans to prosper you and not to harm you,
plans to give you hope and a future.'" (Jer. 29:11)

On September 7, 2016, I began experiencing severe chest pain. Soon I was trembling with chills, wondering what illness was attempting to overtake my body. Even with my strong faith in Jesus Christ, I was quite concerned. Having been born with Ehlers-Danlos Syndrome, there is always a concern for my aorta to develop some sort of malfunction. With the pain being so severe, I honestly considered the possibility of a heart attack.

Before long, the pain subsided a little, so I decided to rest at home to see if it would improve. Then, my dad prayed for me. In this moment of prayer, my fear and doubt dripped away like the condensation on the outside of a glass of ice-cold lemonade on a sweltering hot day. The pain was still present, but I no longer was anxious concerning my physical health. Instead, I had confidence that Jesus Christ would heal my body of all disease, just as He healed those who were sick in Galilee (Matt. 4:23).

The next morning, I sat in the doctor's office, once again worrying about what the diagnosis would be. Having had a heart rate of 130 earlier in the morning, I literally wondered if I would end up in the hospital before the day was over. The nurse had already mentioned the emergency room when I first said the words, "chest pain." Following the initial evaluation by the doctor, the nurse performed an electrocardiogram (EKG). As I lay there on the table connected to the EKG machine, I thought about how fast life can change. One day, I was fretting over paperwork at my workplace and housework at home. The next day, I was undergoing a medical procedure to see if there was a problem with my heart. I prayed the results would bring good news. As I silently prayed, I felt the worry melt away. I knew God would keep His promise to restore my health (Jer. 30:17).

The best words I heard that day were, "Your EKG is normal." What a blessing to know my heart was not only okay; it was normal! Although I was still experiencing discomfort in my chest, it seemed as if God reassured me that all was well. I immediately gave thanks to God for His healing touch. I claimed First Peter 2:24, which says, "'By his wounds you have been healed.'" Instantly, I felt a peace I cannot explain overwhelm me. God's peace continues to help me through trials every day, even in the middle of the night.

In the fall of 2017, I awakened at four o'clock in the morning with a throbbing pain in my lower back. Unable to go back to sleep, I lay in my bed praying until it was time to get up for work. Thinking I may have pulled a muscle or something, I went to work all day, progressively getting worse by the hour. That evening, I was a running a high fever, dealing with persistent pain in my back, feeling quite nauseous. The next morning, my heart rate and blood pressure had escalated as well. By this point, I wondered if I needed to go directly to the emergency room. It seemed something was attacking my body, causing my condition to worsen. My dad and I were both very concerned.

First, I used the Internet as my source for health information, using symptom checkers to attempt a self-diagnosis, something I definitely do not recommend! Satan tried to tell me something was truly wrong with me. Reading about various diseases had me on high alert, for many of the things I read about did not have a good prognosis. At that moment, I rebuked Satan and cried out to God for healing and for peace. Through much prayer, I felt a peace about staying home that day. I knew God would heal me. Following several visits to the doctor's office and two rounds of antibiotics, my severe kidney infection began to subside. After five consecutive nights of high fevers and over a week of discomfort and pain, God healed my body. I knew there was no need to worry, for God has always proven faithful. All I needed to do was go to the throne of grace. God will always help us in our time of need (Heb. 4:16).

Many times, we allow the worries and cares of this world to overtake us. Instead, we need to maintain a perspective realistic to the limitations of our human capabilities, while keeping our focus on Jesus Christ. We cannot assume the world will stop turning on its axis if we take thirty minutes of our day to pray for those

Stop looking at the circumstances threatening to break your heart. Instead, start looking at the One who heals broken hearts.

who are ill or hurting and to seek God's Word for answers. In fact, we will likely find this time spent alone with the Lord will ultimately strengthen our faith and make us stronger.

We have to remember that God will keep us from all harm, not just today, tomorrow, or next week, but forever. Psalm 121:8 says, "The LORD will watch over your coming and going both now and forevermore." When we feel overwhelmed by illness, we must remember the Lord will heal "every disease and sickness" (Matt. 9:35). If troubles come in other forms, such as the loss of a job, a car accident, or a broken marriage, we need to commit to memory the words of Jesus: "'In this world you will have trouble. But take heart! I have overcome the world'" (John 16:33). With God on our side, there is nothing too big for us to handle.

Stop looking at the circumstances threatening to break your heart. Instead, start looking at the One who heals broken hearts

(Ps. 147:3). What Satan meant for evil, Jesus wants to change for your good, as we read in John 10:10: "'The thief comes only to steal and kill and destroy; I have come that they may have life, and have it to the full.'" Jesus does not want you to live a life of worry; He wants you to live a life of joy! We need to fix "our eyes on Jesus, the pioneer and perfecter of faith" (Heb. 12:2). Then, we can handle any situation that comes our way, as we dwell on the "peace of God, which transcends all understanding" (Phil. 4:7).

The Big Picture

You may have read the first part of this chapter and thought of your own life, contemplating questions such as these: *Will God ever give me a miracle? Why am I still sick? Why did my loved one have to die?* While I definitely do not have all of the answers, I can tell you one thing is certain. God will never fail. Just as David told his son Solomon, the same message applies to us today: "'Do not be afraid or discouraged, for the LORD God, my God, is with you. He will not fail you or forsake you'" (1 Chron. 28:20). Even when times are tough, God will always see you through.

God has performed many miracles throughout my young life, the first one being when He raised me from the dead when I was born prematurely. He rescued me from death's door again as a teenager. He has delivered me from illnesses that could have proven life-threatening as an adult. Yet there are prayers I have prayed earnestly, later realizing God would not answer them according to my requests. I prayed He would spare the lives of my mom and my baby brothers. I prayed for Him to allow my Papa Sig, Papa Joe, and Grandma Ethel to live longer. I have prayed for breakthroughs and blessings that often came in some other form than what I expected. Even though God has not always answered my prayers the way I had hoped, I know God is a sovereign God. He has a master plan for our lives. I learned this at a very young age.

I have fond memories of dancing around my grandparent's kitchen table and all through the house, pulling a little dog-shaped wooden pull toy. My Papa Sig had a turtle that he would pull around as we listened to some of my favorite children's songs. What fun we had! We made so many memories together, from visiting the Sponge Docks in Tarpon Springs to enjoying delicious meals at the Kapok Tree and Casa Lupita, two of my favorite restaurants when I was a little girl.

Other times we would join my Grandma Lucille and Papa Sig at their vacation condominium in Fort Myers, Florida. Taking morning walks on the beach with Grandma and Mama was so special. Looking for sand dollars with Papa and Daddy in the Gulf of Mexico was like finding treasures. On the last day of the trip, we would all have to eat one or two ice cream bars, since they would not make the long trip home! Whether we were vacationing together or simply enjoying one another's company at one of our homes, family time was always special.

When I was ten years old, my Papa Sig passed away. It happened on a Saturday night. Even though I was quite young and the details are a little unclear in my mind, I remember my parents and I were at home, eating a nice spaghetti dinner, when the telephone rang. He had a heart attack; there was no opportunity to say goodbye. When I look back on that night, I could not understand at the time why God had taken one of my grandparents. Twenty-seven years later, I still cannot explain the *why*, but I can tell you with calm assurance that God's timing is simply different from our own.

My Grandma Ethel and Papa Joe both went to be with the Lord when I was in my teens. Although we had the opportunity to say our goodbyes to my Grandma Ethel, due to the fact she was battling cancer under Hospice care, there were no goodbyes spoken with my Papa Joe. He was supposed to come home soon from a hospital stay due to pneumonia, but we received a call one night from the hospital. I was in my bed, awakened by my parents delivering the heartbreaking news.

My dad's parents lived next door to us, so I saw them most every day. Sometimes I would be over there visiting when they were ready to eat dinner. Grandma would always convince me to eat a bite with them, and then I would come home and have dinner with my parents. It is a wonder I was not obese as a child! I guess pulling a wagon full of baby dolls, pet bunnies, or my orange and white cat burned a few calories here and there. Grandma would often make her chocolate pound cake for dessert, and my Papa Joe would make his homemade ice cream. Both recipes are still family favorites to this day.

I miss those carefree days of being a kid, hanging out with all four of my grandparents and both of my parents. Losing one grandparent is hard enough, but losing three of them during my childhood was extremely tough. However, losing one parent as an adult was even more taxing on my emotions. Still, I know God has everything under control.

If God is concerned about the tiny sparrows falling from their nest, you can have full confidence that He is concerned about you.

God does not think the way we do. The Lord said, "For my thoughts are not your thoughts, neither are your ways my ways'" (Isa. 55:8). When we are worried about what to make for dinner or what clothes to wear to work or school, God could be thinking about where we will be in twenty or thirty years. When we cry over the absence of a loved one, He is standing with open arms, embracing us with unconditional love and perfect peace. When we worry about whether or not someone we love will receive healing, He could be more concerned about his or her salvation. Even God's Word says the thoughts of the Lord are "profound" (Ps. 92:5). Ultimately, God knows everything about our past, present, and future. His perspective is much different from our own. He sees the big picture.

Imagine looking out a window. As you gaze through the glass panes, you can only see a limited amount of what exists outside. If you strain your neck to see what is on the far left or the far right, your view is still incomplete. You cannot see through walls, beyond trees, or past other obstructions within your line of sight. Even if you go outdoors, you will find that you still cannot see the complete picture that lies before you. God is omnipresent. He can see everyone and everything.

God knows everything about you, even the number of hairs on your head. Jesus questioned, "'Are not two sparrows sold for a penny? Yet not one of them will fall to the ground outside your Father's care. And even the very hairs of your head are all numbered. So don't be afraid; you are worth more than many sparrows'" (Matt. 10:29–31). If God is concerned about the tiny sparrows falling from their nest, you can have full confidence that He is concerned about you.

Perhaps you feel as if God has abandoned you. You may be questioning God's plan for your life. Even Moses questioned God's overall plan, saying, "'Ever since I went to Pharaoh to speak in your name, he has brought trouble on this people, and you have not rescued your people at all'" (Exod. 5:23). Moses could not understand why God would not lead them out of the land of bondage right that very moment. However, God had a much more complex plan than Moses could have ever dreamed.

Through many plagues, God used Moses and Aaron as messengers to help at least temporarily soften Pharaoh's hardened heart. Moses remained faithful, obeying God's commands, even when he could not understand what the Lord was doing. Many years later, God allowed 600,000 Israelite men, as well as women and children, to be freed from slavery in Egypt, and even provided them with abundant provisions (Exod. 12:36–39). Some people might say that 430 years is a long time to wait for liberation from the hand of the Egyptians. Just as God's thoughts are not our own, neither is His timing.

While we measure time in days, weeks, months, and years, God's schedule is quite different, as we read in Second Peter 3:8: "With the Lord a day is like a thousand years, and a thousand years are like a day." Therefore, we must be patient, waiting for His purpose to be fulfilled in every aspect of our lives. Instead of complaining, we need to "be still before the LORD and wait patiently for him" (Ps. 37:7). Then we will find deliverance, just as God brought the Israelites out of Egypt. Even in the midst of the most trying circumstances, God will protect us from harm.

Plans Can Change

While we examine the bigger picture of life, we must realize that plans can often change. For ten years, I was greatly involved with an agricultural youth organization. Through my involvement in this program, I grew as a public speaker, increased my knowledge of agriculture, and honed my leadership skills. From serving as a county and district officer to competing at the state level, my experiences within this organization are ones that I will always recall with great fondness.

One of my favorite activities was livestock judging. I am not sure if it was the actual judging of the animals, the opportunity to travel throughout the state to various farms and competitions, or the livestock judging coach I held with high regard, but all of these factors combined certainly had a lot to do with piquing my interest. One of my favorite livestock judging memories was when I competed on an enormous ranch in Alachua County, Florida. The awards ceremony was inside one of their barns, designed as a small arena with bleacher seating. The barn was so ornate that it had carpet where the cattle would walk and a chandelier adorning the ceiling! The best part was that my parents were able to come with me and share the experience of visiting this elaborate agricultural complex.

On another occasion, I remember my first time competing at the Florida State Fair. For this competition, team members had to give oral reasons. In short, this is where you stand before a judge and orally tell them your justification for ranking the animals in a particular order. While I generally was not nervous talking in front of people, walking into the office with a stern looking gentleman, wearing a cowboy hat and lacking a friendly disposition, was somewhat terrifying. The entire time I was in there, from "hello" to "thank you," he said absolutely nothing, no reaction at all. Despite the fact that I have no recollection of what I said that day, our team ranked in the top three.

While there were many exciting judging events, there was one particular day when my enthusiasm for judging livestock nearly cost me my life. One afternoon, I was due in town to attend a livestock judging practice. Before getting ready to go, I rode my adult-size tricycle down our grassy driveway to retrieve the mail. As I was heading back toward the house, I hit a rut in the driveway, sending the tricycle one direction and me in another, right into the barbed wire fence. Somehow, I managed to pick myself off the ground, turn the tricycle right side up, and slowly make my way back to my dad's workshop. Yes, you read that right. Not the house, where I would find bandages, antiseptic, and of course, my mom, who could help me survey my injury. Instead, I went to the utility sink in our outbuilding. I thought I would wash it off real quick, so I could still go to judging practice. I had the false impression that a bit of water and a couple of paper towels should be good enough.

As soon as I got in the house, my mom practically panicked. The barbed wire had cut a deep gash in the side of my neck, dangerously close to my jugular vein. Yes, the critical vein, which carries life-giving blood from the head to the heart. My mom applied pressure on it and drove me to the doctor right away, where my dad met us in town. Our family physician cleaned out the wound and stitched it up. In case you wondered, I ultimately missed judging practice that day.

While I did not learn about surveying livestock that day, I did learn a valuable lesson. I learned the importance of putting God's plan ahead of my own. In my haste to maintain my plan for the afternoon, I further jeopardized my health by going to our outbuilding before going straight to the house. Instead of considering my well-being, I focused on what I wanted to do. My own desires could have cost me my life. I thank God for His mercy and grace, in healing me, preventing infection, and protecting me from sustaining a more serious injury.

As an adult, I strive to be more in tune with God's still, small voice. I am more interested in following Him where He leads, rather than blazing my own trail, for He always knows best. My dad and I occasionally watch reruns of classic, family-friendly television sitcoms. One of my favorites is *Father Knows Best*. I think it is because I identify with the two daughters in the show, Betty and Kathy, since I have always been a "Daddy's Girl" (and a "Mama's Girl" as well). The title of this show fits my own dad very well. My dad has a wealth of knowledge and good advice. Nevertheless, my Heavenly Father is the One who knows best in any and every situation. He is the One in whom I put my trust.

Trusting God's Plan

Growing up, I decided I would be married by the age of twenty-five, with a gorgeous two-story home, complete with an elevator, an island kitchen, and a great room featuring a set of ornate French doors leading out to an inviting patio. Not to mention beautiful hardwood floors, granite countertops, and stainless steel appliances. Now, as a thirty-seven-year-old young woman, I realize I was a little off course when orchestrating adulthood in my young adolescent mind. According to my original "plan," I am twelve years late getting married with no prospects in sight. Even so, I know God has a master plan far greater than anything I could ever dream.

People often ask me if I plan to get married. Even close friends have hinted at the notion of setting up a date for me. While I know they mean well, I have little desire to interfere with God's plan for my life. If it is God's will for me to marry, I know He will guide and direct me, as He has done for thirty-seven years. I do not need to search high and low for the person God may have selected for me, for God knows exactly where to find me at His appointed time. My primary desire is to follow His leading, with the knowledge that He will order my steps according to His perfect will.

Psalm 37:23 (NLT) tells us, "The Lord directs the steps of the godly. He delights in every detail of their lives." God cares about every aspect of our lives. I trust Him completely. My life does not depend on where I want to go and what I want to do.

God has a master plan for our lives, not just today, but for all of eternity.

Whether it is getting married, adopting a child, ministering in a foreign land, or a myriad of other opportunities that may arise, I want to be in the center of God's divine will. Only then will I find true peace. Only then will I be under the shadow of His wings. Only then will I find joy unspeakable and full of glory. My desire is not to follow my own path, but to go where the Lord leads. His plans will always far exceed my own.

God's master plan is not only for a select few. He has mapped out the intricate details of my life, your life, and the lives of every other person on this planet. Yet it is up to us to seek His wisdom and follow the path He has set before us. As I can tell you from personal experience, the path may not always be smooth. You may wonder why the God who loves you would allow you to endure hardship. God's ways are perfect, but we often stray from His will. The imperfect nature of this world will try to draw us in, seeking to destroy our ties to the Lord altogether.

The enemy comes around "looking for someone to devour" (1 Pet. 5:8 NLT). We must pray for God's protection, asking Him to shield us from all evil. Unlike the evils of the world, everything God does and everything God says is perfect. Second Samuel 22:31 says, "The LORD's word is flawless; he shields all who take refuge in him." God will be our refuge in times of trouble (Deut. 33:27). He plans to prosper us and to give us hope and a future (Jer. 29:11). So do not fear. Trust God in all you do. God has a master plan for our lives, not just today, but for all of eternity.

Chapter Ten

Mountains of Faith

"If ye have faith as a grain of mustard seed, ye shall say unto this mountain, Remove hence to yonder place; and it shall remove; and nothing shall be impossible unto you." (Matt. 17:20 KJV)

One of my favorite places to visit is Washington State. In the Pacific Northwest, it seems even the most perceptive photographer or the most astute artist could never capture the miles-long mountain vistas adequately. Following a picturesque cruise to Alaska, we visited Mount Rainier National Park, where we spent a few nights at Paradise Inn. Built in 1916, this lodge is one of the "Great Lodges of the West."[1] The only thing more beautiful than the lodge itself is its surroundings. For this particular lodge sits in the shadow of Mount Rainier, a majestic mountain crowned with a snow and glacier covered peak year-round. No matter where you stand in and around the lodge, there are captivating views of mountain vistas. The lobby décor includes gorgeous woodwork, hand-painted lampshades, and enormous stone fireplaces. The dining hall serves succulent dishes that would satisfy the taste buds of the most discerning palette. Of course, the main attraction will always be the mountain. God's handiwork always outshines man-made monuments.

The first time I laid eyes on Mount Rainier, I was in awe. The atmosphere is so clean and fresh, with the smell of Evergreen trees permeating the air. The views are breathtakingly beautiful. The name of the inn is fitting because it truly does feel like you have stepped into paradise. I have traveled to several locations in my life where I felt entirely safe, where I was virtually stress-free, and where it seemed like nothing could jolt the peace filling my soul. While our entire stay at Paradise Inn certainly fit these criteria, we encountered a major interruption on the way to the airport, for this seemingly perfect day that started with a huge smile on my face would transform itself into one where my eyes were streaming with tears.

As we were driving between Mount Rainier National Park and the Seattle-Tacoma International Airport, a mother deer charged toward the front end of our vehicle. We swerved, braked, and did everything we could do to avoid hitting the deer, but it was no use. When we finally came to a complete stop, I looked back at the deer in the middle of the road. Although my first thought should have been one of gratefulness for our safety, I happened to notice a couple of fawns standing on the other side of the road in the grass, looking toward what appeared to be their mother lying there, still and unmoving. The fact they would have to go through the rest of their lives without their mother overwhelmed me. With this thought in mind, tears began to stream down my face.

You see, I was not only grieving over the deer; I saw myself in those precious fawns. One moment, they were walking with their mother, having a perfectly good day. The next moment, their lives turned upside down. The shock, the sadness, and the disbelief all came back to me in a wave of emotion, reliving the moment my mom went to be with the Lord. I had cried before, but this time it was different. In this moment, I let the tears flow like a river. Somehow, I feel as if God used these tears to cleanse the sorrow that attempted to overshadow everything I did. Through this experience, God showed me that life goes on. He showed me that even though life would never be the same, my dad and I could find a new normal.

Since that day, I realized several things were not apparent to me in the midst of those circumstances. First, God sent His angels to protect us, bringing our vehicle to a complete stop. Neither my dad nor I received any injuries. The air bags did not even deploy. How much worse it could have been! The volunteer firefighter we spoke to before heading back to Seattle said a local family could use the venison from the mother deer and he was hopeful that another deer would adopt the two orphan fawns. While none of these things on their own made this a good experience, I see now that God did take this unfortunate situation and turn it around for good. Through this detour on our journey, God provided food for a family's table, and God reminded my dad and me that He had not forgotten us.

Perhaps you are struggling to find emotional healing from a detour in your life that has left you battered and scarred. Is there an insurmountable mountain you cannot seem to climb? God will move the mountain out of your way. Have faith and believe. Jesus said, "Whosoever shall say unto this mountain, Be thou removed, and be thou cast into the sea; and shall not doubt in his heart, but shall believe that those things which he saith shall come to pass; he shall have whatsoever he saith" (Mark 11:23 KJV). God's Word says we can move mountains through our faith in God.

Before you start jumping to conclusions, this does not mean we will actually be sitting atop a gigantic piece of machinery, transferring dirt, rocks, and gravel from one place to another. Likewise, I realize that no matter how hard I try, I cannot physically pick up a mountain by my own strength. Nor can I bring a mountain home from any of the scenic mountainous regions I have had the opportunity to explore. A mountain is just a little too large to set in the back of my SUV or pack in my suitcase. Yet Mark 11:23 says we can tell a mountain to jump into the sea if we truly believe what the Lord has said.

In life, there are mountains we must climb over, dig through, or go around. They do not have trees, streams, and waterfalls covering them. Neither do they have beautiful snow-capped peaks as far as the eye can see. Instead, they have illnesses, financial crises, and other difficult situations, which arise, creating obstacles for us to traverse. Yet even in the face of adversity, when the sun is going down, our alternate light source burns out, and we still have not made it to the top of the mountain, God will lead us. He will walk each step ahead of us to ensure no danger ensnares us. He will be our guide, over mountains and through valleys. If we have faith, we will see the mountains step aside!

You may question how you could possibly tell a mountain to move. It is very simple. Jesus said we need to have faith as small as a mustard seed (Matt. 17:20). With God on our side, we can do anything! Nothing is impossible for us, *if*—yes, it is that annoying little word *if* that frequently seems like one of the biggest words in the English language—*if*, we have faith. Now, the good news is that God can take a little bit of faith and make it go a long way. One mustard seed of faith can move a mountain. If you believe God can work a miracle in your life, He will move the mountains out of your way.

You cannot change the past, but you can seek a new future. Jesus wants to give you everlasting hope and eternal life. Whatever you are suffering from, whether it is drug or alcohol addiction, verbal or physical abuse, grief over the loss of a friend or family member, or any other problem you face, Jesus will meet you right where you are. He loves you more than life itself. That is why He gave His life for you (1 John 3:16). Call on Jesus Christ. He will help you climb the mountains of life.

The Eye of the Storm

Having traveled to Western North Carolina for nearly two decades, I have vivid memories of being in the midst of the lofty peaks of the Great Smoky Mountains as storm clouds rolled in overhead. There is something oddly fascinating about listening to the booming echoes of thunder rumbling across the mountain ranges. On one occasion, though, we were hiking on Sunkota Ridge near Bryson City, North Carolina, when a cloudburst formed in the sky above our heads. The thunder roared loudly. The lightning flashed brightly. The rain poured down from the heavens, creating streams across the formerly dry trail. We prayed for God's protection as we walked through the water, dodging lightning bolts as we traveled under the towering trees, in pursuit of a safe haven in which we could hide. In this particular location, the only shelter was our vehicle at the bottom of the ridge.

You cannot change the past, but you can seek a new future.

When I look back on this experience, I cannot help but think how this is the perfect illustration of life. There are moments when we desire safety, yet we must traverse a perilous path in order to reach the place where we will be safe. Throughout our journey, Satan may place obstacles in our path to distract us from the end goal of reaching our safe destination. He will try anything to get our eyes off Jesus Christ: an unforeseen illness, the loss of a lucrative job, a totaled car, a fire-ravaged home, a death in the family, or a myriad of other attacks. Through it all, we must have faith that God will see us through every storm. God is the One who will bring us through the storm, shielding us from Satan's grip, comforting us in our time of need.

Ephesians 6:10–11 says, "Finally, be strong in the Lord and in his mighty power. Put on the full armor of God, so that you can take your stand against the devil's schemes." We must "take up the shield of faith," so we "can extinguish all the flaming arrows of the evil one" (Eph. 6:16). We do not have to live under Satan's authority. With God's power, we can put out all of the fires the devil sends our way.

Bear in mind, wearing the armor of God provides *protection*, not *perfection*. We will still face many trials. We will encounter rocks in the road. We may even stumble and fall, but God will pick us up and dust us off, helping us continue our journey. If we are not careful, though, the rocks we encounter on the path ahead of us may prevent us from seeing the beauty around us.

One day, I was taking a walk with my dad along the banks of Raven's Fork Branch in Cherokee, North Carolina. Instead of viewing the awe-inspiring scene, I was focusing all of my attention on the trail itself. I painstakingly examined each rock, leaf, and uneven patch, so I would not lose my footing and fall over the edge. For some unknown reason, on this particular day, I was paying extra special attention to the terrain. All the while, my dad was telling me about the beautiful autumn trees that were on display. The leaves were brilliant shades of red, orange, and yellow. God had used His paintbrush to produce a breathtaking landscape. If I had continued to focus on the rocks in my path, instead of finally looking around me, I would have missed the beauty of God's handiwork. I would not have been able to absorb the enormity of the unique rainbow of colors God used to decorate the mountainside.

The parallel between the literal rocks in my path and the figurative rocks we encounter on a daily basis is remarkable. Just as I focused on the rocks in my path, we may set our focus on something we lack rather than thanking God for something He has already given us. When we have such a narrow focus, we may miss a blessing from God. Instead, we should try to see things in an entirely different light.

There is a commonly told story of a young boy whose father took him to a rural area. His father wanted him to see how well off they were financially, so he thought he would do so by showing him how a local farming family lived.

On the way home from their tour of the farm, the dad asked

the son, "What did you learn today, son?"

"Well, Dad," the young boy began. "I learned that we have a backyard that goes to our fence, but they have a backyard that reaches as far as the eye can see. I noticed we have one dog, but they have three dogs and many other animals. Oh, and we have a small swimming pool made out of concrete, but they have a creek that has no end. We get our food at the grocery store, but most of their food is fresh from their farm. We have a security system and a fence to protect us, but they are surrounded and protected by loving neighbors and friends."

After contemplating the response he had given his father, the child said, "Thanks, Dad, for showing me how poor we really are!"

Contrary to his dad's belief that his son would be able to see how wealthy they were, the young boy did not see the figurative rocks this family had to step over on a daily basis. He did not recognize the fact he and his family might have been driving a more expensive car or wearing nicer clothes. He did not take into account the things his family had, which cost more money. It did not matter to him that they lived in a ritzier neighborhood. His perspective was that his life paled in comparison. He saw the benefits of a simpler life focused on the more valuable things money cannot buy. He was looking at the beautiful brilliant leaves, not the jagged rocks in the road.

When you are in a proverbial sunset, you will encounter rocks. There may even be moments when those rocks seem like colossal, immovable boulders. However, God will never give you rocks without giving you something bigger and better than you ever imagined. Have a fresh perspective. Rather than staring at the rocks, gaze at the trees.

Remember the words of Paul: "I have learned the secret of being content in any and every situation, whether well fed or hungry, whether living in plenty or in want" (Phil. 4:12). You will be glad to know Paul did not keep the secret of being content to himself. In the next verse, he wrote, "I can do all this through him who gives me strength" (Phil. 4:13). In order to be content, regardless of your circumstances, you only need to remember one thing. You can do all things through Jesus Christ! He will give you strength to overcome every mountain you face!

If you find yourself looking at the problem instead of the solution, you are not alone. Even the disciples found themselves concentrating on their dilemma instead of their deliverer. A storm came upon the lake, threatening to sink their boat. They were extremely afraid and ran to Jesus, saying, "'Master, Master, we're going to drown!' He got up and rebuked the wind and the raging waters; the storm subsided, and all was calm" (Luke 8:24). Instead of putting their complete trust in Jesus to keep them safe from harm, they focused their eyes on the storm itself instead of the One who calms the storms.

Even the disciples found themselves concentrating on their dilemma instead of their deliverer.

Jesus asked the disciples, "'Where is your faith?'" (Luke 8:25). Even Jesus wondered why they were so afraid. Here they had the King of kings and Lord of lords on board with them, yet they still became completely frazzled by stormy seas. Additionally, the disciples questioned, "Who is this? He commands even the winds and the water, and they obey him'" (Luke 8:25). Jesus' disciples had seen blind eyes opened, the lame made to walk, and the dead raised to life. So why did it amaze them that He could also command the winds and waves to obey Him?

Although the disciples had seen Him perform many miracles, we have to remember they were human beings just like you and me. Their natural bodies experienced pain, their minds were fearful at times, and they regularly became filled with doubt. Still, Jesus exhibited unparalleled patience with the disciples, taking every opportunity to teach them how to trust God fully. One such instance is when Jesus rebuked the fig tree, and it withered away. Jesus explained, "If ye have faith, and doubt not, ye shall not only do this which is done to the fig tree, but also if ye shall say unto this mountain, Be thou removed, and be thou cast into the sea; it shall be done. And all things, whatsoever ye shall ask in prayer, believing, ye shall receive" (Matt. 21:21–22 KJV).

It is the Great Commission, not the great suggestion.

While the disciples may have marveled at some of the things Jesus did, illustrations like these served to help them better comprehend the vast potential that comes from faith in God. He wanted them to realize the power that only comes from the one true living God. Not only that, but He wanted them to understand their mission in life. Their calling far exceeded being a disciple of Christ, gaining wisdom from His teachings and following His footsteps. Jesus affirmed their great responsibility when He said, "'Go into all the world and preach the Gospel to all creation. Whoever believes and is baptized will be saved, but whoever does not believe will be condemned'" (Mark 16:15–16). You and I have the same responsibility. Our task is to carry the message of the Gospel to all who will believe.

The Great Commission was not exclusively for the disciples, but for everyone who believes. Furthermore, it is the Great Commission, not the great suggestion. Jesus was not simply hoping we would find time to accomplish this mission. He gave us this directive as a command. When we become followers of Christ, we simultaneously become messengers of Christ. Our job is to tell others about the way, the truth, and the life, for the only way to receive salvation is through Jesus Christ (John 14:6). From the homeless person on the street corner to the wealthy executive in the corporate office building, everyone needs Jesus.

Fulfilling the Great Commission requires more than knowledge of this critical task. We must believe in the Lord Jesus Christ, convinced that He will help us in every aspect of our lives. This belief is not manifest without complete faith. God's Word says, "But let him ask in faith, with no doubting, for the one who doubts is like a wave of the sea that is driven and tossed by the wind. For that person must not suppose that he will receive anything from the Lord; he is a double-minded man, unstable in all his ways" (James 1:6–8 ESV). We cannot doubt, for if we do, we will likely not receive anything. We must trust in God, that He will meet our every need. When we fully rely on God, our faith will strengthen. When we speak the name of Jesus, He will even restore broken lives. One of my dad's songs, "Speak His Name," exemplifies the restoration power of the name of Jesus.

A man was held in bondage
In the midst of the town.
No help for his suffering
Had ever been found.
Then, one day, a stranger came
From over the sea.
He whispered the name
That sets captives free.

Chorus:
Speak His name; speak His name,
The name above all names.
Jesus, Redeemer,
The risen Son of God.
Speak His name to someone

Whose life is all broken.
There's hope in His mercy,
His healing, and love.[2]

There is life-changing power in the mighty name of Jesus. It should be our daily desire to share the name of Jesus Christ with every single person we meet. God has chosen us to represent the Savior of the world. Jesus said, "'You did not choose me, but I chose you and appointed you so that you might go and bear fruit—fruit that will last—and so that whatever you ask in my name the Father will give you'" (John 15:16). Jesus said if we ask in faith, the Father will give us what we need. Yet we cannot doubt, for then we will receive nothing at all.

Faith is necessary to please God. Hebrews 11:6 says, "And without faith it is impossible to please God, because anyone who comes to him must believe that he exists and that he rewards those who earnestly seek him." This verse expounds on the fact that we must have faith; otherwise, we cannot please God. Furthermore, it says we must believe God exists. Even the devil and his angels believe God exists. What good is that to us? We must go a step further and take time to seek Him sincerely.

God is not waiting, ready to grant our every wish. Even so, God promises to provide everything we need, since He already knows our needs. Matthew 6:8 says, "'Your Father knows what you need before you ask him.'" He wants to give us our heart's desires, and He wants fellowship with us as well. We must seek Him through songs of worship, through the study of God's Word, and through diligent prayer.

If we ask our Heavenly Father to move the mountains in our lives, we must have faith that they will actually move (Matt. 17:20). God does not need any help. Yet some people tend to think it is their duty to "help God out." They want to meddle in areas they should leave alone. They want to make decisions before they go to the throne of grace for wisdom. Whether they are buying a new home, looking for a better job, or deciding whether to start a family, some people think they know best. Nowadays, people who consult the Internet on a myriad of topics think they become experts after surfing the web for a short time. Running a symptom checker online does not make you a doctor; no more than consulting the Bible makes you a theologian. Regrettably, this world is full of people who believe they are more knowledgeable than God Himself.

In Romans 1:28, we read of people who were in a similar position: "Just as they did not think it worthwhile to retain the knowledge of God, so God gave them over to a depraved mind, so that they do what ought not to be done." When individuals determine they no longer need the wisdom of God, then they become immoral, corrupt, and wicked. They often lose their ability to reason, to show compassion, and to make sound decisions. When humankind believes they know more than God does, society goes into a tailspin leading to total demise. In all actuality, we have crossed this threshold once again. The world in which we live is full of violence and corruption. Nonetheless, we must have faith that God will see us through the vilest storms and that He will make the sun shine again. Otherwise, we may fall victim to the "depraved mind" mentioned by the apostle Paul in the book of Romans.

Faith is not just something your grandparents practiced that you no longer need.

Some individuals live as if faith is an unnecessary part of life, as opposed to a lifeline to God's amazing grace. Faith is not just something your grandparents practiced that you no longer need. In fact, we need faith just as much in the twenty-first century as they did in their early years. Without faith, it is impossible to please God. We cannot see, smell, or touch faith, yet we can know for sure it exists. Faith gives us "assurance about what we do not see" (Heb. 11:1).

Just as sure as we are certain the sun will set this evening and rise again in the morning, we need to have the same level of confidence that faith in Jesus Christ is the only way we will be able to stand against the wiles of the devil (1 Pet. 5:8–9). Faith is the only way to move mountains out of our way (Matt. 17:20). Faith is the only way to inherit eternal life, which only comes through Christ Jesus. Cast aside your doubts and fears. Have faith in Jesus Christ!

Living Water

When I was a teenager, my dad and I embarked on an all-day hike to the Sand Cave, a popular landmark in the Cumberland Gap National Historical Park located in the state of Kentucky. Joined by several of our cousins, we packed the essentials in our backpacks and drove to the trailhead before daybreak. The prospect of seeing a natural cave covered in countless vibrant colors of sand left us in great expectation. The added bonus of walking atop the enormous White Rocks made this the ultimate mountain expedition.

As we prepared for this daylong adventure, we were sure to ask many questions of those who had previously made the trek. Since they told us there would be plenty of streams and waterfalls along the way, we took a supply of water that would get us to the top, expecting to fill our bottles for the descent. Along the winding path, we saw many beautiful towering trees and native plants. So many beautiful scenes of nature, except there was one thing missing. Instead of flowing with clean water, the streams were stagnant with a muddy composition.

When we reached the Sand Cave, we were pleased to know there would be a waterfall awaiting us. Imagine our disappointment when we only found a trickle of muddy water coming down from the rocks above. Straining the water through the bottom of my shirt, we managed to obtain enough water to make it down the mountain. Even though it was not what we expected to find, we were very grateful to have something to sustain us for our descent to the valley below.

The Sand Cave is not the only place in the world where the water may become contaminated. When I think of discolored water, I immediately think of the river that winds its way through my home county. The iconic Suwannee River is the second largest river system in Florida, flowing for 246 miles.[3] The river has a tannic color, caused by decaying vegetation in the Okefenokee Swamp. There are an estimated 197 freshwater springs that feed into the Suwannee River basin. The Suwannee River Water Management District has the highest concentration of freshwater springs than any other region in the United States. Most of these springs have crystal clear water that comes from Florida's aquifers, the source of drinking water for approximately ninety percent of Floridians.[4]

Despite these millions of gallons of clear water flowing into the river, the brown tint of the river is unchanged. Likewise, when we allow the world to corrupt our minds with its evil schemes, we begin to take on a worldly appearance. Like the water from the springs, which cannot overpower the dark water of the Suwannee River, the secular things surrounding us may overshadow the light of Jesus Christ within us.

Entertainment, like video games and movies, may subconsciously fill individual's minds with violent images and malevolent notions. Careers often sequester people's thoughts with their minds fixed on gaining a promotion, relocating closer to home, or securing a better retirement plan. Routine tasks like cleaning the house, buying groceries, and washing the car may even compete for someone's attention. Instead, we must all put Jesus Christ first in our lives. If we seek His will first, then all of the burdens of life will become much lighter. Instead of blending in with the world, we need to ensure the light of Jesus shines brightly within us, like a lighthouse on the sea.

Whether you live on a mountain or in a metropolis, water sustains life. Yet there are times when water is scarce, like it was on the top of the mountain during our hike. When a hurricane approaches, the grocery store shelves become void of bottled water. Sometimes, though, water is an even more precious commodity. I have been to countries where men and women carried buckets of water from a river with a yellowish tinge, in order to have water for drinking, cooking, and cleaning.

While it is true that we must have water in order to survive, the water we drink on this earth will never fully satisfy. Whether it is water from a mud-laden waterfall or water from the most pristine water source in the Swiss Alps, a glass of water from either location will not indefinitely quench one's thirst. Nonetheless, you will be relieved to know there is one type of water that will satisfy your thirst eternally.

A Samaritan woman encountered Jesus one day at the well. While she spoke to Him of the physical water in the well, Jesus introduced her to living water. Jesus told her, "'Everyone who drinks this water will be thirsty again, but whoever drinks the water I give them will never thirst. Indeed, the water I give them will become in them a spring of water welling up to eternal life'" (John 4:13–14). By using water as a metaphor for salvation, Jesus showed her the way to everlasting life.

When you confess your sins and accept Jesus Christ as your personal Lord and Savior, you will always have an overflowing supply of life-giving water. Jesus said, "'Whoever believes in me, as Scripture has said, rivers of living water will flow from within them'" (John 7:38). Regardless of what season of drought you may find yourself in, take solace in the knowledge that Jesus will supply your every need. The apostle Paul wrote, "My God will meet all your needs according to the riches of his glory in Christ Jesus" (Phil. 4:19). If you need peace, God will grant you peace beyond all understanding (Phil. 4:7). If you need strength, the joy of the Lord will strengthen you (Neh. 8:10). If you are thirsty, He will shower you with living water (John 4:10).

God will provide all of your needs. He will lead you through every valley, across every river, and over every mountain. When you completely put your trust in the Lord, then He will guide you every day of your life. Pray for God to strengthen your faith, so you can watch the mountains move!

Chapter Eleven

Jesus Gave His Life for Love

"This is how we know what love is: Jesus
Christ laid down his life for us." (1 John 3:16)

In my family, Christmas has always been a cherished time of year. My mom would make dozens of Christmas cookies, my dad would prepare a delectable dinner, and our family would gather for a delightful holiday. My mom and I would trim the tree, and my dad and I would set up the train set around the evergreen. The songs of the holiday would ring through the house, including some of my favorites, such as "Light of a Million Mornings" by the Brooklyn Tabernacle Choir, "Come On, Ring Those Bells" by Evie, and "Beautiful Star of Bethlehem" by Betty Jean Robinson, along with many beloved Christmas carols like "Away in a Manger" and "Silent Night." One thing that always remained the same was the fact that Jesus Christ was the center of this beloved annual celebration.

As a little girl, my mom and dad instilled in me valuable knowledge, which has helped shape who I am as an adult. Through their godly influence, I fully understood as a child that Jesus was not simply a character in the Bible, but He was my best friend. He was living and would walk with me, talk with me, and love me forever.

My parents taught me about Jesus Christ when I was very young. They read the Bible to me, prayed with me, sang songs about Jesus, and helped me develop a relationship with my personal Lord and Savior. I asked Jesus to come into my heart at the young age of four years old. My mom, who was serving as the children's church director of our local church, baptized me a few years later at a special children's baptismal service for children who had committed their lives to Christ. God gave me a marvelous gift when He gave me loving parents who introduced me to my best friend, Jesus Christ.

The love of Jesus is greater than any gift given in the history of humanity.

Jesus truly is the reason I am alive today. Without His healing touch, I would have never made it home from the hospital when I was born. My heart started to beat again because Jesus raised me to life. I will forever be grateful to Jesus Christ for showering upon me His unconditional love through the most precious gift of life. The love of Jesus is greater than any gift given in the history of humanity.

Jesus extends the gift of eternal salvation to every single man, woman, boy, and girl. He did not give such a priceless gift only to benefit a small, exclusive group of people. Nor did He give His life in an effort to improve His reputation. Christ gave His life because He loves us more than we could ever begin to understand. First John 3:16 tells us that the sacrifice Jesus made for us is the very definition of love itself. When I think about unconditional love, I not only think of my Heavenly Father's love, but also the love my dad has for me. He would do anything he could to keep me healthy and safe. My dad loves me unconditionally, but his love pales in comparison to the incomprehensible love of our Lord and Savior, Jesus Christ. As a song I wrote says, "Jesus Gave His Life for Love."

A parent loves their child
More than life itself.
Nothing would be spared

To keep them in good health.
How much more love did it take
For God to love the world?
So much to give His only Son
To show us how He loves.

Chorus:
Jesus gave; He gave His life for love.
The perfect sacrifice
Sent from Heaven above.
Jesus gave; He gave His life for love.
He died upon the cross
To show us how He loves.
Jesus gave; He gave His life for love.[1]

Along with the agony Christ endured on the cross of
Calvary, consider the anguish His Father must have felt. God
sent His only Son to suffer and ultimately die for the sins of the
world. Most parents would never even consider giving their
child's life in order to save the life of someone else, even if the
person had an unblemished reputation. Yet, Romans 5:8 (NASB)
says, "But God demonstrates
His own love toward us, in
that while we were yet
sinners, Christ died for us."
God did not give us
something of little value, or an
unwanted gift that He was
trying to give away. God gave
His only Son to save the sins
of the entire world.

God gave His very best,

even when we deserved

the very worst.

God gave His very best, even when we deserved the very
worst. He knew we are sinners and fall short of His glory (Rom.
3:23). He knew it would take a perfect sacrifice to cleanse our

sins. He knew the only road to redemption was through the precious blood of Jesus Christ. Because God knew we could not save ourselves, He gave us the most selfless gift of all. God, the Creator of the universe, revealed His love to us by giving us His most special treasure, His only Son, Jesus Christ.

Hope Beyond a Holiday

Christmas has always been a special time to me, but I must admit, Christmas has changed quite considerably over the years. Ever since my mom left this world to be with Jesus, along with many other loved ones, the dining room table has fallen victim to many empty chairs. There are still dozens of Christmas cookies baked by yours truly, and my dad continues to prepare a delectable holiday meal. One of our favorite things to do at home is to cook together, whether we are making a traditional holiday meal or preparing many other types of dishes throughout the year, such as my dad's cheese and onion enchiladas, chicken and dumplings, or fettuccine Alfredo, and my smothered chicken with garlic mashed potatoes or tuna pasta salad. We also love to bake, with my dad making artisan bread, homemade bagels, and his famous deep-dish pizza, and for dessert, I enjoy making a wide assortment of homemade cookies, cakes, and brownies. I suppose you could call us, Chef Dad and Sous Chef Daughter. Although the holiday season still keeps our kitchen extremely busy, the way we observe this special time of year drastically changed a few years ago.

As a young girl, my parents ensured our family Christmas celebration always centered our holiday traditions on the birth of Christ. Reflecting on the past, we did still tend to have an overabundance of gifts surrounding the tree, although many were inexpensive. Of course, my parents also gave me the courtesy of letting me know they had purchased the gifts, not Santa. We did not observe the Santa tradition in our home at all. My parents were concerned with the notion of telling me that both Santa and Jesus knew everything I did, as this is misleading to children when they find out the Santa story is make-believe. Combining truth and lies is not a very good idea, especially in the training of children. Deuteronomy 6:5 (ESV) commands us to love the Lord with all of our heart, all of our soul, and all of our might. Additionally, this passage says, "'And these words that I command you today shall be on your heart. You shall teach them diligently to your children, and shall talk of them when you sit in your house'" (Deut. 6:6–7 ESV). Our responsibility is to teach children the truth of God's Word, not deceptive myths. I am thankful for parents who took this scripture to heart.

Now, as a young woman, I look back with fondness at Christmas celebrations past. Still, I must acknowledge the fact that many aspects of Christmas are not biblically sound. Sadly, nearly every culture in the world integrates traditions based on pagan practices. Even the days of the week have pagan names. Unfortunately, Christmas is no different, especially since the date stems from the ancient pagan rituals of the Romans who celebrated the winter solstice with a celebration lasting several days. The early church in the book of Acts did not celebrate Christmas. Neither did the Puritans and pilgrims who settled in America. They felt the Church of England had strayed far beyond the teaching of Christ and had established too many human traditions. In fact, Christmas did not become a formal celebration until a declaration from Pope Julius I in AD 350. Yet there is no instruction in the Bible to observe the birth of Christ, but rather to observe His sacrificial death (Luke 22:19) and resurrection.

Although millions of people celebrate Christmas on the twenty-fifth of December, many theologians acknowledge that Jesus was not likely born in the winter. We simply do not know the date and moving the modern holiday known as Christmas to an alternate location on the calendar is not exactly an option, considering the vast commercialization of this economically driven season.

As Christmas gifts and even church-sponsored programs move in a more secular direction, I feel the Spirit of God drawing me in the opposite direction. Instead of the man-made customs of Christmas, I want to place my focus on Jesus Christ. He is "Christ in you, the hope of glory" (Col. 1:27). Through Jesus Christ, we have hope beyond a holiday. Jesus is the "hope of glory." Worldly traditions can never give such hope.

As I have grown older, I have come to realize that the reason to celebrate Christmas has less to do with a particular day of the year and more to do with the desire I have to witness to others about my Lord and Savior, Jesus Christ. My dad and I still exchange a few small gifts, but we have redirected more of our giving to help others in need. One of the highlights of the season for me is to visit shopping malls and Christmas markets, sharing the love of Jesus with everyone God places in my path. During the holiday season, people seem to be more receptive to the Gospel as I pass out tracts my dad and I have written, telling people about Jesus and the reason He came to earth. Giving gifts has no value compared to giving the greatest message of all.

Through Jesus Christ, we have hope beyond a holiday. Jesus is the "hope of glory." Worldly traditions can never give such hope.

Jesus came to earth to save us. Matthew 1:21 says, "'She will give birth to a son, and you are to give him the name Jesus, because he will save his people from their sins.'" God did not send His Son to earth, so the men, women, and children He created would have something to celebrate during the month of December. Neither did God send His Son to be born in a manger, just so He could receive gifts of gold, frankincense, and myrrh. God owns the cattle on a thousand hills (Ps. 50:10). He has no need of any material items on earth, for "'he himself gives everyone life and breath and everything else'" (Acts 17:24–25). God sent His Son to come to earth to live and dwell among us. He sent His Son to be the Savior of the world.

The Priceless Gift

For some people, Christmas is all about the gifts they receive. Granted, I have received much-appreciated Christmas packages from family and friends over the years. I fondly recall opening things such as plaid pajamas with a matching nightgown for my baby doll, as well as the beautiful mandolin I received as a gift from my parents. One Christmas, my parents gave me a shiny red go-kart for Christmas. When my dad drove it home in the back of our Volkswagen Rabbit, my eyes lit up when I first laid eyes on it! Being the special father that he is, my dad let me "test drive" it before Christmas when he brought it home from the local lawnmower shop where he purchased it. How awesome it was to take a spin around the yard with my new set of wheels, even before they were officially mine! Over the years, I have had the blessing of many memorable surprises.

From clothing and jewelry to trinkets and books, I am grateful for the thought that went into every single one of these carefully selected items. Yet sometimes the greatest gift is one not expected at all. I have always told my dad that my favorite time to receive flowers is when it is for no reason at all. Not a gift of flowers for a birthday, Christmas, or some other holiday, but instead, the gift of a bouquet of flowers, *just because.* It makes my heart leap for joy!

Gifts are a special way of showing a person how much you care, but the greatest gift ever given in the history of the world did not come wrapped in the finest wrapping paper or tied with a fancy bow. The greatest gift ever given was an infant child wrapped in swaddling clothes and laid in a manger, inside a lowly stable (Luke 2:7). Jesus Christ was born one glorious night. Our Lord and Savior came to earth a little over two thousand years ago.

So how did we get from the humble birth of the King to a commercialized, multi-billion dollar celebration? From cutout cookies to dazzling decorations, all of the activity throughout the holiday season leaves little time to focus on the true reason for Christmas. While I enjoy many aspects of Christmas, it is my hope and prayer that we can all slow down a bit, amid the busyness of Christmas, and remember that special night.

On the night Jesus was born, there were no last-minute holiday sales. No one wrote Christmas cards to one hundred of their closest relatives and friends, and no one wrapped gifts for the annual office Christmas party. These traditions have nothing to do with Emmanuel, God with us (Matt. 1:23). A bright star lit up the heavens, announcing the birth of the King of kings and Lord of lords. That special night, while quite unassuming compared to the fanfare we have today, was the moment that changed the world forever. Although Jesus Christ was born in a manger, He grew up to save the world.

Every Christmas, I am striving more and more to keep my eyes on Jesus Christ. Even as I select special items to give to my family and friends, I want these items to remind them of my love for them and in turn, the immeasurable love Jesus has for all of us. To me, the greatest joy in giving a gift is sharing my love with someone else. Nevertheless, our giving is small and the gift of God's love and grace is great. He gave us His only Son, Jesus Christ. You may wonder why God gave His Son. The answer is simple. God gave His Son out of love (1 John 4:10).

Following His Father's example, Jesus gave of Himself by healing the sick, raising the dead, and performing many miracles. God's Word says, "Jesus also did many other things. If they were all written down, I suppose the whole world could not contain the books that would be written" (John 21:25 NLT). Jesus helped others more than we will ever know. Then, when Jesus was thirty-three years old, He made the ultimate sacrifice by giving His life, so we could receive the gift of eternal life (John 3:16).

When you think about it, Jesus' level of giving sort of makes that beautiful silk scarf you bought for your grandmother, or the deluxe train set you handpicked for your children, seem frivolous. Jesus gave His all, expecting nothing in return. He emptied Himself (Phil. 2:7). Even now, He does not expect any form of repayment. We will accept or reject His priceless gift of grace, which God freely extends to every man, woman, boy, and girl. While God gives us the liberty to choose, those who reject this precious gift will not live eternally in Heaven. John 3:36 says, "Whoever believes in the Son has eternal life, but whoever rejects the Son will not see life, for God's wrath remains on them." Choose Christ today. It will be the most important decision you will ever make.

Our giving is small and the gift of God's love and grace is great. He gave us His only Son, Jesus Christ.

No matter the season, my prayer is that you will embrace the love of Jesus. Without the birth of Christ, Christmas is nothing. Without Christ, the world would be lost. The birth of Jesus brought love, peace, and joy to the world. On that special night, hope was born; eternal hope found only through Jesus Christ.

I Often Wonder

Several years ago, I wrote a song titled, "I Often Wonder." The lyrics reflect on the perspective of Jesus as He was growing up.

While we do not know everything Jesus did as He was growing up, we know Mary and Joseph provided a safe, loving home for the Son of God. Joseph taught Him the carpentry trade. Mary likely taught Him how to wash His clothes, make His bed, and cook a meal. Jesus grew up living in an ordinary family, even though He had an extraordinary purpose.

Although there is no way to know what thoughts went through Jesus' mind as a young boy and later as a teenager, the Scriptures do tell us that He understood more than His own parents could comprehend. When Jesus was twelve years old, He and His parents went to Jerusalem for the annual Passover celebration. As His parents were on their journey home, they realized He was not with their friends and relatives as they originally thought. Upon returning to Jerusalem to look for Jesus, they found Him in the temple courts, amazing the teachers with His profound wisdom and understanding.

Our focus should not be on a holiday known as Christmas, but on Christ, the Savior, who gave His life for us.

When Joseph and Mary approached Jesus and asked Him why He stayed behind, He questioned, "'Why were you searching for me?'" (Luke 2:49). Then Jesus asked them, "'Didn't you know I had to be in my Father's house?'" (Luke 2:49). Even in His youth, Jesus obviously knew something His parents did not. Luke 2:50 says, "But they did not understand what he was saying to them." Even though He might not have known every intricate detail of the future God had in store for Him, Jesus was fully aware of His calling. He knew His first priority was to fulfill His Father's plan for His life.

One day when He was older, Jesus was with His disciples,

who were trying to convince Him to eat something. Jesus told them, "'I have food to eat that you know nothing about'" (John 4:32). Once again, Jesus indicated that even the people who were closest to Him did not have knowledge of the magnitude of His calling in life. John 4:34 says, "'My food,' said Jesus, 'is to do the will of him who sent me and to finish his work.'" Jesus was not born in a stable just to be a good man. God sent Him to this earth to live and die for the salvation of the world.

As Jesus stood before Pilate, He said, "'The reason I was born and came into the world is to testify to the truth'" (John 18:37). Jesus knew why He was born; He was born to do the will of His Father. Even before He was crucified, Jesus said, "'Father, if you are willing, take this cup from me; yet not my will, but yours be done'" (Luke 22:42). Jesus came into this world to conduct His Father's business. If that meant suffering and giving His life on a cross for you and me, He was willing to fulfill His Father's plan. This is why God sent Him into the world.

On the night Jesus was born, a host of angels notified a group of shepherds in a field of His miraculous birth. Wise Men saw a star in the east, later guiding them to the Christ child. The Wise Men brought gifts of gold, frankincense, and myrrh, which were appropriate gifts, especially considering Jesus' future. Frankincense was an ingredient in incense used as perfume to anoint someone's body. Myrrh was a resin often used to prepare a body for burial, which foretold of Jesus' death on the cross. Gold was a fitting gift for the King of kings. The celebration did not require fanfare; it only required reverence for Jesus.

Let us all strive to move our focus away from the festive nature of the holiday season and instead, place our eyes on Jesus. Jesus Christ is the Lord of lords. He is the Messiah, fulfilling more than three hundred prophecies. He is Emmanuel, God with us (Matt. 1:23). Our focus should not be on a holiday known as Christmas, but on Christ, the Savior, who gave His life for us. He deserves all of our attention, all of our glory, and all of our praise.

God placed us on this earth to worship and adore Him! Not just at Christmas, but all year through.

One of my favorite Christmas carols is "O Come, All Ye Faithful." Like many other Christmas carols, this song was originally written to be a hymn sung year-round in the church. The message of this song overwhelms me with a renewed joy, due to the gratefulness in my heart for the love that Jesus Christ has shown to me every day of my life. That is why I do not see this song as a Christmas carol, but instead, as an anthem for all seasons. We need to praise Jesus Christ 365 days a year.

Originally written in Latin by John Francis Wade in the nineteenth century, Frederick Oakeley is the one credited with providing the English translation as we sing it today. The first verse and chorus express complete adoration for our Lord and Savior:

O come, all ye faithful,
Joyful and triumphant,
O come ye, O come ye to Bethlehem;
Come and behold Him
Born the King of angels;

Chorus:
O come, let us adore Him,
O come, let us adore Him,
O come, let us adore Him,
Christ, the Lord.[2]

The glory of Christmas does not stem from the twinkling lights or lavish gifts. The wonder of Christmas comes solely from the miraculous birth of the King of all kings. We should celebrate the wondrous gift God gave to the world. Let us behold Him in all of His magnificent glory. Let us adore Jesus Christ, our Lord and Savior! The word *adore* originates from the Latin word *adorare*, which means "to worship."[3] We need to spend time worshiping Jesus Christ. He alone deserves our adoration and our praise.

Jesus Christ was born so He could give His life for you and me. He came to earth so we could receive salvation through Him. Now He sits at the Father's right hand. Jesus loves us more than we could possibly fathom, and He will never stop loving you and me. Let us worship Him forevermore. O come, let us adore Him!

Chapter Twelve

Life Is a Mission Field

*"He said to them, 'Go into all the world and
preach the gospel to all creation.'" (Mark 16:15)*

One evening in 2014, my phone rang unexpectedly. A friend
called to tell me how the Florida Worship Choir and Orchestra
would be traveling to New York City to share the Gospel of
Jesus Christ through song. When I heard words like Central Park,
Times Square, Carnegie Hall, and Brooklyn Tabernacle, I was in
awe of the doors God had opened for this particular ministry. I
never expected then that God would provide a way for me to be
a part of this incredible mission trip.

God walked ahead of us every step of the way, from the
moment we began making travel plans. Through this trip, I
developed a deeper understanding of how we are a reflection of
Christ to everyone around us. People look at us to see if we are
smiling or if we look angry, if we are kind or rude to others, and
if we really love our neighbors as ourselves. We do not have to be
on a mission trip to witness to others. We are living testimonies
of God's redemptive grace. Life itself is a mission field.

The moment I arrived at the airport, the excitement began to
build. New York City is one of my favorite cities to visit. Even
though my hometown is a small rural community in Florida, I
love the hustle and bustle of this populous metropolitan area.
This time, though, I began to look at people more closely. I saw
more clearly the hurt in their eyes, the brokenness of their spirits,
and the longing for something more. I talked to young and old
alike about the love of Jesus Christ. I prayed God would use me

to encourage everyone around me. I wanted this trip to be more than an enjoyable trip to the Big Apple. I wanted this to be a life-altering experience. While I was praying that God would change other people's lives, I did not even realize He was changing my life as well. I came home with a newfound boldness of faith. God rejuvenated my spirit and strengthened the desire in my heart to tell others about the saving love of Jesus Christ. This is what I was born to do.

We took the bus from John F. Kennedy International Airport in Queens directly to Central Park in the heart of Manhattan. We each received a bundle of tickets for our Carnegie Hall concert, including a tract featuring the profound words from John 3:16. As I handed them to strangers strolling through the park, I prayed they would not toss it aside, but carefully consider its message. During the concert at the Naumberg Bandshell, I saw people from nearly every tribe and tongue represented. Tears streamed down my face as we sang the song, "This Blood," written by Rita Springer and Paulette Wooten. The lyrics of this song declare the Gospel message in such a remarkable way. To see people who looked so desperate for answers, and to know we were presenting the Gospel of Jesus Christ, the answer to all of life's problems; it was overwhelming. I knew right then that this was not going to be an ordinary choir tour.

We do not have to be on a mission trip to witness to others. We are living testimonies of God's redemptive grace. Life itself is a mission field.

On Sunday, we had the opportunity to divide into smaller groups, ministering to twelve churches in the New York metropolitan area. I had the privilege of singing at Christian Bible

Church in Yonkers, New York. Pastor Todd Brandt and his family began pastoring this church in 2011. The people were so gracious, and it was a joy to worship with them. One of my favorite parts of the day was the Prayer Walk through downtown Yonkers. Stopping to pray along the Hudson River, inside the train station, and at other locations was a very special experience. I pray God will encourage them in their ministry, and I hope our paths cross again one day.

Another incredible door that opened for us was the flash mob in Times Square. Imagine 350 choir and orchestra members gathering in the midst of the "Crossroads of the World" to sing praises to Jesus Christ! What a blessing to know we had an estimated one hundred thousand people within earshot of us that evening. After the flash mob, one woman asked if I was a Christian. I gladly told her that I loved Jesus Christ with all of my heart. She asked me to sing for her. I sang the chorus to my song, "There's Sunshine Awaiting You." The woman who had been so excited about the flash mob turned quite serious and said my song touched her heart. God knew I was supposed to meet her. He knew she needed encouragement. I am so grateful to know God could use me, even in the midst of tens of thousands of people.

Every year, God continues working in my life. It still amazes me to know that the little girl who sang in Atlanta for the first time in public would end up singing on stage at Carnegie Hall. The Florida Worship Choir and Orchestra had the opportunity to sing on this prestigious stage, debuting our recording, *Almighty God*. What an honor to worship Jesus Christ in this historic building. I believe all of the members of the choir and orchestra would agree that we did not just present a musical performance, but we had church at Carnegie Hall!

One of my favorite places in New York City is the Brooklyn Tabernacle. We had the privilege of singing at the Tuesday evening prayer service during our time in New York. What a joy to minister to the congregation and to worship Jesus Christ with them! The anointing of the Holy Spirit was present throughout the entire service. My heart was overflowing with joy after spending quality time in the presence of the Lord. We went there to minister, and we received a tremendous blessing ourselves.

As I look back on our mission to New York, I stand amazed when I think of the unexpected blessings God bestowed upon us, even before we left home. I stepped out on faith and requested donations online to help cover the cost of the trip. Three days later, God provided funds, which exceeded my original goal. The very moment I reached my goal, God reaffirmed the fact that He was the One who had called me to participate in this mission trip.

Just as He called me, He is calling you to the mission field as well. Everywhere around us, there are people who need to know everything is going to be okay. They need a smile, a hug, or a word of encouragement. They need to know the Almighty God loves them beyond measure. You do not have to be on a mission trip in a foreign land, or even in another state, to tell someone that Jesus loves them. You could be at the grocery store, riding the subway, or talking to a colleague at work. Every person on this earth needs everlasting hope. Tell someone today that there is eternal hope in Jesus Christ!

Looking Beyond

Every single day, I yearn for God to swing wide the doors of opportunity for me to minister to even more people around the world. Like me, do you long for something more in life? Is there a tugging at your heart to accomplish something bigger than you and your surroundings? Beyond our occupation, our family, and our friends, we are all here for a greater purpose. God has placed us on this earth to fulfill a divine calling in our lives. We are here to tell others about Jesus Christ and His love. Just as we look beyond a picturesque sunset and anticipate the dawning of a brand new day, we must look beyond our current circumstances and fix our eyes on Jesus Christ.

Virgil Prentiss Brock penned the lyrics for the song, "Beyond the Sunset," following an inspiring conversation one evening in 1936. The topic of conversation revolved around an unusually gorgeous sunset in Winona Lake, Indiana. Virgil's cousin, Horace Burr, who was blind, commented that it was "'a wonderful sunset.'"[2]

Someone mentioned how he always talked about seeing. Horace replied, "'I *can* see. I see through other people's eyes, and think I often see more; I see beyond the sunset.'" The phrase, "'beyond the sunset,'" struck Virgil deeply. Later that evening, Virgil and his wife, Blanche, sat down at the piano to write the words and music to this beautiful hymn.

Prayer should be our first course of action, not our last resort.

What an astonishing story; a man who could not see ultimately had greater vision than those with perfect eyesight. Through his family's description of the beauty set before them, Horace saw more than a lake and a sunset. He could look beyond the physical limitations of this world in order to catch a glimpse of something that seemed almost heavenly.

How many times in life do we look at our current situation and begin to succumb to a state of hopelessness and despair? Perhaps you see your children hanging out with the wrong crowd. Instead of asking God for help, your mind first goes into a tailspin of the possible outcomes. Will they try drugs, participate in underage drinking, have sex before marriage, or be imprisoned? Even worse, will they put themselves in a predicament that costs them their life? After you evaluate the myriad of possibilities, then you finally stop to pray about it.

Since when did prayer become the last possible course of action? Prayer should be our first course of action, not our last resort.

We need to stop dwelling on the problems of this earth. Instead, we need to pray and have faith that God is working all things together for our good (Rom. 8:28). Jesus Christ is the answer to every problem in life. Hebrews 12:2 says we should fix our eyes on Jesus. It does not say to look around the world to see if there is a better alternative. This verse clearly tells us to look at Jesus, the "pioneer and perfecter of faith." Even when we do not see a way out and our own vision clouds our view, He will strengthen our faith. We must look beyond our circumstances and keep our focus on Jesus Christ. Only then will we be able to fulfill the calling the Lord has placed on our lives.

Follow His Call

You may feel you do not have a calling, only because you are not currently serving as a pastor, Sunday school teacher, musician, singer, choir director, or deacon. Nevertheless, God has placed a special call on each of our lives. This calling may not require us to have a leadership role within our church. Your individual mission may be to visit and encourage shut-ins, clean the church sanctuary, or contribute financial gifts to the Lord's work. Your calling may be to write notes of encouragement for those who are grieving, to crochet blankets for nursing home residents, or to help serve meals at the local soup kitchen. You could serve the Lord countless other ways. God may be calling you to be a prayer warrior, going to the throne of grace on behalf of people who are suffering from illnesses, battling addictions, or enduring heartache of some kind. Ask God to show you what He wants you to do. He will reveal His purpose for your life.

When I think of someone who follows the call of God, I remember a special woman of God who attends the Brooklyn Tabernacle in New York. When people visit this church for the first time, they are likely to have the opportunity to meet this dear lady. When they do, she will hand them a Gospel tract, but this is no ordinary tract. She painstakingly handwrites every single one of them on a small spiral bound notepad, filling each page with her testimony and scriptures. She is a remarkable example of someone who recognizes her calling and pursues it with fervor.

Perhaps you feel as if you do not have the qualifications to fulfill the will of God in your life. You may feel inadequate. I want to reassure you. When we feel inadequate, God is more than enough! He has given each of us the gifts and talents we need to follow the call He has placed on our lives. In Romans 12:6–8, Paul wrote, "We have different gifts, according to the grace given to each of us. If your gift is prophesying, then prophesy in accordance with your faith; if it is serving, then serve; if it is teaching, then teach; if it is to encourage, then give encouragement; if it is giving, then give generously; if it is to lead, do it diligently; if it is to show mercy, do it cheerfully." No matter what task God has assigned to you, He has also given you the tools you need to accomplish the assignment.

God has given you a special ability unlike that of any other individual on this planet. First Timothy 4:14 says, "Do not neglect your gift." Do not be like Jonah, running away from the Lord's call. His calling was to preach to the people of Nineveh because of the wickedness in their region (Jon. 1:2). Jonah ignored God's command. The Bible says, "Jonah ran away from the LORD" (Jon. 1:3). He did not even contemplate the pros and cons of going to Nineveh. Instead, he embarked on a ship bound for Tarshish. God sent a storm upon the sea. When the sailors realized he was using their ship as a method of escape, they cast Jonah into the sea following his confession.

Instead of having the opportunity to enjoy a fish dinner, Jonah nearly became a fish dinner. After being swallowed by a large fish, God gave him three days and three nights under the sea to reflect on the error of his ways (Jon. 1:17). After being spewed out of the fish's belly onto the shoreline, Jonah was commanded a second time to go to Nineveh. Apparently, the inside of a sea creature is less than inviting, for without hesitation, Jonah 3:3 says, "Jonah obeyed the word of the LORD and went to Nineveh."

Would it take three days in the belly of a fish to convince you to obey God's call on your life? Are you running away from the Lord, hoping He will not be able to find you? Stop running. God has a job for you to do. It is not because He wants to make

We need to share the Good News with everyone we meet, whether we are standing on the platform at church or standing in the checkout lane at the grocery store.

you work, but because He wants you to live a purposeful life. He has a purpose for you on this earth, much greater than anything this world has to offer. Not only that, but He has given you a special gift to use for His glory. The Bible says, "Each of you should use whatever gift you have received to serve others, as faithful stewards of God's grace in its various forms. If anyone speaks, they should do so as one who speaks the very words of God. If anyone serves, they should do so with the strength God provides, so that in all things God may be praised through Jesus Christ" (1 Pet. 4:10–11). Everything we do on this earth should be for the glory of God.

When we follow the call God has placed on our lives, we will have true joy and lasting peace. God will give us authority to overcome the evils of the world. When Jonah finally went to Nineveh, the Ninevites immediately agreed with the words he preached. Jonah told them God's wrath was upon them unless they decided to change their evil ways. Upon receiving his message, "The Ninevites believed God" (Jon. 3:5). Jonah had a compelling message and God gave him the gift of articulating this message to the Ninevites. When God calls someone to the ministry, He ensures they have the talents, the gifts, and the tools they need to succeed. God will never ask you to do more than you are able. However, He does require us to use these abilities for His divine glory.

When we get to Heaven, individuals who have a personal relationship with Jesus Christ will hear the words, "Well done, good and faithful servant" (Matt. 25:23 KJV). What does a servant do? They work hard for their master. In the same way, we should devote our lives to the work of the Lord. The Bible says we should do everything as unto the Lord (Col. 3:23). Everything we do should be for God, not for man. Whether we are mowing the lawn for our neighbor, donating items to the church clothes closet, or providing aid for a family who lost their home due to a natural disaster, we should always complete the task as if we are serving our Heavenly Father. He gave His only Son to die on a cross for our sins. He gave His very best, holding nothing back. We should strive daily to give our best to Him in return.

We need to share the Good News with everyone we meet, whether we are standing on the platform at church or standing in the checkout lane at the grocery store. Considering recent news headlines, it is imperative that we tell people how they can receive the gift of salvation through Jesus Christ. The return of Christ is closer than ever before, yet so many people do not have this blessed hope. We should be "looking for that blessed hope, and the glorious appearing of the great God and our Saviour Jesus Christ" (Tit. 2:13 KJV). Our primary goal in life ought to be sharing this eternal hope with everyone we meet. This is the greatest message we could ever convey.

Perhaps you believe witnessing to others is a job for your local pastor, or maybe you feel an evangelist would be able to explain the Gospel more eloquently. What about the people in your community who refuse to go to church or attend a revival? How can they hear about the Lord unless someone tells them? Will you be the one to answer the call God has placed on your life? Will you take time to visit someone, to write to someone, or to talk to someone? Will you tell them about the abundant grace of Jesus Christ? You are the only Bible some people will ever read. If you do not tell them about Jesus, they may never know the joy of looking beyond the sunset. Set your eyes on Jesus Christ. Allow Him to use you according to His perfect will. Your life will never be the same when you look beyond the shortcomings of this world and focus on the amazing plan God has for your life! Your mission field is waiting.

Chapter Thirteen

Be Still

"Be still, and know that I am God."' (Ps. 46:10)

Think about the last time you sat still for a long length of time. You may have voluntarily chosen to relax in tranquility for a while. Perhaps you spent time at the beach, soaking up the sun-kissed rays, or sat poolside in a remote location, indulging in the pages of a good book. On our river cruise through Europe one summer, if you sat perfectly still out on deck, you could hear the birds singing their sweet melodious songs in the nearby trees on the banks of the Danube River. What a delight it was to enjoy such a calm, serene setting!

Conversely, there are times when being still is not a choice, but an inescapable predicament. Although I love traveling to Europe, it seems the flight becomes longer with each trip across the pond. Sitting still in a cramped airplane seat is not exactly my idea of fun, but it is definitely worth the inconvenience, considering the payoff when we land safely on the ground, eager to enjoy everything this continent has to offer. The beautiful landscapes, historic sites, scrumptious food, and best of all, the delightful people we have encountered on our European journeys make the seven or more hours of flight time completely worthwhile.

Sometimes we must sit still at the dentist's office or at an extremely long red light at an intersection. Many individuals have to stay in one room for an indefinite length of time when they are ill in the hospital. Those convicted of a crime must remain in prison for the duration of their sentence. Often, it is difficult for us to sit still, having knowledge of everything going on around us. Worry may overtake us, despite our best intentions not to let anxiety overwhelm us.

Moses knew the secret to being still. He had confidence God would protect him and the Israelites, even as the Egyptian army was closing in on them. However, the Israelites were not too convinced and became filled with apprehension. Moses said to the Israelites, "'Do not be afraid. Stand firm and you will see the deliverance the LORD will bring you today. The Egyptians you see today you will never see again. The Lord will fight for you; you need only to be still'" (Exod. 14:13–14).

Imagine! An army was ready to kill them and Moses said, "'You need only to be still'" (Exod. 14:14). Some of them likely thought Moses had truly lost his mind. They may have said things like, "He's been in the desert too long," or "He must be delirious from this long journey!" Instead of being still, they probably wanted to run like the wind!

The Israelites thought they were destined to die as they cried out to the Lord in sheer terror. I am sure the last thing they wanted to do was be still. They said, "'It would have been better for us to serve the Egyptians than to die in the desert!'" (Exod. 14:12). The Israelites had given up on Moses, and their faith in God was wavering as well. Having to stand still as the Egyptian army drew nearer doubtless used up their last ounce of patience with Moses and his unusual response to this imminent danger.

Even so, Moses was unafraid. He put his faith in God, trusting He would deliver them from the hands of Pharaoh and his army. He obeyed the Lord. The Lord said to Moses, "'Raise your staff and stretch out your hand over the sea to divide the water so that the Israelites can go through the sea on dry ground'" (Exod. 14:16). Moses did not question the Lord. He did not ponder the physics of what God said was going to happen. Instead, Moses sprung into immediate action when he "stretched out his hand over the sea, and all that night the LORD drove the sea back with a strong east wind and turned it into dry land. The waters were divided, and the Israelites went through the sea on dry ground, with a wall of water on their right and on their left" (Exod. 14:21–22).

Because Moses did exactly as the Lord commanded, hundreds of thousands of Israelites found safe passage by walking through the Red Sea. Now this was not your average little creek running through a quaint little valley between the continents of Africa and Asia. The Red Sea is 220.6 miles wide at its broadest point and the average depth is 1,608 feet deep.[1] Scientists have tried to prove otherwise, but only God could perform a miracle so great that it would allow hundreds of thousands of people to walk through this enormous body of water.

As soon as the Israelites were safely across, the Lord told Moses to stretch out his hand, so the water would flow back into place. Exodus 14:28 says, "The water flowed back and covered the chariots and horsemen—the entire army of Pharaoh that had followed the Israelites into the sea. Not one of them survived." Through His miraculous power, God saved the lives of Moses and all of the Israelites whom He led out of bondage.

Are you living in fear as the Israelites were? Do you feel as if you want to give up on your job, your family, or maybe even your life? Does it seem the chains of bondage have you bound permanently? I have good news for you. The same God who freed the Israelites will bring freedom to your life. He will lead you to your own promised land.

Whatever has its hold on you, God is greater. Sickness, disease, abuse, drugs, alcohol, depression, or any other problem you face; nothing is impossible for God. You may be thinking, *You just do not understand. My situation is different. I do not deserve God's love. I have made too many mistakes. God could not possibly love me.*

God created you. He loves you unconditionally. He has known you since before you were born. Psalm 139:13 says, "For you created my inmost being; you knit me together in my mother's womb." Before you were born, God knew your name, where you would live, and even where you would be at this precise moment in time. You are "fearfully and wonderfully made" (Ps. 139:14). Our Creator has set you apart. God made you in His image (Gen. 1:27).

God created you for a purpose. He has a plan for your life. He wants to give you a future filled with hope. Jeremiah 29:11 says, "'For I know the plans I have for you,' declares the LORD, 'plans to prosper you and not to harm you, plans to give you hope and a future.'" God does not want you to live a hopeless life. If you feel like you are sinking into a pit of despair, be encouraged. God has not forgotten you. Just as He delivered the Israelites, God will also bring deliverance to your life.

God will never fail you. The Bible tells us, "The faithful love of the LORD never ends! His mercies never cease" (Lam. 3:22 NLT). God's love for you will never run out. The reason you are alive today is that God wants you on this earth for a purpose. Just as God called Moses to lead the Israelites to the Promised Land, God has a calling for you. Be still and listen to God's voice.

Only One Thing Is Needed

People often ask me what occupation I would choose if I was not a schoolteacher. Primarily, my heart's desire is to serve in full-time ministry and missionary work. I could also see myself being the host of my own travel show, or even a professional writer, photographer, lawyer, or interior designer. Another job I would like to have would be serving as an event planner. For two consecutive years, I had the privilege of putting together the end-of-year luncheon at the school where I teach. Even picking out the napkins and plates was exciting to me. My love of event planning likely comes from my mom, who loved to plan birthday parties, graduation celebrations, and any other special event she had the joy of hosting.

In the Bible, we read of Martha, who resembled one of the first event planners of her day. She was busily preparing all of the necessary aspects of hosting Jesus as a dinner guest in her home. Even though she wanted everything to be perfect, her worry overshadowed the most important parts of the occasion, even the guest of honor.

First Peter 5:7 says, "Cast all your anxiety on him because he cares for you." Although this world will attempt to fill our minds with turmoil, we need to focus on Jesus Christ and His matchless love. Amid all of the worry, He will bring lasting peace. Martha learned this the hard way when Jesus visited her home.

God's Word says, "Martha was distracted by all the preparations that had to be made. She came to him and asked, 'Lord, don't you care that my sister has left me to do the work by myself?'" (Luke 10:40). The food preparation and other tasks that needed to be accomplished all sidetracked Martha, causing her to disregard the true reason she was making preparations in the first place.

If we examine this passage of scripture according to modern-day standards, we could imagine the following: Martha is busily making sure the napkins are color coordinated with the tablecloth, the silverware is polished, the hors d'oeuvres are ready, the appetizers, entrees, and desserts are all set, and that each glass has the perfect balance of ice to liquid. Not to mention the personalized place cards, elaborate floral centerpieces, and tranquil background music. A beautiful gathering, for sure, yet I hope I never become so engulfed in event preparation that I disregard the actual event, especially one which includes a divine appointment.

During the time Martha was fretting over unimportant details, Martha's sister, Mary, was in the presence of the King of all kings. Mary fully realized the significance of the extraordinary, honored guest in their home. Instead of worrying about all of the domestic duties, Mary sat "at the Lord's feet listening to what he said" (Luke 10:39). All the while, Martha scolded Mary for sitting there and even complained to Jesus.

Jesus responded to Martha, "'You are worried and upset about many things, but few things are needed—or indeed only one. Mary has chosen what is better, and it will not be taken away from her'" (Luke 10:41–42). He was not concerned with whether or not the dishes matched, if the bread was warm, or if the floor was clean. He had valuable, heart-stirring words to share with these two sisters. In fact, He told Martha only one thing was necessary. The one thing was for Mary and Martha to listen to Him (Luke 10:39). Instead of listening, Martha focused on things that were of little importance, especially when compared to gleaning wisdom from the Lord Jesus Christ.

How true this is in our own lives! Think about the many hours we spend on our smartphones, watching television, or surfing the Internet. Countless things consume our time on a daily basis. Yet how much time do we spend listening to the voice of our Heavenly Father? Jesus told Martha the only thing that mattered was for Mary to sit at His feet and to listen to what He said. Nothing has changed, for "Jesus Christ is the same yesterday and today and forever" (Heb. 13:8). Jesus longs for you and me to listen to His voice, just as He wanted Martha and Mary to listen to Him. Jesus desires for us to spend time with Him, just as we would spend time with our friends and family.

Jesus said, "'Here I am! I stand at the door and knock. If anyone hears my voice and opens the door, I will come in and eat with that person, and they with me'" (Rev. 3:20). If we hear His voice, He will share a meal with us. He is waiting with open arms, knocking on the door of our hearts. The King of kings wants to fellowship with us! All we have to do is open our hearts and listen to His still, small voice.

If you feel you have made an erroneous error in talking when you should have been listening, you are in good company. Just as

Jesus corrected Martha, God chastised Peter while he was talking to Jesus. Peter said, "Lord, it is good for us to be here. If you wish, I will put up three shelters—one for you, one for Moses and one for Elijah'" (Matt. 17:4). Instead of listening to what Jesus had to say during the Transfiguration, Peter was getting ready to move to the top of the mountain. Jesus' Transfiguration was taking place right before his very eyes, yet Peter was preoccupied with possible thoughts of hiring a construction crew to help build three separate dwellings! While this sounds somewhat preposterous, I am certain there are times in our own lives when we have equally insignificant ideas. Instead of listening to Jesus, we make our own plans, which we think will satisfy the Lord. Instead of acting on our own desires, we should seek the Lord's will, fully trusting His master plan.

While Peter was still speaking, God said, "'This is my Son, whom I love; with him I am well pleased. Listen to him!'" (Matt. 17:5). Imagine how Peter felt when a brilliant cloud came over him, and God told him to listen to His Son. I am sure Peter was a little embarrassed, wishing he had petitioned for a mountaintop neighborhood at a more opportune time. All God asked was for the disciples to listen to Jesus. The parallel between Martha's encounter with Jesus and Peter's encounter with God is striking. They both are worried about infinitesimal details. They became distracted by earthly concerns. Through their encounters, they discovered the importance of being still and listening to our Savior. Like them, we need to listen to the still, small voice of our Heavenly Father.

Instead of acting on our own desires, we should seek the Lord's will, fully trusting His master plan.

Complete Surrender

One of my favorite scriptures is Psalm 46:10 (KJV), which says, "Be still, and know that I am God." God could have plainly said, "I am God." Instead, He began this statement with the words, "Be still." This command comes from the Hebrew word *raphah*, which means "to let go."[2] God said we should surrender ourselves to Him, with complete knowledge that He is God. This means we must turn loose of our worry, fully relying on God.

God is our deliverer, our shelter, and our firm foundation. No matter what is going on in the world around us, we must put our complete trust in Him. There is no need to worry over the miniscule details of life, for God has everything under control. Lay aside your financial struggles, your workplace woes, your physical battles, and every other thing that contributes to your anxiety.

You could be at a breaking point right now. You may feel as if one more little pothole in the road of life will be the straw that breaks the camel's back. No matter how hard it is to hold on to that last thread of hope, do not let go. Hang on. God will rescue you. He will always give you strength to endure every trial. Wait upon the Lord, and He will sustain you.

Abraham and Sarah knew precisely what it meant to wait upon the Lord. Abraham was nearing one hundred years old; Sarah was ninety years old. Sarah had never borne a child, yet God had promised she would conceive. Even though "Sarah was past the age of childbearing," Sarah knew God was faithful (Gen. 18:11). After she waited many years, God sent word to Sarah that she would conceive. Although they trusted the Lord, Abraham and Sarah's first response was to laugh. Imagine, a couple who had nearly two hundred years between them having a baby! The idea was truly absurd. Even so, when Abraham was one hundred years old, their son Isaac was born (Gen. 21:5). God may require us to wait, but God will always fulfill His promises. His Word is forever true.

You may feel as if God has not heard your prayers, as He did for Abraham and Sarah. Or you could feel as if God has given you too much responsibility, which is increasing your stress levels to the point where you find it difficult to function and perform daily routine tasks. First Corinthians 10:13 says God will help us when we feel overwhelmed: "God is faithful; he will not let you be tempted beyond what you can bear. But when you are tempted, he will also provide a way out so that you can endure it." Through every problem we face, God will provide an answer, a way out. Do not carry your burdens any longer. Surrender your life to Him. When you completely surrender to the Lord, your load will be lighter. Your nightmares will transform into dreams. Your sunsets will turn into sunrises. Your hopelessness will be replaced with hope!

Even Abraham had to completely surrender to God. He was tested to the point of offering his son Isaac as a sacrifice. God told Abraham, "'Take your son, your only son, whom you love— Isaac—and go to the region of Moriah. Sacrifice him there as a burnt offering on a mountain I will show you'" (Gen. 22:2). I am sure the majority of people would simply ignore such a command, but Abraham was not like most people. He got up early the next morning, prepared items needed for the sacrifice, and made the journey to the mountain.

Abraham did not question God. Nor did he try to make excuses for why he could not possibly sacrifice his only son. I am sure he was saddened. In his human nature, he likely hoped for some other solution. Yet he was obedient, even to the point of being willing to give his son's life as a sacrifice to God. I cannot begin to imagine the thoughts that went through Isaac's mind as his father "laid him on the altar, on top of the wood" (Gen. 22:9). Abraham told him God would provide a lamb, but I am sure Isaac never dreamed he would be the one placed on the altar.

Abraham took out the knife to slay his son, "but the angel of the LORD called out to him from heaven, 'Abraham! Abraham!'" (Gen. 22:11). The angel said, "'Do not lay a hand on the boy. . . . Do not do anything to him. Now I know that you fear God, because you have not withheld from me your son, your only son'" (Gen. 22:12).

Abraham was completely devoted to God. He was not going to hold anything back, not even his son Isaac. After the angel spoke to him, Abraham looked over and saw a ram caught in the thicket. Abraham named this place, "The LORD Will Provide" (Gen. 22:14). Just as He provided a lamb for Abraham, God will always provide our needs. He is Jehovah Jireh, our provider. The Lord will prove faithful, every single time.

God will provide all of our needs, if we seek Him first.

God already knows what we need, even before we ask. Matthew 6:31 (KJV) says, "Therefore take no thought, saying, What shall we eat? or, What shall we drink? or, Wherewithal shall we be clothed?" We do not have to worry about these things, for our Heavenly Father knows we need these things (Matt. 6:32). From food and clothing to perfect peace, God has not left one provision out of the equation. He will provide everything we need to complete a task, to overcome our fears, and to live life to the fullest.

God will provide all of our needs, if we seek Him first. Jesus said, "'But seek first his kingdom and his righteousness, and all these things will be given to you as well. Therefore do not worry about tomorrow, for tomorrow will worry about itself'" (Matt. 6:33–34). When we fully yield our lives to the Lord as Abraham did, completely relying on God for everything we need in life, we have no need to worry. We have no need to fear. We have no need to do anything except to seek the Lord and to listen to Him. Be still and know that He is God!

A Wee Little Lamb

When I was a little girl, tiny baby lambs fascinated me. I used to tell my parents that I hoped Jesus would give me a baby lamb as a pet in Heaven. Although I have never owned a lamb as a pet, I have enjoyed seeing them at petting zoos. One such petting zoo will always hold a special place in my heart, since it was where I received my first pygmy goat named Joey. The owner of the petting zoo at the county fair said he could not afford to have one of his workers feed the baby goat multiple times a day, since its mom had died. I volunteered to feed this precious little animal on several occasions during my time as a Fair Ambassador, since I had also become friends with the owner's granddaughter.

Toward the end of the fair, the kind, grandfatherly man who owned the petting zoo informed me that Joey was mine to keep. Imagine my amazement as I cradled my very own baby goat in my arms. I thanked him profusely, promising to give an update on Joey when we saw each other again. A year or two later, I bought two nanny goats from him at another fair, which led to a herd of pygmy goats running around our family farm.

Raising pygmy goats was very exciting, but it resembled a roller coaster ride, as it certainly had its share of ups and downs. When one of the nannies gave birth to healthy offspring, it was a joy to watch little kids jumping around the pen. On the contrary, there were times when I went out to their pen only to discover that a mother or baby had died during the birthing process.

One time I found myself sitting on the ground with my arm up inside a doe, trying to save the life of her and her unborn little one. Still, it was worth all of the blood, sweat, and tears. From showing them in the county fair to hand feeding them as if I had my very own petting zoo in my backyard, there were moments when I would not have wanted it any other way. God's creatures are incredibly complex. To know He had entrusted me with a precious herd of goats was a wonderful blessing.

In some way, I felt as if God had given me the desire that had filled my young heart as a little girl. Although I wanted a baby lamb, God gave me a baby goat. When we pray, God always answers our prayers. He may answer yes, no, or wait. Another possibility we often overlook is the fact that God may answer yes in a different way than we could ever imagine. Inevitably, God's answer will prove perfect in the end. We need to realize God truly knows what is best for our lives. He is like a shepherd looking out for His sheep.

King David wrote, "The LORD is my shepherd, I lack nothing" (Ps. 23:1). While we are not physical sheep, we do have a loving shepherd who is watching over us every single day of our lives. He loves us unconditionally, not wanting any of us to stumble along life's journey. Without a shepherd to guide us, we may encounter danger, enduring unnecessary hardships. We need the Good Shepherd to keep us from going astray. He will always guide us, while providing our every need.

Even when Jesus was ministering throughout many towns and villages, He was concerned about people. Matthew 9:36 tells us, "When he saw the crowds, he had compassion on them, because they were harassed and helpless, like sheep without a shepherd." Jesus longs to be our shepherd. On more than one occasion, He referred to Himself as the shepherd: "'I am the good shepherd. The good shepherd lays down his life for the sheep'" (John 10:11); "'I am the good shepherd; I know my sheep and my sheep know me'" (John 10:14). Not only does Jesus know who we are, but He also knows everything about us, from our greatest qualities to our deepest, darkest sins. In spite of our many inadequacies, Jesus loves us so much that He laid down His life just for us. First John 3:16 says, "This is how we know what love is: Jesus Christ laid down his life for us." The King of kings loves us more than we could even begin to comprehend.

One of my favorite stuffed toys as a child was a pastel yellow plush lamb I had as an infant. It has a small silver crank sewn into the fabric, and when it is turned, it plays the lullaby, "Jesus Loves Me." I still have this simple, yet tangible reminder of the way Jesus has loved me since before I was even born. Children and adults alike, from all around the world, sing the beloved words, "Jesus loves me, this I know, For the Bible tells me so."[3] The Bible tells us all about the love of Jesus Christ. Still, simply knowing about the love of Jesus is not as precious as openly receiving the love of Jesus with our whole heart.

Jesus does not want a part-time relationship with weekend visitations. He wants to fellowship with us daily and for us to worship Him continually.

Jesus is our loving shepherd who knows us by name. He wants us to listen to Him and to follow Him. Jesus said, "'My sheep listen to my voice; I know them, and they follow me'" (John 10:27). Jesus wants to be our shepherd, our companion, our guide, and our friend. Jesus does not want a part-time relationship with weekend visitations. He wants to fellowship with us daily and for us to worship Him continually.

You may be wondering how you could possibly manage this with your hectic schedule. Your first thoughts may be, *I work forty hours a week, my family needs me when I am home, and I barely find time to take a shower in the mornings.* I completely understand. As a full-time public school teacher, with many other responsibilities, I also find myself pressed for time, amid everything from lesson plans to laundry. While we must complete necessary daily tasks, we can always find time to praise the name of Jesus.

We could talk to the Lord in the car during our commute to

work. Surely, a conversation with the Lord would be more uplifting than the local radio talk show or latest news headlines. That shower we fret over would be the perfect time to talk to God. While it is important to spend time duly in prayer, we do not have to kneel at an altar with our hands folded in prayer every time we want to talk to our Heavenly Father. We can talk to God everywhere we go. I do not believe God will be offended if we talk to Him while we wash the dishes or walk to the mailbox. He simply wants to hear from us.

Likewise, we need to learn to listen to His voice. There are several times in the Bible where Jesus told a crowd of people, "'Listen to me'" (Mark 7:14). It is hard to believe that Jesus would have to request the people to listen. When I see Jesus face-to-face one glorious day, I believe I will not be able to utter a word at first, for complete joy shall fill my heart, soul, and mind. I will likely bow down at His feet, in humble adoration. No matter my reaction, I know He will not have to tell me to listen, for He will have my undivided attention. Yet when He walked on earth, He often had to tell people to listen.

How many times in life are we distracted by the worries and cares of this world to the point where we miss hearing His still, small voice? I certainly never want to find out later on in life that I missed a divine message from God, simply because I was checking my email, watching television, or engaged in some other unimportant task that caused me to miss hearing precious words from my Lord and Savior.

Sometimes, messages from God are audible. Other times, they come through scriptures, dreams, or even other people. No matter what method God chooses to use to speak to us, we can rely on the fact that He will deliver the exact message we need the very moment we need to receive it. Just as a shepherd knows what their sheep need to survive, God knows our every need. He knows where we are, even if we have gone off course. We are never out of the reach of the love of Jesus Christ, for the Bible says nothing "will be able to separate us from the love of God that is in Christ Jesus our Lord" (Rom. 8:39).

Jesus desires for us to have a relationship with Him. He wants us to receive salvation through Him. He said, "'I am the gate for the sheep. All who have come before me are thieves and robbers, but the sheep have not listened to them. I am the gate; whoever enters through me will be saved. They will come in and go out, and find pasture. The thief comes only to steal and kill and destroy; I have come that they may have life, and have it to the full'" (John 10:7–10). Satan comes around placing negative thoughts in our minds, similar to a pack of wolves preying upon a flock of sheep. Jesus wants us to have a full, abundant life, free from the dangers that seek to ensnare us. All we have to do is enter into a victorious life through Jesus Christ.

Jesus told His disciples, "'I am the way and the truth and the life. No one comes to the Father except through me'" (John 14:6). He is the only way to receive salvation. Do not wander around like a sheep gone astray. Run to God, our Heavenly Shepherd. Listen to His voice. He loves you more than life itself; that is why He gave His life for you.

Chapter Fourteen

When the Sun Rises

"The steadfast love of the LORD never ceases; his mercies
never come to an end; they are new every morning;
great is your faithfulness." (Lam. 3:22–23 ESV)

Millions of people enjoy spectacular sunrises every year. Whether viewed over the endless horizon of an ocean vista, the simplicity of a picturesque little lake, or the expanse of a grassy field covering hundreds of acres, there is something soothing about a sunrise. A couple of years ago, I was in Cocoa Beach, Florida, where I had a front row seat to marvel at God's creation as the sun peeked above the horizon, its bright and shining rays reflecting on the waves below. Though I had seen many sunrises before, I stood speechless as the sun ascended toward the heavens. The beauty was overwhelming. Once I had captured the scene in several dozen photographs, I meandered along the shoreline.

Even though I have lived in Florida all of my life, I will always stand in awe of the vastness of the ocean, the waves lapping on the shore, the seagulls soaring overhead, and of course, the quest for the perfect seashell. That morning, I had only walked maybe a dozen or so steps along the sand when I found the quintessential shell. I was so excited. When I turned it over in my hand, I was stunned. Someone had written on the inside of the shell, "Trust Jesus." What a wonderful way to encourage others!

A moment later, a woman walked by and handed me a seashell. Thinking she had seen me picking up a shell, I thought she simply wanted to give it to me instead of keeping it herself. Imagine my surprise when I turned it over and found it also said, "Trust Jesus." As she briskly walked down the beach, I wanted to run after her and learn her story. Instead, I stood there motionless, realizing there would be no way to catch her as she began jogging along the water's edge.

While I completely put my trust in Jesus, I was in awe that someone would take the time to carefully write on each shell and place them inconspicuously along the beach. I pray God will help her continue this ministry, as I am sure it will encourage the individuals who find the special shells along the beach. Sometimes, those with the greatest ministry in life will never fully know the impact of their influence here on earth.

Even if only one person comes to know Jesus Christ, it makes an eternal difference in the life of that person. The oft-repeated story based on an essay by Loren Eiseley introduces two people who were going for a walk along the beach. As they were strolling along, they encountered a large number of starfish that had washed up on the shore. One of them bent down, picked up a starfish, and tossed it back into the ocean.

The other person asked, "What good did that do? Look at all of them. That did not make a difference."

The person who saved the starfish replied, "It made a difference to that one."

Even if only one person comes to know Jesus Christ, it makes an eternal difference in the life of that person.

Would you pick up a starfish and cast it back into the sea? God may be calling you to make a difference in one person's life. He could be leading you to purchase a bag of groceries for the family next door, taking the opportunity to share the Gospel with them. Perhaps God has laid it on your heart to provide a bottle of water and a Bible for someone you pass each morning as you travel to work. God may want you to phone a friend to encourage them or to smile at someone who seems discouraged. Many of us would jump at the chance to go on a mission trip to the other side of the world, or to provide clothing, household items, and food for a family who lost everything they owned due to a horrific storm. While these things are certainly worthwhile causes, we need to make sure we do not lose sight of the daily ministry opportunities God places in our path.

Recently, my dad and I visited one of our favorite restaurants. Upon receiving a pager, we soon started a conversation with a pleasant couple who were also waiting for a table. After exchanging pleasantries, occupations, and the like, with this couple, the hostess escorted us to our booth. While we enjoyed our conversation with these two strangers who had seemingly become new friends, we thought little more about it as we placed our order. It was not long before we realized God had a blessing in store for us that evening.

As my dad went to pay the bill, the server informed him that someone had already taken care of our meal that evening. A moment later, the gentleman we had been talking to as we waited for a table came by to give us a fifty-dollar bill, in addition to the amount he covered for our meal. He said he wanted to bless us.

We could afford to pay. In fact, we even had a gift card we received as a Christmas present. Yet this couple chose to bless us by paying for our meal. No one asked them to; the Holy Spirit prompted them to pay it forward. They wanted to be a blessing. Their simple act of kindness was not so they could obtain bragging rights, but to make a difference in the Kingdom of Heaven. In return, we were able to be a blessing to our waitress as well. The Bible says whenever we bless someone; we are doing it as unto the Lord. Here on this earth, we are the hands and feet of Jesus. We must work diligently until He comes.

When Jesus returns to this earth, He will say, "For I was an hungred, and ye gave me meat: I was thirsty, and ye gave me drink: I was a stranger, and ye took me in: Naked, and ye clothed me: I was sick, and ye visited me: I was in prison, and ye came unto me" (Matt. 25:35–36 KJV). The righteous will ask when it was that they saw him hungry, thirsty, or needing compassion (Matt. 25:37–39). Jesus will reply, "Inasmuch as ye have done it unto one of the least of these my brethren, ye have done it unto me" (Matt. 25:40 KJV).

When we help another individual, it is as if we are helping Jesus. So the next time you make a phone call to check on someone, pay for someone's meal, or share an encouraging word to brighten someone's day, remember, you are doing it for Jesus. It may seem insignificant at the time, but it is significant to God. Even the smallest action, like tossing a starfish back into the water, can make a huge difference in someone's life. In the case of the starfish, it not only changed its life, but also saved it.

Living in Sunshine

On our first visit to Boston, Massachusetts, our journey included a walk along the iconic Freedom Trail, where we saw more than a dozen historic sites, from Boston Common to Bunker Hill. Walking past the Old North Church, from which the famous "one, if by land, and two, if by sea" signal guided the midnight ride of Paul Revere, I felt as if we had stepped inside my American history textbook from when I took Dr. McMahon's class in junior college. Touring the USS Constitution, I began to ponder what it must have been like to live and work on this naval vessel back in the heyday of "Old Ironsides." This trip back in time, so to speak, was very enjoyable, but one of my favorite parts of the trip was the time we spent outside of the city limits.

One day, we rented a car and drove to Walden Pond. As someone who majored in English, I was eager to see this noteworthy landmark, where many literary authors have gleaned inspiration from this incredible setting. Looking out over the sixty-one acres of natural beauty known as a "pond," I was mesmerized at the way the pines and maples along the 1.7 miles of shoreline proudly stood tall as their reflection shown on the water's surface. Nothing quite compares to the gorgeous golden rays of sunshine shining down upon the surface of a glistening body of water.

Without a source of light to shine upon the water, though, there would be no reflection. Without the sun and moon to lighten the earth below, the amazing world God created would be dark. In darkness, beauty begins to fade. The absence of light makes it impossible to see the sparkle in someone's eye, the special flowers blooming beneath a shade tree, or the raindrops falling from the sky. Light gives life to everything it shines upon, from a baby's sweet innocent smile to a butterfly's graceful pattern of flight. Although darkness creates an ideal environment in which to get some much-needed rest, darkness is not conducive to many different activities. It would definitely be difficult to mow the grass at night with zero sources of light!

If you want to experience complete, utter darkness, journey into the deep underground recesses of a cavern. My dad and I have toured numerous caves all around the world. One of the most memorable was the Caves of Drach on the island of Mallorca, Spain. This cave tour ends with a concert on the shore of Lake Martel, one of Europe's largest underground lakes. The musicians perform on floating vessels. Hearing the beautiful melodies echo through the cave system was a tremendous experience.

Another outstanding cave excursion was one my dad and I took in Mexico. We had the opportunity to go swimming inside of a cave near Playa del Carmen, Mexico. This particular cave was a popular place to explore, with guides who took you to a whole other world, swimming right among the stalactites, often only a few inches above your head. The entire experience was incredible, from everything below the earth's surface to the authentic Mayan meal they prepared for us in a cavern-enclosed dining area.

When the storms of life seek to overwhelm you, God will make the sun shine again.

The guide gave us a flashlight that was waterproof, warning us that the light would cost approximately sixty dollars to replace, if we dropped it into the depths of the cavern along the way. Thankfully, we managed to emerge from the subterranean waters with the flashlight still in hand. What a stunning reminder of how quickly darkness can replace light when the guide requested everyone to turn off the flashlights at the same time. I could not even see my hand in front of my face! Without doubt, light was an essential piece of equipment to guide us back to the surface safely, for it would have been quite challenging to navigate the narrow passageways in absolute darkness.

While caves feature stunning stalactites and stalagmites, the numbers of plant and animal life decrease rapidly as you venture farther into the depths of the earth. While there are temporary cave residents near the mouth of the cave and troglobites dwelling inside the cave, the majority of living things cannot survive without light. Light is a vital aspect of life. Yet there is only one light source, which will last for all eternity.

Jesus said, "'I am the light of the world. Whoever follows me will never walk in darkness, but will have the light of life'" (John 8:12). This world is full of darkness. You may be living in darkness right now, whether in the shadows of depression, the clutches of addiction, or another difficult storm in which you find yourself. Turn away from the darkness; focus your eyes on Jesus Christ. He will be your light in the darkness.

King David knew the vital importance of the Lord's light. He wrote, "The LORD is my light and my salvation; whom shall I fear? The LORD is the stronghold of my life; of whom shall I be afraid?" (Ps. 27:1 ESV). Even when the sunset seems it will be eternal, you can rest assured that God will be your light. He will save you from the depths of desolation. He will give you strength. Although the dark clouds may seem unbearable, the dawn will break forth once again. Psalm 30:5 (ESV) says, "Joy comes with the morning." Be faithful to the One who created you. When the storms of life seek to overwhelm you, God will make the sun shine again.

After the Sunset

How splendid it is to marvel at a beautiful sunrise announcing the dawning of a new day! Yet before the sun can rise, first it must set. The beauty of a sunset is in the eye of the beholder. One person may be viewing a gorgeous sunset while on vacation. Another could be seeing a sunset shrouded in storm clouds, from the window of a hospital room. Both are sunsets; nevertheless, they are vastly different. Sunsets could be literal or figurative ones, clouding our view when it comes to realizing true joy.

In life, we will encounter many trials. During these difficult times, we may even attempt to put up a wall to guard our emotions. We try to hide our fears, our worries, and our disappointments behind a façade, hoping no one will notice. Trying to mask our emotions is very similar to an attempt to conceal unsightly blemishes.

Reflect back to a time when you tried every product on the shelf to try to cover up all of those annoying pimples. Sure, some products may have eased the discomfort or appearance, but the imperfections still showed on the surface. Alternatively, consider this: try painting over an unattractive patterned wall with only one coat of thin latex paint. Surely, some aspect of the pattern will still stand out. Likewise, no cosmetics, paint, or other pretense will permanently conceal whatever it is you wish to hide inside your mind, your heart, or your soul.

Nonetheless, people continually look for ways to mask their faults, whether they are internal or external. People jump on the bandwagon every time a new product comes along to bust belly fat, smooth wrinkles, or restore hair loss. There are also products that will numb pain, lessen anxiety, and ease depression. While some of these products may prove beneficial to some, others still find themselves battling their symptoms. Other people are dealing with deep emotional scars caused by abuse, addiction, loss, or some other horrifying reality with which they are trying to come to grips. There are moments when they try to hide all of this baggage, putting up a front that unconvincingly projects the message, "All is well." They walk around with the knowledge that everything is falling apart, but the words on their lips say, "I'm fine, *really*."

Is this you? Do you act as if nothing is wrong, holding back your emotions for fear of looking weak to your family, your friends, or your colleagues? Does it seem like a struggle just to get out of bed each morning? God does not want you to live in fear or misery. He wants you to give Him your burdens, trusting Him to give you strength and to fill you with peace. Psalm 62:8 says, "Trust in him at all times, you people; pour out your hearts to him, for God is our refuge." Do not hold back your emotions any longer. Pour out your heart to the only living God, who loves you more than you could imagine. He will be your refuge, even in the midst of discouraging situations.

Even Jesus Christ, the only perfect individual to walk on the face of this planet, found Himself in the midst of troubling times. One valley Jesus had to walk through was the loss of His friend, Lazarus. Lazarus had been gravely ill. Jesus arrived four days after Lazarus passed away. When Jesus was led to the gravesite, the Bible says, "Jesus wept" (John 11:35). It does not say Jesus put up a front, trying to conceal His emotions. He did not try to maintain His composure. He was not afraid to cry. Even though He knew Lazarus would soon miraculously walk out of the tomb, Jesus was troubled in His spirit when He saw Mary weeping (John 11:33). Jesus felt compassion for His loved ones.

Jesus understood human emotions. He experienced sorrow in this world firsthand. He suffered many things in this world, even to the point of being despised and rejected among men, and ultimately being crucified on a cross, as we read in Isaiah 53:3: "He was despised and rejected by mankind, a man of suffering, and familiar with pain." Jesus, the King of kings and Lord of lords, was "a man of suffering." Imagine how it felt to know some of the people you were sacrificing your life for were also some of the ones who were driving the nails into your hands and your feet. Yet Jesus did not put His thoughts and feelings into a box. He was open and honest, even on the cross.

Darkness overshadowed the land for three hours as Jesus was hanging on the cross on our behalf (Matt. 27:45). God's Word says, "About three in the afternoon Jesus cried out in a loud voice, 'Eli, Eli, lema sabachthani?'" (Matt. 27:46). Translated, these words mean, "'My God, my God, why have you forsaken me?'" (Matt. 27:46). Even God's own Son felt as if God had abandoned Him. Still, I am sure Jesus knew deep down that God was in control. He knew His Father would not fail Him, in spite of the agony He was enduring. He knew the darkness would not last forever and that a bright new day awaited Him. Three days later, God revealed His resurrection power when Jesus rose up from the grave to life everlasting!

I want to assure you that God is our Heavenly Father as well. He always watches out for His children. He loves us more than we could ever comprehend. That is why He sent His only Son to die on a cross for us, for the forgiveness of our sins. He knew we needed a Savior. He knew we could not bear all of the burdens of life. He knew we could never make it on our own.

Whatever you are going through, you are not alone. God will be your anchor. He will give you unwavering hope. Jesus questioned, "Did I not tell you that if you believe, you will see the glory of God?'" (John 11:40). Just as Jesus spoke these words to Martha, He would say the same to you. Let go of your worries, your cares, and your doubts. Know that the sun will rise again. Believe and you shall see the glory of God at work in your life today. A magnificent day shall break forth when the sun rises!

Chapter Fifteen

Heaven Ever After

"And so we will be with the Lord forever." (1 Thess. 4:17)

From the moment I filled out my college application, I knew I wanted to be a teacher. Following my parent's example, I prayed God would use me to impart academic knowledge to my students, but more importantly, to give them some moral guidance as well. During my growing up years, my mom and dad were my teachers. My dad was the principal of a private school when I was very young and has been teaching high school mathematics at a public school now for nearly thirty years. Additionally, he teaches college algebra and statistics for the local community college via dual enrollment. My mom served as children's ministry director at our church. They were both my teachers as well, which is something I will always cherish. Being homeschooled had a positive impact on my life in many ways.

Learning at my own pace, receiving one-on-one instruction, and having the opportunity to spend more quality time with my family meant that I also had more time to focus on the Lord. From playing hymns on the piano and reading the Bible to watching Christian programs on television, like *Gospel Bill*, *Circle Square*, and *Joy Junction*, I was always reminded how much Jesus loves me. Even my curriculum was scripture-based. My parents are the ones who encouraged me to build my foundation upon the solid Rock, Jesus Christ. I put my trust in Jesus, for He is the only One who can provide an eternal foundation. As the beautiful hymn written by Edward Mote in 1834 says, "On

Christ, the solid Rock, I stand; All other ground is sinking sand."[1]

Through the years, I have often heard criticism of my parents choosing to homeschool. People have said homeschoolers lack socialization skills and have no academic prowess. For some of them, this may be true. For me, this was simply not the case. Talking to people has always been one of my favorite pastimes. Considering I achieved a 4.0 GPA on completion of my master's degree, I know homeschooling was the perfect choice for me academically as well.

In many ways, I can see how God definitely had a part in my parent's decision to homeschool. I know the loss of so many loved ones, my hospitalization when I was a teenager due to a perforated colon, and my mom's hospitalizations and health concerns through the years were all easier to cope with as a homeschooler. Surely, my studies would have been lagging behind drastically if I had been a traditional student at a public or private school. By working at my own pace, I was able to work ahead when time allowed and slow down when life threw curveballs that called for a flexible schedule for education.

Certainly, many of my experiences as a homeschooler helped inspire me to be a teacher. In addition to having two wonderful role models, my parents, I enjoyed many interdisciplinary activities. My parents provided scientific equipment so I could perform experiments in my own home kitchen. I explored the enormity of space using our telescope. Trips to the library were almost a weekly occurrence, and we frequently visited the local history museums. Living on a farm offered many educational moments as well. Of course, music was a part of the schedule every day, even on weekends and holidays.

Vacations even became an educational experience, whether we were learning about the geography of the Great Smoky Mountains National Park, the history of the Appalachian culture, or the science behind the formation of stalactites and stalagmites on one of our many ventures into underground caves, such as the

Lost Sea or Ruby Falls. Living history museums, hands-on science museums, and other educational destinations were a part of the itinerary as well. Homeschooling provided countless interactive experiences, causing the academic concepts to seemingly leap off the pages of my textbooks and come to life.

Following my high school graduation from Christ Fellowship Academy, I attended Florida Gateway College (formerly known as Lake City Community College). As a homeschooler who had never attended public school, I wondered if I would be successful in a college setting. Soon I discovered that the zoology professor believed I should be a scientist, the history professor thought I was a history buff, and the professors who taught English, Spanish, and education courses became close friends. I even had the privilege of taking my dad's statistics course, one of the two most special memories I have of my college career. The other treasured memory was taking a web design course with my mom. I earned the only A in Mr. Rigsby's physical science class, and I was a member of the Phi Theta Kappa International Honor Society. Clearly, I had no reason to be concerned about my academic progress.

When I graduated with my Associate in Arts degree, I had the distinct honor of delivering the commencement address. In my speech to faculty, staff, parents, and students, I spoke of the Lord, even in the midst of this secular setting. How awesome it was to share my faith with everyone in attendance. I encouraged my fellow graduates and their families to "value life and live a life of value," something I strive to do every day.

Since that moment, I have graduated two additional times. I received my second college degree when I earned my Bachelor of Arts degree in English with a minor in general education from the University of Florida. Then, I graduated summa cum laude from Nova Southeastern University with a Master of Science degree in English education, achieving a perfect 4.0 GPA on all of my graduate level studies.

Every single educational experience I enjoyed was like a piece of a giant puzzle, each one being put in place by God Himself, all leading to the day when I became an English teacher in August 2006. The very first class I ever taught was an intensive reading class. Having been under the impression that I would be shadowing another teacher, I found myself in a classroom with no books, no lesson plans, and no assignments. I had a couple of dry erase markers and a room filled with eleventh and twelfth grade students staring at me intently. Some of them looked as if they wanted to hear what I had to say; others seemed like they were shooting daggers in my direction with their eyes. Immediately, I knew I needed to begin building a relationship with them straight away.

Therefore, I began by writing the words *confident* and *confidante* on the board. Although I do not recall all of the wisdom I tried to convey to them that day, I know I explained how I wanted them to be confident in their learning. Most of all, I stressed to them how I was their confidante, along with their other teachers, parents, guardians, and mentors. I told them I wanted the best for them, not just in school, but in life as well.

Even bumpy roads can have beautiful scenery along the journey.

I cannot say my first year teaching was as smooth as silk. It was truly a bumpy road for many reasons. Yet even bumpy roads can have beautiful scenery along the journey. While there were students who threatened to inflict bodily harm if they saw me "out on the streets," others daily expressed their appreciation for the way I was helping them be successful in their studies. All along, I knew I became a teacher for a purpose. Thirteen years later, my goal is still to make a difference in the lives of my students. I want to teach them new things relating to my subject area, but I also strive to impart moral values and life lessons.

As I meet young people in the classroom, I am always concerned about their spiritual well-being and relationship with Christ. When I talk to students and hear their stories, I find out that a large number of them put their trust in Jesus Christ. Many others are lost, practicing false religions or even no religion at all. During my teaching career, I have encountered young people who are heavily involved in witchcraft, atheism, and cults. Some believe whatever society tells them. How sad that people can be so deceived to the point where they choose to believe such lies.

In the name of political correctness, the government hinders teachers from openly sharing the Gospel of Jesus Christ with students. When my ancestors came to the New World in the early 1700s, they made the arduous journey in search of freedom *of* religion, not freedom *from* religion. Furthermore, people originally established schools in America to ensure that students would be able to read the Bible.[2]

Although it is against school board policy to tell students about Jesus or to pray with them, I am grateful to God for the way He uses my life to shine forth as a testimony to my students and colleagues. Without my prompting, students often tell me how they found my website and listened to one of my songs or watched an episode of *Be Encouraged*. The fact that God would direct them to my website and use it to minister to them is quite humbling. Additionally, students often comment on how I smile, even when I am dealing with an unpleasant situation. I pray they always see something different about me. Through the Holy Spirit, may they quickly come to the realization that this difference is all because of Jesus Christ.

The World Needs Jesus

When I was younger, I regularly sang a song written by Phil

McHugh and Greg Nelson titled, "People Need the Lord." In the thirteen years I have been teaching, the decline of civilization has become blatantly evident within the classroom. Behavioral issues are at an all-time high because of a society, which is spinning out of control. Many children do not understand the importance of obeying their parents, and others lack any parental support whatsoever. Then there are demanding millennials, entitlement groups, and those with a mindset of pure rebellion. Other people fall into temptation and sin against God. Instead of crying out to Him for mercy, many individuals are running away from God at a rapid pace.

Sadly, many of these people are running away from the only One who can save them. In many cases, morality is no longer important. People follow their own desires, allowing Satan to overshadow their moral principles. Rather than giving in to their sinful nature, they need to cry out for the Lord to help them. We all have an inherent need for the Lord. He is the only One who can keep us safe from the enemy.

First Peter 5:8 says, "Your enemy the devil prowls around like a roaring lion looking for someone to devour." We must be alert, always ready to resist the devil. The Bible says, "Submit yourselves, then, to God. Resist the devil, and he will flee from you" (James 4:7). We do not have to listen to Satan's lies, nor do we have to act upon his evil schemes. As an alternative, we can resist him in the name of Jesus, and he will flee. What a difference it would make if every single person would turn away from evil and turn toward the only living God! He is the only lasting hope on earth. What this world needs is Jesus Christ.

Because of the continuous threat of violence throughout the world, countless individuals live in a world of trepidation, yet they long for a world of peace. Many people are afraid to venture beyond the four walls of their home due to the threat of terror ensuing wherever they go. Tears often replace laughter, and fear surpasses hope. There are so many dangers lurking around us.

From accidents to addictions, people often place themselves in imminent danger. Frequently, perilous times come without warning, due to natural disasters or people who have evil bound within their hearts.

Although the world seems torn apart and divided, the vast majority of countries band together when tragedy strikes. When a disaster occurs on one continent, the entire world grieves for the loss of life, as seen by the ways people pay homage to the affected city or country via special profile pictures and hashtags beginning with #prayfor on social media channels. However, this peaceful nature is short-lived. People come together briefly and then go about their daily lives. Those who may post a #prayfor hashtag one week may be posting vulgar obscenities a week later. Instead of promoting peace, innumerable people are breeding a hostile environment.

There have been shootings and bombings at dozens of so-called "soft targets," including marathons, malls, and movie theaters. Many terror attacks have occurred at concerts, sporting events, and popular tourist destinations. Additionally, nations are rising up to declare their absolute power over one another. Occurrences like these leave people perplexed. They want to know why God allows these things to happen, and they wonder why someone does not stop these violent acts. Jesus told the disciples about the violence that must take place before His return. He said, "'When you hear of wars and rumors of wars, do not be alarmed. Such things must happen, but the end is still to come. Nation will rise against nation, and kingdom against kingdom. There will be earthquakes in various places, and famines'" (Mark 13:7–8). Moreover, He said everyone who stands firm, trusting in God completely, will be saved (Mark 13:13).

God does not desire for people to endure heartache. Yet this world consists of such iniquity, even to the point of killing innocent, precious children. It is extremely disturbing to hear of individuals who murder babies in their mother's womb. For those who believe an unborn baby is not a human, the Lord said, "'Before I formed you in the womb I knew you, before you were born I set you apart'" (Jer. 1:5). Before conception, God knows us by name.

The moment of conception, a new life begins. Therefore, abortion ultimately ends a life and is brutal murder. Truly, killing an unborn child is no different than murdering any human being, whether young or old. God gave us the Ten Commandments, which include His command, "'You shall not murder'" (Exod. 20:13).

While there may be isolated cases where a mother's life is at stake, millions of infants lose their lives every year only because the mother does not desire to raise a newborn. Millions of babies killed, even though there are a large number of potential parents who would love to adopt a son or daughter. Abortion is a selfish act, which disregards human life. Every child, whether born or unborn, is a human being and deserves the right to live.

Before conception, God knows us by name.

An estimated fifty-six million induced abortions occurred each year worldwide, from 2010 through 2014.[3] Since many locations around the globe are not required to report abortion statistics, this number is likely a low estimate. How can we justify killing approximately twenty-five percent of all babies conceived? Sadly, this has become the "norm" in society today. Many people no longer value human life.

When you consider abortion, take a moment to thank God that your mother did not decide to abort you, in order to move on with her life and avoid the responsibilities and joys of motherhood. Imagine how God feels when He sees people engaging in this type of disgraceful behavior. According to God's

Word, the world will continue to be in a state of decline until the moment God restores true peace and morality.

Until Jesus Christ returns to this earth, treacherous things are going to happen. Nations will fight horrifying wars. Earthquakes are going to violently shake the very ground we walk upon. Some families will even turn on each other to the point of death. Yet individuals who put their complete trust in Jesus Christ will find eternal salvation. If you are a follower of Jesus Christ, you do not have to fear the future.

The apostle Paul wrote, "If God is for us, who can be against us?" (Rom. 8:31). There is no power in the world that is greater than God Almighty. Nothing can separate us from His mighty hand or the great love He has for us (Rom. 8:38–39). Regardless of what obstacles we face, "'All things are possible with God'" (Mark 10:27). Nothing will be impossible with God on our side.

A Strong Tower

In the book of Genesis, we read about a man who thought he did not have an innate need for God. Instead of depending on the power of God Almighty, he thought all things were possible without God. He decided to lead the charge for the construction of the Tower of Babel, so he might display his own power. The people of the city, who were also desiring power, said, "'Come, let us build ourselves a city, with a tower that reaches to the heavens, so that we may make a name for ourselves; otherwise we will be scattered over the face of the whole earth'" (Gen. 11:4). The sole purpose of this tower was so Nimrod and the citizens of the city could "'make a name'" for themselves. Nimrod desired wealth and notoriety. He wanted people to notice him and all of his underlings. What better way to do this than to build one of the first skyscrapers of their time!

This displeased the Lord greatly. The Lord said, "'If as one people speaking the same language they have begun to do this, then nothing they plan to do will be impossible for them. Come, let us go down and confuse their language so they will not understand each other'" (Gen. 11:6–7). God knew unity among this determined group of people could result in great power. He also knew dependence on each other could negate a need for their dependence on God. Since the Lord knew Nimrod and all of his compatriots had an intrinsic need for eternal salvation, He caused great confusion among them, changing the universal spoken language to many different languages.

Merriam-Webster defines the word *babel* as "a scene of noise or confusion."[4] The construction of this great tower came to a halt, due to the scene of organization transforming itself into one of complete and utter chaos. Nimrod never fully realized his plan to build a tower to reach the heavens because his desire for power exceeded his desire for God. The people exalted themselves instead of exalting the One who created them. Even so, God was merciful and saved them from themselves.

Nimrod and his followers were not the only ones who have sought to build a tower of power. In Germany, my dad and I saw many towers built during the middle ages. The purpose of these patrician towers was to signify power. The family who built the tallest tower could control the town. In the town of Regensburg, the Golden Tower, built in the year 1260, stands nine stories tall. Some people declare it the highest medieval residential tower north of the Alps.

Oddly enough, some of these towers have faux floors and windows with exterior architectural features made to look like it has additional stories. Back then, it was not about how many floors you had or how many square feet of living space you had. What mattered is that you ruled the city skyline with your towering structure.

Honestly, nothing has changed since Nimrod walked the earth or since thirteenth century aristocrats competed to see who could build the tallest tower. In the present day, multibillion-dollar corporations consistently seek renowned architects to design the most technologically advanced skyscraper in the city, so their corporate logo can grace the city skyline as an indication of economic power. Likewise, people are just as eager to climb the ladder of success. Some people hunger for power more than they hunger for food. They awaken in the morning without even giving thanks to God for their breakfast. Instead, they start their day wondering how they will earn their next hundred, thousand, or even million dollars.

Individuals spend their lives trying to obtain a "big break," which will garner fame and fortune. Their dream may be to become a movie star, a CEO, or a self-made millionaire. Their quest for power overwhelms them. When they finally obtain the power they seek, they often find it does not fill the longing in their heart. Numerous celebrities have earned millions of dollars, owned lavish mansions and the most expensive cars, adorned themselves with designer clothing, and attended the ritziest celebrations. Yet their children were wayward, their marriage was failing, and you could see the sadness in their eyes. Although they seemed to "have it all," none of their worldly possessions could provide genuine happiness. Earthly power and wealth only bring temporary contentment.

The riches and wealth in this world will not last forever. God's Word says, "'Lay up for yourselves treasures in heaven, where neither moth nor rust destroys and where thieves do not break in and steal'" (Matt. 6:20 ESV). The things we have on this earth are only temporary, but the things we do for the Lord will last for all eternity.

Not every act of kindness we perform in the name of Christ will receive recognition on this earth. Nevertheless, one day we will have a greater understanding of the way our Heavenly Father was keeping record. God's Word says, "Whatever you do, work at it with all your heart, as working for the Lord, not for human masters, since you know that you will receive an inheritance from the Lord as a reward. It is the Lord Christ you are serving" (Col. 3:23–24). Every kind word spoken, every caring gesture made, every prayer uttered; God keeps track of every single one of them. For all of the positive things we have done in the name of the Lord are being kept like shining jewels by Christ our Savior.

We should not strive to be a household name. Our most important mission in life is to share the most excellent name with every household in the world.

Every day, we should strive to care for others and be an example to those around us. It does not matter if you are a housekeeper at a hotel or the CEO of an entire resort. God has called every one of us to serve others, just as a shepherd cares for their sheep. The Bible tells us what we should do: "Be shepherds of God's flock that is under your care, watching over them— not because you must, but because you are willing, as God wants you to be; not pursuing dishonest gain, but eager to serve; not lording it over those entrusted to you, but being examples to the flock. And when the Chief Shepherd appears, you will receive the crown of glory that will never fade away" (1 Pet. 5:2–4). Take care of the people God places in your life. Do not be greedy; share your abundance with others. Live your life as an example for others to follow. Ephesians 5:1–2 (ESV) says, "Therefore be imitators of God, as beloved children. And walk in love, as Christ loved us and gave himself up for us." Show love to others, as God loves you. Endeavor to be like Him. Then, when Christ returns, you will receive a "crown of glory that will never fade away" (1 Pet. 5:4).

We should not strive to be a household name. Our most

important mission in life is to share the most excellent name with every household in the world. Jesus Christ is the name above all names. He is our strong tower. Jesus will give us power when we are weak. He will protect us when we encounter danger. He will be our stronghold. The towers built by human hands will one day crumble to the ground, but "the name of the LORD is a strong tower; The righteous runs into it and is safe" (Prov. 18:10 NASB).

Running the Race

You may wonder how you could possibly share Jesus Christ with the entire world. Your mind may be telling you that nothing you do could have a positive impact. Perhaps you feel as if there is too much corruption, too much greed, and too much violence. While I do agree that this world seems to be growing more and more rebellious, there is something each of us can do. Not only that, but Jesus gave us power to be able to accomplish this vital assignment.

Jesus gave us our marching orders, so to speak, in the Great Commission. Before Jesus ascended into Heaven, He told the disciples, "'Therefore go and make disciples of all nations, baptizing them in the name of the Father and of the Son and of the Holy Spirit, and teaching them to obey everything I have commanded you. And surely I am with you always, to the very end of the age'" (Matt. 28:19–20). Jesus did not tell the disciples this was something they could pursue if they felt like it, or if they were not too busy doing something else. He commissioned them to go forth and share the Good News with all nations, and this commandment still applies to us today.

Unfortunately, many people do not want someone to tell them what to do. In my teaching career, there have been numerous times when a student was insubordinate and did not want to complete an assignment. On the road, people choose to drive recklessly rather than follow the rules of the road. To complicate matters, they engage in texting while driving and even driving under the influence. Driving while intoxicated accounts for approximately one-third of the traffic-related deaths in the United States each year.[5] All because people have an addiction and do not want to listen to authorities regarding safe driving practices. The defiant attitudes of people only add to the pain and suffering we must endure on this earth.

Jesus knew corruption would fill this earth. He knew this world needed a Savior. That is why He gave His life on Calvary, to save us from our sins. He also knew many people would not choose the road to eternal life. Jesus said, "'For wide is the gate and broad is the road that leads to destruction, and many enter through it. But small is the gate and narrow the road that leads to life, and only a few find it'" (Matt. 7:13–14). Sadly, many people in the world think they do not need Jesus; however, the complete opposite is true. You need Jesus. I need Jesus. The entire world needs Jesus.

When I look around the world, I see things that break my heart. Millions of babies never even have the opportunity to enjoy life on this earth, all because someone decides to end their life. People engage in immoral activity, unreservedly disregarding the sanctity of marriage. Still others are living in sin through other kinds of wicked behavior, destroying their bodies, their families, and their lives. People seem to have misplaced their moral compass. They are following the evil forces of this world instead of listening to the very One who created them.

Looking back in history, this type of corruption is not exclusive to the modern world. In fact, there was one time when the world became corrupt to the point that God wished His creation did not even exist. There was so much wickedness on this earth, the Bible says, "The LORD regretted that he had made human beings on the earth, and his heart was deeply troubled" (Gen. 6:6). Think about it. The humans on earth had become so sinful that their very own Creator regretted creating them in the first place. God's Word goes on to say, "But Noah found favor in the eyes of the LORD" (Gen. 6:8).

"But Noah"—those two little words changed a family's life forever. Noah was different from the rest of the population, not engaging in immoral sins, but keeping his eyes on God. God saw something special in Noah and his family. Genesis 6:9 says, "Noah was a righteous man, blameless among the people of his time, and he walked faithfully with God." I am sure Noah was not perfect. He probably slammed a few doors in his day, and he may have gotten upset if one of his sons did not do their chores. All the same, he was righteous in God's sight, and he did not engage in wicked deeds and sinful ways. Noah trusted God and knew the Lord would take care of him and his family.

What would you do if God came to you and said He was going to destroy the earth because of the destruction people had brought into the world (Gen. 6:13)? Would you make a phone call, post an update on Facebook, or just sit down and cry? Noah did not question God. He did not even tweet about it or text his best friend to tell them the news. Instead, he listened intently to all of the instructions, detailing the size of the ark he was to construct,

You need Jesus. I need Jesus.

The entire world needs Jesus.

what animals to bring aboard, how much food to pack, and all of the other tasks that were to be completed. This was a massive undertaking. Instead of having a panic attack, the Bible says, "Noah did everything just as God commanded him" (Gen. 6:22). Noah did not just do half of the job and then sit down to watch his favorite program on television. He did not believe he had a better way to build the ark. He did not delegate someone else to do the job. He did exactly what God asked him to do, paying meticulous attention to detail.

Frequently, we complain about jobs the Lord asks us to do. Sometimes, we are tired and it is hard to find energy to get the job done. Other times, people try to discourage us, even though we know God has enabled us for the task. I am sure Noah was discouraged when people laughed at him for building an ark. They had never seen a flood like that before. There was no rain in the forecast. They must have thought Noah had lost his mind. Someone might have said, "Look at Noah, building that atrocity and bringing all of those animals so close to where our children play! Someone needs to put a stop to such outlandish behavior!"

What would your neighbors think if they saw you building a gigantic boat in your front yard, standing tall at approximately forty-five feet high? I am sure the Neighborhood Beautification Committee would have something to say about such a project at their monthly meeting! Not to mention the jarring noises of a construction site extending in to the wee hours of the night and the potential for air pollution from the thousands of animals in one confined location. Surely, a judge would find you guilty of multiple violations!

Even so, God asked Noah to accomplish a monumental task. Noah ignored the backlash from the opposing side and immediately obeyed God. He did not tell God he had to fit it in between watching the Sunday afternoon football game and improving his golf swing at the range on Saturday. He did not tell God he lacked the energy and would maybe get around to it next week. He did not even explain what was going on to his neighbors. He just got the job done. Oh, and Noah did not try to cut corners when building the ark. He accomplished the task precisely as God commanded. Noah did all of this without complaining, even at the age of six hundred years old.

God provided a lifeboat, so to speak, for Noah and his family, along with seven pairs of every kind of clean animal, one pair of every kind of unclean animal, and seven pairs of every kind of bird, "male and female, to keep their various kinds alive throughout the earth" (Gen. 7:2-3). Because Noah found favor in the eyes of the Lord, God spared him and his family.

God told Noah that the rainbow was a sign of the covenant between God and all life on earth, and He promised never to destroy the earth by floodwaters again. The rainbow is a promise not only to Noah and his family, but also to you and me. God will

God will be our protection

from the coming storm.

be our protection from the coming storm. As this world spirals out of control, we have a safe haven in the midst of the tumultuous seas.

God's Word says, "'Just as it was in the days of Noah, so also will it be in the days of the Son of Man. People were eating, drinking, marrying and being given in marriage up to the day Noah entered the ark. Then the flood came and destroyed them all'" (Luke 17:26–27). If you look at the headlines today, it is easy to see that we are living in times very similar to the days of Noah. People are living as if there really is no tomorrow, yet they have no regard for the harsh reality that eternity may only be one day away. Just as God provided a way out for Noah and his family, God has provided us with an escape from the evilness in this world.

God promises salvation to every single person, young and old, who confesses their sins and puts their trust in Jesus Christ. God's Word says, "For God so loved the world that he gave his one and only Son, that whoever believes in him shall not perish but have eternal life. For God did not send his Son into the world to condemn the world, but to save the world through him" (John 3:16–17). God is not looking for revenge. He is looking for reverence. He desires that everyone should not perish, but live forever. That is how much He loves us.

Jesus Christ is coming back to this earth one day very soon. It is our responsibility to tell others about His imminent return before it is too late. Jesus Christ is the only way to receive salvation, a gift freely given to all who will believe. If you do not have a personal relationship with Jesus, I urge you to make today the day of salvation (2 Cor. 6:2). Call on the name of Jesus Christ, and you shall be saved (Rom. 10:13).

God spoke this very world into existence. He created you to be more than a failure, more than a statistic, and more than an outcast. Romans 8:37 states, "In all these things we are more than conquerors through him who loved us." You are more than a conqueror through Jesus Christ, who loves you more than you could ever truly imagine.

God is not looking for revenge.

He is looking for reverence.

If you put your trust in Jesus Christ, you will have the peace and joy that only come from knowing the King of kings and Lord of lords. With all of its troubles and trials, life is certainly not a fairy tale. Yet it will have a happy ending, if you have a personal relationship with the author who has written the pages of your life story.

In Heaven, all of the anguish we have experienced on this earth will fade away: "And God shall wipe away all tears from their eyes; and there shall be no more death, neither sorrow, nor crying, neither shall there be any more pain: for the former things are passed away" (Rev. 21:4 KJV). Keep your eyes on Jesus, for He is "the author and finisher of our faith; who for the joy that was set before him endured the cross, despising the shame, and is set down at the right hand of the throne of God" (Heb. 12:2 KJV). Jesus died, so we might live. Now He sits at the right hand of God, interceding on our behalf (Rom. 8:34).

In spite of the hardships we endure, we must persevere, "for our light and momentary troubles are achieving for us an eternal glory that far outweighs them all" (2 Cor. 4:17). Esther Kerr Rusthoi expressed this verse in a special way when she wrote the song, "When We See Christ." When we see Jesus, we will not be pondering the calamities we experienced on earth. We will not be thinking about the disappointments in life, the times when tearstains covered our pillow, or the moments we struggled to put one foot in front of the other. Instead, all of the heartache we have endured on this earth will suddenly vanish. So be brave. Run the race. When we see Jesus Christ face-to-face, Heaven ever after will only have just begun.

Chapter Sixteen

The Spirit of God

"And in him you too are being built together to become
a dwelling in which God lives by his Spirit." (Eph. 2:22)

On our Mediterranean cruise, my dad and I had the blessing of traveling to Greece. On one of the city tours, our guide escorted us into a large gothic style cathedral in the center of town. When we entered through the door and followed the other visitors and local people to the front of the church, though, I felt something was quite unusual about the uncustomary procedure of dozens of people being ushered through a small door on the right side of the platform. As we approached this tiny entrance, I led the way with my dad following close behind me.

The first thing I saw was an ornate silver casket, which I quickly assumed held a patron saint's remains. The people before me were kissing the mummy's feet as part of a ritual, while two monks stood on either side, chanting words that were indecipherable to me. All along, something did not feel right within my spirit. In spite of the fact that some people held this patron saint in high regard, a deceased individual has no power to bless, to heal, or to save. No one should idolize any other human being, living or dead. The man's soul had departed, and the mummified body was simply the earthen vessel left behind.

Therefore, when I approached the casket, I did not stop nor bend down to kiss the feet. All of the sudden, the two monks immediately halted their ritualistic chanting, slammed the lid of the casket down abruptly, and rapidly exited through a secret door in the wood paneling as fast as lightning. They seemed insulted by my refusal to observe the customary practices.

First John 4:1 says, "Do not believe every spirit, but test the spirits to see whether they are from God, because many false prophets have gone out into the world." As I quietly left the room, I thought about how the world has many false prophets and idols. When I tested the spirits in that room, I knew they were not from God. I knew the Spirit of God living inside me was at odds with the spirit and traditions of men at work in that place. I pray these two men will put their trust in the one true living God who loves them unconditionally.

Another time, my parents and I were out for a late afternoon fishing expedition on the Suwannee River. We decided to take our small boat up a creek that fed into the river. As we headed up this narrow waterway, all three of us had a troubled feeling. While we did not see anything strange, something did not feel right. Although we were uncertain what activities were taking place in that area at the time, we were quite certain it was not of the Lord. As such, we promptly turned back to resume our journey along our original route.

I am so grateful to God for giving us the ability to discern the Spirit of God from destructive and deceptive spirits. Even at a young age, I knew God is the One who dwells within my heart and soul. My desire is that the Holy Spirit will work through me, so I can be a witness for Jesus Christ everywhere I go. Sometimes we do not have the opportunity to tell someone about Jesus, but we need to ensure

People instantly need to see something different about us. We need to shine like a beacon in the night to a lost and dying world.

our lives are a testimony of the grace of the Lord Jesus Christ. People instantly need to see something different about us. We need to shine like a beacon in the night to a lost and dying world.

Picture a tempestuous sea at night. A ship's captain would surely run aground if not for the lighthouse keeper, tending the life-saving beam of light all through the night. The light shines, warning ships of impending danger, urging them to change their course and to avoid the perilous rocks lingering just below the water's surface.

Many people in this world are like ships, sailing through turbulent waters, with no light guiding their way. Some of them do not even have a captain, allowing the pull of other people to tug them along, like the blind leading the blind. Others are coasting through life without a final destination in mind. They are unprepared, lacking the provisions they need for the detour they are taking in life. In Matthew 5:14, Jesus said, "'You are the light of the world.'" He has called us to be a light that shines bright in a world of darkness. We need to be the ones to help guide the lost safely home before it is too late.

Perhaps you are one of those people, sailing around in circles amid a sea of turmoil. You feel as if there is no way out. You may have given up on life. Thoughts of jumping overboard and ending your life could have entered your mind. Do not throw in the towel. Hold on a little longer. Your life has value. You are precious in the eyes of God, the One who created you. He loves you so much that He gave His only Son for the forgiveness of your sins and to give you eternal life (John 3:16).

Your past does not define you. The abuse you endured does not define you. The affair you had does not define you. Your scars from the past do not define you. The abortion you had does not define you. The damaging substances you poured into your body do not define you. Your immoral lifestyle does not define you. Nothing you have done and nothing someone else has done to you defines you.

God created you for a purpose. Psalm 139:16 (NLT) says, "You saw me before I was born. Every day of my life was recorded in your book. Every moment was laid out before a single day had passed." God has always been looking out for you, even before you were born. He created you in His image (Gen. 1:27). You were born to live for His glory!

You may think, *No, I am just not good enough. I am not rich enough. I am not smart enough. I am not beautiful enough.* Stop thinking those thoughts this very moment. Even with our shortcomings, God is more than enough! He knew we could never make it on our own, which is why He provided a Savior. God knew it would take a perfect sacrifice to redeem you and me, which is why He gave the most precious gift of all, His only begotten Son (John 3:16).

God did not pay for you with gold bonds or write a check to save you. First Peter 1:18–19 (NASB) says, "You were not redeemed with perishable things like silver or gold from your futile way of life inherited from your forefathers, but with precious blood, as of a lamb unblemished and spotless, *the blood* of Christ." God went beyond any sacrifice ever given. He gave His only Son, whom He loved dearly, to save the sins of the entire world. He did it out of love, knowing some people would not even love Him in return. That is what God did for you.

You do not have to live in your dark past any longer. God has secured a bright future for you, filled with the light of Jesus. He loves you beyond imagination. He longs to be a part of your life. Give the broken pieces of your life to Jesus. He will put them back together and make you whole.

God Loves You

You may be ready to put this book down, determined that no god could ever love you. Like many people in the world today, you may have only heard about a god of hate, rather than the

God of love. I have met individuals who never knew real love until they met Jesus Christ as their personal Savior. For some of them, no one had ever shown them love, so the whole concept of receiving or giving even the smallest amount of love was foreign to them.

You may be like these individuals, uncertain of what love truly means. God loves you so much that He gave His only Son to die for the forgiveness of your sins. John 3:16 says, "For God *so* loved

> **God does not want you confined to a prison of doubt, denial, or disappointment.**

the world" (emphasis added). God does not just love you a little; He loves you a lot. Our Creator loves you beyond measure!

God loves you more than you could ever fully comprehend. God sent His only Son to purchase salvation for your sins. The blood of the Lamb has pardoned your sin. Through God's unmerited favor, you can receive eternal life in Heaven.

First Thessalonians 5:9–10 says, "For God did not appoint us to suffer wrath but to receive salvation through our Lord Jesus Christ. He died for us so that, whether we are awake or asleep, we may live together with him." God does not desire for you to suffer on this earth. God does not want you confined to a prison of doubt, denial, or disappointment. He wants you to find freedom through Christ.

The Spirit of God is not limited to one person, one church, or one nation. God is not going to listen to the prayers of an internationally known speaker or evangelist instead of listening to you. He will listen to all of His children. He loves us all the same. He knows we need His unconditional love and He knows we need His guidance through all of the difficulties we encounter on the road of life. That is why He sent the Holy Spirit to comfort us. God uses the Holy Spirit to guide us and to change lives miraculously, such as the way He transformed the life of Saul.

Saul had threatened to murder Jesus' disciples. He also desired to take Christians as prisoners. However, God had other plans. A brilliant light flashed from Heaven, blinding Saul as he was traveling on the road to Damascus. Saul "fell to the ground and heard a voice say to him, 'Saul, Saul, why do you persecute me?'" (Acts 9:4). When Saul questioned the identity of the mysterious voice, he heard these words: "'I am Jesus, whom you are persecuting'" (Acts 9:5). Jesus did not give up on him, despite the fact that Saul turned his back on God. Blind for three days, the Lord spoke to Saul through a vision, informing him that a man named Ananias would visit him.

When Ananias entered the house where Saul was staying, Ananias said, "'Jesus, who appeared to you on the road as you were coming here—has sent me so that you may see again and be filled with the Holy Spirit.' Immediately, something like scales fell from Saul's eyes, and he could see again" (Acts 9:17–18). The Spirit of God entered Saul's heart and mind, instantaneously restoring his eyesight and completely transforming his wayward life. Saul went from wanting to kill Christians to being a follower of Christ, "speaking boldly in the name of the Lord" (Acts 9:28).

Instead of singing to the congregation, we should sing to an audience of One, Jesus Christ.

God will do the same for you. Whatever evil seeks to overtake you, God is greater than any power on this earth. He will deliver you from depression, addiction, fear, loneliness, or any other thing that has you bound. God freely offers a new life through Christ: "Therefore, if anyone is in Christ, the new creation has come: The old has gone, the new is here!" (2 Cor. 5:17). Call on Jesus

Christ today. Do not allow your past to control you any longer. When you invite the Spirit of God to live inside you, the old things pass away, and your life becomes new!

God Is Great

One evening at home, my dad and I were watching a video featuring Terry MacAlmon and Phil Driscoll leading worship in Berlin, Germany. Terry was leading the congregation in the praise song, "You Deserve the Glory," written by Gary Sadler and Aaron Keyes. The lyrics of this song proclaim the greatness of God, while singing to the Lord Himself.

While there are many praise and worship songs sung today, nothing warms my soul like a worship song sung directly to our Heavenly Father. Instead of singing to the congregation, we should sing to an audience of One, Jesus Christ. Psalm 48:1 says, "Great is the LORD, and most worthy of praise." Jesus is the only One who is worthy of our praise and adoration.

Sadly, many churches have turned their focus away from worshiping God, replacing exalted praise with entertaining performances. Some platforms on Sunday morning now incorporate light shows, smoke machines, and secular-inspired music. The Gospel is frequently an afterthought, and worshiping God is more about developing a flawless program as opposed to allowing the Lord to direct the service according to His perfect will. Congregants may pay more attention to the worship team than the One whom they worship.

In the secular world of music, fans raise their hands toward the performers, idolizing the vocalists and musicians on stage. God said, "'You shall have no other gods before me'" (Exod. 20:3). Worshiping other humans is no different than worshiping other gods. Yet many fans even idolize well-known Christian performers, seeking photo opportunities and autographs. While there is certainly nothing wrong with taking a photograph with someone or getting a book autographed, there is a fine line between admiring a person's zeal for the Lord versus idolizing them for their own personal attributes.

My dad and I have visited ancient Olympia, Greece, the site of the very first Olympic Games. The museum there houses many artifacts, including hundreds of hand-fashioned idols, from miniature ones that would fit in your shirt pocket to giant statues that would require a crane to lift them. Many people revere these so-called gods to this day. In one section of the museum, a curator chastised people for taking photographs of a marble statue. While it was permissible to take photos in this museum, apparently they did not give permission for visitors to take a picture of this particular statue, since they considered it a god. As I walked out of that room, I immediately had a burden on my heart for the man who was so deceived. I pray he has called on the name of Jesus since the time of our visit, for the god he was worshiping then has no power to save him or anyone else.

Although there are many gods worshiped in the world today, there is only one true living God. All of the other gods are either in a grave somewhere or else they were never truly alive in the first place. I do not put my hope in a graven image, nor any other human being. I put my hope in Jesus Christ. He is the reason I sing. He is the reason I worship. He is the reason I live.

There is only one true and living God. First Timothy 4:10 says, "That is why we labor and strive, because we have put our hope in the living God, who is the Savior of all people, and especially of those who believe." I strive every day to share the love of Jesus with everyone I meet. He is the Savior of our souls; Almighty God is He! I have put my complete hope in Him, for there is no one else who can save me, redeem me, or love me like Jesus. I owe my life to Him.

We should live our lives as a living sacrifice, offering all of our glory and praise to the One who deserves to be glorified. Romans 12:1 says, "Offer your bodies as a living sacrifice, holy and pleasing to God—this is your true and proper worship." May we all devote ourselves to worship, offering our highest praise to the One who died on a cross for the forgiveness of our sins. Jesus Christ alone is worthy. There is no one else like Him. Let us worship Him forevermore!

Chapter Seventeen

When Opportunity Knocks

"Be very careful, then, how you live—not as unwise but as wise, making the most of every opportunity." (Eph. 5:15–16)

Thomas Alva Edison once said, "Opportunity is missed by most people because it is dressed in overalls and looks like work."[1] How true this is, especially in today's society. Even so, what if the work God calls us to do is the key to a life-changing experience for another individual? Would we refrain from completing a task with such profound significance?

Many of us work at least five days a week. Although we put a lot into our careers, we often count down the days until our next vacation. Whether we simply need a break to rejuvenate ourselves or to maintain our sanity, most people enjoy having a day off. Although I enjoy being a teacher, I cherish holidays and weekends when I can spend more quality time with my family and spend time doing things I love to do, such as writing, baking, and playing the piano. Nevertheless, one job requires us to be "on-call" 365 days a year. While this might sound a little extreme, it is the most important position we could ever fill.

Jesus said, "'Go into all the world and preach the gospel to all creation. Whoever believes and is baptized will be saved, but whoever does not believe will be condemned'" (Mark 16:15–16). He has called us to share the Gospel of Jesus Christ everywhere we go. Jesus did not tell us only to preach the Gospel five days a week, or solely to share the Good News at church on Sunday.

Moreover, He did not make this commandment optional, for it does not say go into the world and preach the Gospel if you feel like it. Jesus knew the importance of spreading the Gospel. Whoever believes will receive the gift of salvation and eternal life in Heaven. The alternative is condemnation to an eternal hell. Certainly, you would do everything you could to save someone from a burning building. Likewise, we should strive every day to save others from the eternal fire of hell.

As followers of Christ, our Heavenly Father has called us to share the love of Jesus Christ with everyone we meet. Perhaps you believe you lack the training or the knowledge to be able to share the message of the Gospel. That is the beauty of the Good News. The primary qualification to share the Gospel is to believe the Gospel. If you have a personal relationship with Jesus Christ, you qualify for the job.

What's more, there is urgency when it comes to sharing the message of salvation. When you read the newspaper or watch the evening news, it is evident that Christ's return is imminent. My dad wrote a song a few years ago titled, "Christ Will Return." The second verse reminds us that we do not have to be concerned about the troubles of the world.

Don't be troubled by
The day we're living in.
When violence fills the earth,
You know we're near the end.
For nation shall rise against nation,
With sin on every hand.
But we have this blessed assurance
That Christ will come again.

Chorus:
Christ will return;
We'll see His glory face-to-face.
Christ will return,
The One who saved me by His grace.

Sickness and death must go;
Our tears He'll wipe away.
I'm watching and waiting,
For this could be the day.[2]

One day soon, a trumpet will sound and the "dead in Christ will rise first. After that, we who are still alive and are left will be caught up together with them in the clouds to meet the Lord in the air. And so we will be with the Lord forever" (1 Thess. 4:16–17). Our mission is to share this glorious news with others before it is too late. Not only that, but it is critical that this message be shared with as many people as possible.

First Thessalonians 5:2 declares, "The day of the Lord will come like a thief in the night." Sadly, many people will not be ready for His return. People often put it off, saying they will accept Christ tomorrow, next week, or even next year. They want to wait until a more "convenient" time. Yet the return of Christ could be today.

Meanwhile, many people who have accepted Christ think they do not have enough time to witness to others. Jesus knew this would be the case, even two thousand years ago. Jesus told His disciples, "'The harvest is plentiful but the workers are few'" (Matt. 9:37). Jesus knew millions of souls would need redemption, yet most people would be too busy to show them the way to receive salvation. He knew people would often refrain from sharing the greatest message that anyone could ever share.

Just as Edison said most people missed opportunities, we often miss opportunities to share the Gospel. God's Word says, "Be wise in the way you act toward outsiders; make the most of every opportunity" (Col. 4:5). God places people in our path, if we slow down long enough to notice them. We could encounter someone on an airplane, at the grocery store, in a hospital, or any other location where we may find ourselves. Instead of rushing on past them, let us make a concerted effort to speak to them, telling them that Jesus Christ loves them unconditionally.

I can tell you from personal experience that these encounters truly make a difference. I have talked to people in many different countries about my Lord and Savior, Jesus Christ. Not too long ago, I witnessed to a family on a cruise ship, only to find they had already put their trust in Jesus Christ. As I shared my testimony with them, I knew God ordained the crossing of our paths. When I began speaking to them, I soon found the meeting was of shared value, since we all left the dinner table with uplifted spirits. As Christians, we are not only called to share the Gospel with nonbelievers, but to also "encourage one another and build each other up" (1 Thess. 5:11).

When opportunity knocks, you could be the one to lead a lost soul to Christ.

I thank God for the friendship that blossomed between Debbie, her family, and me, for our online communication has proven to be a continual stream of reciprocated encouragement and prayer support. When we meet new friends along life's journey, we may never see them again on this earth, but we need to pray that we will see them again in the life to come. Every time we sow a seed, the Lord will send someone along to water that seed. Whether God calls you to sow the seed or nurture the seed, be sure to put forth your best effort. Share the Gospel with everyone you meet.

Never miss the opportunity to work for the Kingdom of God. Luke 16:9 (NLT) says, "'Use your worldly resources to benefit others and make friends. Then, when your possessions are gone, they will welcome you to an eternal home.'" We need to do all we can to share the Gospel. The friends we make on this earth will one day be our friends in Heaven, if they have committed their lives to Christ. When opportunity knocks, you could be the one to lead a lost soul to Christ. If you are contemplating whether you should share Jesus Christ with your supervisor, a store clerk, or even your neighbor across the street, let nothing stop you. Ask God to give you wisdom. Then go forth and proclaim the Good News! Tell someone about the love of Jesus Christ today! Be a harvester!

Balcony Friends

I will always remember the time my dad and I had the special honor of sitting in box seats when we heard the Vienna Symphonic Orchestra in concert at the Konzerthaus in Vienna, Austria. The opportunity to purchase these premium seats at a drastically reduced last-minute price was too good to turn down. From our vantage point, we were close enough to the musicians that we could almost read their sheet music. It was such a joy to listen to their musicianship and the intricate artistry of the guest pianist.

Other times, we have had the privilege of sitting in the front row of a balcony for a concert, a church service, or another type of program. Each time I sit in a balcony, I am reminded how blessed we are to have special people who stand on the balcony of our lives, so to speak, cheering us on. In her book by the same title, Joyce Landorf Heatherly refers to these types of friends as "balcony people." God uses these special people in our lives to provide constant encouragement and support.

I am not talking about the acquaintances you only hear from once a year via a standard Christmas greeting. These are the God-given people who constantly inspire you. They listen to you diligently and impart words of wisdom. They are always eager to agree with you in prayer for whatever concerns you. Friends like these weep with you and rejoice with you. They live out the scripture that tells us to "encourage one another day after day" (Heb. 3:13 NASB).

God has blessed me with several balcony friends. Some of them live nearby and some of them live on the other side of the globe, yet our friendships know no distance. I am thinking of one particular friend, Maria, who lives in the Canary Islands, and another friend, Mari, who lives in Romania. It is a joy to keep in touch with them. Sharon, a dear friend from California, always brings a smile to my face. Although we do not get to see each other very often due to living on opposite coastlines, we are always close at heart. I have cherished friends who live close by, like Angie, Evelyn, Carla, and Goldie, who offer motherly advice just when I need it most. Often friends become a part of our family, like our sweet friend and neighbor, Lucille, whom I have known since I was a little girl. Other precious friends like Karen, Linda, Jan, and Dusty, are scattered throughout the United States, yet they are always eager to take my prayer requests to the throne of grace or offer a word of encouragement. What a blessing that my dad and grandma are close friends of mine as well; they always love and support me in everything I do.

Sometimes, friendships grow and flourish over time. Other times, friendships sprout up very quickly, almost overnight. For there are times when God places encouragers in our lives, even when we least expect it. My dad and I met Abraham in New York City. This precious brother in Christ speaks words of life into our ministry every time we talk to him. Nearly every word he says seems to be a heaven-sent message, tailor-made for us. When I am talking to this grandfatherly gentleman, it is easy for me to recognize that only God could orchestrate such a friendship. He reminds me that some friends resemble angels in disguise, a blessing from Heaven above.

Through these treasured friendships, God showers me with unconditional love through their prayers and encouragement. These balcony friends embody the scripture that says, "A friend loves at all times" (Prov. 17:17). Even Jesus knew it was important to have friends, people who would support Him through His most difficult journey, the journey to the cross. There are multiple examples of Jesus referring to friends in the Bible. He called His disciples friends in John 21:5. In John 15:15, Jesus said, "'I no longer call you servants, because a servant does not know his master's business. Instead, I have called you friends, for everything that I learned from my Father I have made known to you.'" Jesus has called us His friends. He wants a friendship with us.

Jesus has called us His friends.

He wants a friendship with us.

You may wonder how you could ever be a friend to Jesus. Well, what do friends typically do? Although there are many activities friends enjoy doing together, one of the main things they enjoy is talking to one another. When was the last time you talked to Jesus? He is our best friend in life, even closer than our blood relatives are (Prov. 18:24). Whether you enjoy a balcony full of friends on this earth or not, take comfort in the knowledge that one balcony friend is always cheering you on. Make a point to talk to people everywhere you go, introducing them to your closest friend, Jesus Christ. Never miss an opportunity to share the love of Jesus Christ, for He is your forever friend!

Missed Opportunities

Just as I felt a nudging in my heart to witness to the woman on the plane and to the family on the cruise ship, God sends countless opportunities my way that I simply miss. There are times when I second-guess whether I should to speak to someone or not. Other times, I find myself in a hurry and close the door of opportunity in the interest of time. While I freely admit the error of my ways, I do not share these facts lightly. In reality, I am sure it would be disheartening to know the number of times I have missed an opportunity to share the Gospel.

Think about it. Have you ever missed an opportunity to tell an individual that Jesus loves them? Every restaurant server, every hotel or store employee, every coworker—well, you get the picture. God places people in our paths every single day. He will set up the designated meeting time and place, and He will even give us the words to speak. Yet it is up to us to show up to the meeting, ready and willing to speak the words of hope He places inside of our hearts.

Sometimes, we not only miss the opportunity to encourage someone else, but we often miss life-changing opportunities that would influence our own lives. Take the prospective disciples, for example. In Luke 9:59, Jesus said to one man, "'Follow me,'" and the man responded, "'Lord, first let me go and bury my father.'" Jesus replied, "'Let the dead bury their own dead, but you go and proclaim the kingdom of God'" (Luke 9:60). Another person said to Jesus, "'I will follow you, Lord; but first let me go back and say goodbye to my family.' Jesus replied, 'No one who puts a hand to the plow and looks back is fit for service in the kingdom of God'" (Luke 9:61–62). These individuals did not fully grasp the opportunity Jesus offered to them.

Both of these individuals could have potentially become one of Jesus' disciples, yet they missed out because they did not put Jesus first. Yes, they were concerned about their families, all of whom are extremely important. Still, God is even more important. Jesus stated, "'Anyone who loves their father or mother more than me is not worthy of me; anyone who loves their son or daughter more than me is not worthy of me'" (Matt. 10:37). Jesus wants us to surrender our lives to Him. When we give our lives completely to Him, life will be more fulfilling.

James and John, the sons of Zebedee, fully understood this. When Jesus encountered them along the shoreline, they did not hesitate to leave everything behind, so they could devote their lives to Christ: "They were in a boat with their father Zebedee, preparing their nets. Jesus called them, and immediately they left the boat and their father and followed him" (Matt. 4:21–22). These two brothers did not worry about having a bag packed with all of the essentials for an arduous journey, which could last an indefinite number of years. Nor were they fretting over whether or not their family would miss them. Although they loved their family very much, as evidenced by the fact they were spending time with their father when Jesus found them, their love for the Lord was even greater. They showed complete devotion to Christ by following Him without any hindrance.

While God may not call us to leave our families behind, God may call us to leave a comfortable lifestyle to embark on a journey to the mission field, or He may call us to resign from our dream job, so we can pursue a ministry to the homeless, the widows, or the orphans. Our plans are not always the same as God's plans for our lives. Although His plans are perfect, they may not be as glitzy as our human nature may desire. Following God's plan may involve sleepless nights, uncomfortable circumstances, or even dangerous locations. On the other hand, when we live inside the will of God, we have nothing to fear. He will protect us from harm when we walk in His steps.

I recall a time when my dad and I visited Guatemala. We stopped there on a cruise ship, but after our morning tour, we decided to head out on foot. As we approached the gate to the cruise terminal, the officials advised us to refrain from advancing beyond the confines of the secure area. Having brought dozens of sandwich bags holding Gospel tracts, pencils, candy, and toys, I was heartbroken at the thought of carrying these items home, as opposed to sharing them with the children there. Therefore, my dad and I continued to walk past security into the unknown.

Almost as soon as we cleared the secure area, an individual asked us if we needed a ride up into the mountains. He said he knew where to find some children, having overheard us talking to the security officers. Neither my dad nor I felt good about the situation as we quickly walked past him, for we had heard about attempted abductions and other crimes committed in this region. As we walked through a neighborhood, we found a couple of children, but we still had quite a large number of goody bags remaining. I silently prayed that God would lead us to children. He had brought us this far, and I knew He had a plan for bringing us to Guatemala.

As we approached what looked like a dead end, we veered toward the left and spotted a soccer field full of young children. My dad asked one of the coaches if we could give the bags to the team. He said, "Yes." As I watched the children's faces light up as they opened these unexpected gifts, I was nearly speechless. The opportunity to share the love of Jesus Christ with someone is truly extraordinary. I pray God sent someone to water the seeds we planted on that soccer field and that those precious children have come to know Jesus as their personal Lord and Savior.

If we follow God's will for our lives, we will always be ready and willing to answer when opportunity knocks.

Walking back toward the ship, my dad commented that he was glad God kept us safe. I then realized I never once even feared for my safety, although Guatemala is one of the most dangerous countries in the world, based on the annual homicide rate. In this moment, I did not simply quote the Twenty-third Psalm, but I lived out its meaning.

In Psalm 23:4, we read, "Even though I walk through the darkest valley, I will fear no evil, for you are with me; your rod and your staff, they comfort me." Here we were, walking through the middle of unfamiliar streets filled with potential danger, yet I was unequivocally unafraid. I knew God had His hand upon us. At that moment, more than ever before, I fully understood the concept of fearing no evil. The greatest aspect of all was the way I knew in my heart of hearts that the Lord was my shepherd.

When we trust Him completely and allow Him to direct our paths, Jesus will always bring us safely home. Doors will open and doors will close, but if we fix our eyes on Him, we will always be walking on the path we need to follow. When we place our footsteps inside of His, we will never miss an opportunity He has designed for us. If we follow God's will for our lives, we will always be ready and willing to answer when opportunity knocks.

Chapter Eighteen

The Lord Will Go Before You!

"The LORD himself goes before you and will be with
you; he will never leave you nor forsake you. Do not
be afraid; do not be discouraged.'" (Deut. 31:8)

When I was in college, I made the decision to live at home. It
was only about a seventy-five minute drive to the University of
Florida in Gainesville, where I completed my bachelor's degree in
English. Usually, I drove two or three days per week. This
decision cut down on my living expenses drastically, and it
allowed me to spend quality time with my parents, family, and
friends. Besides, the prospect of sleeping in my own bed at night
definitely held more appeal than a dorm room mattress! Other
pros were enjoying home-cooked meals, seeing my pets on a
regular basis, and being able to play my piano every evening as I
have for over twenty-five years. For many reasons, it was a win-
win situation for everyone involved.

While I knew this was the right decision, my parents and I
prayed diligently for my protection on the roads. One morning, I
was running about ten minutes late. Like any other busy interstate
around the globe, the traffic on I-75 fluctuates hourly. I prayed
God would get me to my first class safely, and if possible, on
time as well. As I was driving down the interstate, I saw several
flashing lights in the distance. Thankfully, it was on the other side
of the interstate, so I knew it would not impede traffic in the
southbound lanes. What I saw moved me to tears.

A compact red sports car had crashed. Somehow, the car
had traveled from the southbound lane where I was driving,

crossed the median, and careened up into the trees. All I could see were confetti size pieces, scattered in a broad area. I pray God spared the lives of the passengers inside that car. I immediately called my mom and asked her to pray for them, and to pray for their families, not knowing the outcome of the horrific accident.

Based on the number of first responders, it had likely happened about ten minutes prior. Ten minutes—the number of minutes I was running late. All I could think was how that could have been me. Alternatively, I could have been in the path of that car. Since that moment sitting behind the wheel, I have come to realize that delays are often divine interventions.

If we listen to God's still, small voice, we will be exactly where we need to be at the appointed time.

Sometimes, though, in our haste to be somewhere on time, we determine to drive too fast, or to become angry with the people around us for our own tardiness. We may even be fearful, afraid we will be embarrassed, lose our job, or miss something important due to our lateness. Instead, we need to rely on God. We need to remember that He orders our steps. If we listen to God's still, small voice, we will be exactly where we need to be at the appointed time.

Even at the age of 120 years old, Moses knew God would guide the Israelites to the Promised Land. Though his faith may have briefly wavered, he never gave up. Moses knew beyond any doubt that God would go before them. He knew God would help them conquer this land. Moses told the Israelites to be strong and courageous. He shared the same advice to Joshua, who would lead the charge across the Jordan.

Moses offered the following pep talk, if you will, to Joshua: "'Be strong and courageous, for you must go with this people into the land that the LORD swore to their ancestors to give them, and you must divide it among them as their inheritance. The LORD himself goes before you and will be with you; he will never leave you nor forsake you. Do not be afraid; do not be discouraged"' (Deut. 31:7–8). Though I am sure these words of wisdom provided some level of comfort to Joshua, he was still human. He likely questioned if he was qualified to enter into battle. He may have wondered if their mission was hopeless, considering the time they had spent in this barren land. Moses and the Israelites literally sought the Promised Land for decades. This makes the majority of our wait times today seem like a piece of cake!

Nevertheless, Moses heard from the Lord; he knew God would not fail them. Moses knew with full certainty that God would deliver the land He had promised to them. With great insight, he reminded Joshua that God would be with them, so there was no need to fear. Moses had complete faith and trusted God to keep His promise to never leave them nor forsake them.

Likewise, God will never leave you. Just as Moses encouraged the Israelites, I want to encourage you now. The same God who was looking out for these thousands of people in the desert is the same God who loves you more than you could imagine. He will guide your steps. The Scriptures are a message from God to every single person on earth. God's promises are just as relevant today as they were in the time of Moses. God is telling you through His Word to be courageous. He is fighting your battles for you.

Sometimes, though, we forget to listen to the Lord's voice. We become so wrapped up in ourselves that we forget our inherent need for the Lord. The Israelites became so sure of themselves that they forgot it was God who gave them the power to defeat the enemy in the first place. The Lord said to Moses, "Say unto them. Go not up, neither fight; for I am not among you; lest ye be smitten before your enemies. So I spake unto you;

and ye would not hear, but rebelled against the commandment of the LORD, and went presumptuously up into the hill" (Deut. 1:42–43 KJV). It was not long before they fully discovered the error of their ways. God turned a deaf ear toward them. Their rebellion against God caused them to spend forty years in the wilderness.

As they approached the Promised Land, the Lord told Moses that this land would be given to his descendants; however, Moses would not have the opportunity to set foot on this land. The Lord said, "'I have let you see *it* with your eyes, but you shall not go over there'" (Deut. 34:4 NASB). Moses went to be with the Lord before they entered the Promised Land, only seeing it from afar.

Moses received a word from the Lord concerning his death, which is why he mentored Joshua as the new leader. Joshua served under the leadership of Moses for forty years, and they had been through a lot together. They shared a solid belief that God would not fail the Israelites. They had seen God's power firsthand. God parted the Red Sea, allowing the Israelites to cross on dry land, causing Pharaoh and his army to drown in the sea. God sent a cloud by day and a fire by night to guide them through the wilderness. Moses and Joshua knew God was sovereign and all-powerful. They also knew He would prove faithful.

As the new leader of the Israelites, Joshua heard from the Lord, just as Moses had previously received guidance. The Lord told Joshua to lead the Israelites across the Jordan River (Josh. 1:2). God caused the water to stop flowing, so they could walk across dry land. Just as He told Moses, the Lord told Joshua, "'Be strong and courageous. Do not be afraid; do not be discouraged, for the LORD your God will be with you wherever you go'" (Josh. 1:9).

How would you react if God told you He was going to lead you and thousands of people under your leadership across a river—without a boat or a bridge? Would you be afraid? Likely, you and I would both experience some apprehension in this situation. Nevertheless, Joshua immediately told the Israelites to pack up and prepare for the journey.

Sometimes, it is easy to look at our circumstances in the natural and automatically decide they are impossible. We become fearful of the unknown, not willing to trust God to move in our lives. We need to adopt the fearlessness of Joshua, who led the Israelites across the Jordan. All the while, one of Joshua's greatest tests was still to come.

God commanded him to march with the Israelites around the walls of Jericho for seven consecutive days in order to conquer the city. God told him to march around the city one time each day for six days and on the seventh day, God said, "'March around the city seven times, with the priests blowing the trumpets. When you hear them sound a long blast on the trumpets, have the whole army give a loud shout; then the wall of the city will collapse and the army will go up" (Josh. 6:4–5).

What would you do if you received these marching orders? Think about the city closest to where you live. How would you look if you gathered thousands of people to march around the city limits seven days in a row? People would likely ridicule you and curse you for such an outrageous disruption of their municipality. You may even be arrested for disturbing the peace or lose your life at the hands of a disgruntled or deranged citizen.

Regardless of the unusual directives, Joshua heard from the Lord and there was no hesitation on his part. The Bible says Joshua called the priests and told them, "'Take up the ark of the covenant of the LORD and have seven priests carry trumpets in front of it.' And he ordered the army, 'Advance! March around the city, with an armed guard going ahead of the ark of the LORD'" (Josh. 6:6–7). Joshua did not overanalyze the situation, call a meeting to devise a plan, or establish a board of directors to determine the best way to move forward. He did what God called him to do because he knew the Lord would not fail.

Let us all be like Joshua, listening to God's still, small voice, ready and willing to follow Him wherever He leads. When we obey the Lord's command, miracles happen. Even in the midst of the most disconcerting situations, God is in control.

Through the Fire

On one of our visits to an orphanage in Roatán, Honduras, we arrived at the port, only to find that the person who was supposed to pick us up had not arrived at the scheduled time. Apparently, there was some miscommunication between the driver and the director of the facility. As we had a large number of boxes and supplies to deliver, we decided it best to wait and see if we could find the person with whom we had pre-arranged transportation. In Honduras, it is unwise to jump in a car spontaneously, even if it appears to be a licensed taxicab. Poverty is great in this region of Central America, so the idea that we had hundreds of dollars of valuable supplies made us a target for crime.

My Grandma Lucille, my mom's mother, traveled with us on this trip, so my dad decided to walk to the top of the hill, leaving us with the boxes. Crew members from the cruise ship we were sailing on assisted us in getting everything off the ship to this secure point of our journey. Not long after my dad walked toward the cruise terminal entrance, a taxi driver began loading all of the supplies into his vehicle, without our consent. I repeatedly told him to stop, but he persisted. Unsure of what to do, I prayed God would give us wisdom. While I did not want him to steal all of our donations, I was hesitant of getting into an automobile with someone who seemed so aggressive. However, I felt my grandma and I would be safe inside the protected area. As we neared the spot where my dad was talking to an official, the driver stopped and let us out. Thankfully, he was just trying to be helpful. I thank God for helping us get everything to the children's home safely and for His continuous protection.

When we face a difficult or dangerous situation, we should always strive to keep our eyes on Jesus. He will guide us and direct us. He will keep us sheltered from harm. Even when we are fearful, we need to remember we are not alone. We must rely on God, fully acknowledging that He will keep us safe, just as He kept my family and me safe in Roatán. No matter what dangers come our way, God will be with us, even in the midst of the fire.

Shadrach, Meshach, and Abednego found this out on a physical level. They literally found themselves in the blazing fury of a fiery furnace. King Nebuchadnezzar was infuriated because they would not bow down and worship his image of gold. As such, he threatened to throw them into the fire. They responded, "'If we are thrown into the blazing

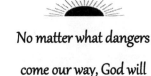

No matter what dangers come our way, God will be with us, even in the midst of the fire.

furnace, the God we serve is able to deliver us from it, and he will deliver us from Your Majesty's hand'" (Dan. 3:17). Their commitment to God was sure, because they knew He was greater than any power on this earth. Why were they so confident? Because they knew, God would never fail.

Notwithstanding, they also knew God's sovereign plan could include a different type of rescue, one that involved a journey to Heaven. They followed their statement with, "'But even if he does not, we want you to know, Your Majesty, that we will not serve your gods or worship the image of gold you have set up'" (Dan. 3:18). Regardless of the possible outcomes, they refused to bow down to a fabricated idol. Their devotion to the one true God was so great; they were willing to give their lives as a sacrifice and example of Christian faith.

King Nebuchadnezzar followed through with his promise. He ordered his soldiers to tie them up and cast them into the furnace, heated to a temperature seven times hotter than usual (Dan. 3:19–20). The furnace was "so hot that the flames of the fire killed the soldiers who took up Shadrach, Meshach and Abednego" (Dan. 3:22). Nevertheless, King Nebuchadnezzar said, "I see four men loose, walking in the midst of the fire, and they have no hurt; and the form of the fourth is like the Son of God" (Dan. 3:25 KJV). At once, he ordered them to come out.

The same fire that killed some of Nebuchadnezzar's soldiers "had not harmed their bodies, nor was a hair of their heads singed; their robes were not scorched, and there was no smell of fire on them" (Dan. 3:27). These three individuals knew the hand of God was upon their lives. They trusted God would be with them, even in the midst of what should have been a fatal fire. They knew something Nebuchadnezzar did not understand; their God had the power to rescue them from the fire. The Lord walked ahead of them, shielding them from all harm, so they might be a testimony of His miraculous power.

How many times have we heard from the Lord and dismissed His call on our lives? How many days have we been so busy with the noisy nature of life that we missed hearing His still, small voice? Have there been times in your life when you knew you should be somewhere in particular, but your personal preferences reigned supreme? That sporting event on television, the movie you and your friends wanted to see at the cinema, the new restaurant that opened last week; these things are well and good, but our priority should be listening to God's voice. God may be calling us to instead visit a shut-in, encourage a friend who is lost, or stay home and study God's Word. God's will is more important than our desires, and it may even save someone's life, quite possibly our own.

If Shadrach, Meshach, and Abednego had not stood firm in

their faith, they would have surely died in the furnace. If Moses had not been faithful to the Lord, the Egyptians on the shores of the Red Sea would have likely murdered the Israelites. If Joshua had not obeyed God's command, the walls of Jericho would not have crumbled to the ground and the Israelites might have spent the rest of their lives in the wilderness. If I had not been running late that day on the way to college, I might not be alive today.

We must put our trust in Jesus Christ, even when life is difficult, for He is the One who will calm our fears. He will give us strength and courage. He will be with us everywhere we go, just as He was with the three Hebrew children in the furnace and just as He was with the Israelites when they marched around Jericho and the walls went tumbling down!

You may assume this occurrence was no big deal, and that some old walls crumbled, probably due to poor construction, not because some people marched around a city. These city walls were unlike most of the ones you might see today. They were six feet thick, twenty-six feet high, sitting atop a forty-six-feet-high embankment. Modern-day archeologists have excavated the site and discovered that the walls did collapse, except for a small section where Rahab and her father's household, along with the Israelite spies, probably exited the city (Josh. 6:25). Only God could have caused this miracle to occur. No other explanation on earth could justify the abrupt crumbling of the walls of Jericho.

The same God who performed miracles in the days of Moses and Joshua still performs miracles today. At times, though, we become as the Israelites, and our arrogance overwhelms us to the point where we feel we do not need God's presence in our lives. The moment we determine our lack of need for God, that is the exact moment when everything will begin to tailspin out of control like a helicopter plunging to the ground due to a broken propeller. We need Jesus in our lives, even more than we need clean air to breathe and fresh water to drink. He is the One who sustains our lives!

Bountiful Harvests

During my lifetime, my dad has grown dozens of different crops, but one particular crop will always stand out in my mind. One summer, we harvested a copious quantity of sweet, succulent watermelons. My dad grew multiple varieties, ranging from small Icebox watermelons to the large, elongated Charleston Grey watermelons. We had so many that we gave them away to nearly everyone we knew. Inevitably, we had more supply than demand. It became difficult to eat them all before they spoiled, with us eventually eating the hearts of the watermelons and feeding the leftovers to the cattle.

When I think of this special memory, a verse from the Bible comes to mind: "'Give, and it will be given to you. A good measure, pressed down, shaken together and running over, will be poured into your lap. For with the measure you use, it will be measured to you'" (Luke 6:38). We had a bounty of watermelons, more than we could possibly use. Although cultivating a crop like this took a lot of hard work, God honored our dedication and poured out His blessing upon our garden. If we had not been willing to water the seeds and tend to the needs of the plants, then we would have missed God's abundant blessings. Similarly, how many times in life do we miss a blessing because we are too busy, too tired, or too unmotivated to reach out our hand and take hold of what God wants to bestow upon us?

In order to receive a blessing from the Lord, we must first realize this truth: without Jesus, we cannot do anything. Jesus said in John 15:5, "'If you remain in me and I in you, you will bear much fruit; apart from me you can do nothing.'" Without Jesus, we are like a fruit tree that does not bear any fruit and never will. Surely, an orchard operator would cut down such a tree, for it would be useless. Instead, we should live for Jesus and listen to His guidance in our lives. Jesus said, "'My Father is glorified by this, that you bear much fruit, and *so* prove to be My disciples'"

(John 15:8 NASB). When we live a life that glorifies God, we will be like a tree laden with fruit, ready for harvest.

When we are walking closely with Jesus, we will have a bountiful supply of God's love, so we can share His love with everyone we encounter on the road of life. When He walked on this earth, Jesus chose twelve apostles to minister with Him and to fellowship with Him. More importantly, He taught them how to share the Gospel with others. God's Word is our training manual. We are God's disciples. We must work hard for the sake of Christ. We cannot allow the fruit God has produced in our lives to spoil. We must share the blessings of God with others on a continual basis.

When we live a life that glorifies God, we will be like a tree laden with fruit, ready for harvest.

If we do not share the blessings God gives us, we will find that all will be for naught. Jesus told the parable of a wealthy man who had a large crop. He decided to tear down his barns, so he could build barns with a higher capacity. Because of his abundance of grain, he thought he could just eat, drink, and make merry (Luke 12:19). However, God responded, "Thou fool, this night thy soul shall be required of thee: then whose shall those things be, which thou hast provided?" (Luke 12:20 KJV). Just as this man could not store up a multi-year supply of grain, we cannot store up good deeds. Just because we pray faithfully for one week does not mean we no longer need to pray the rest of the month or even the rest of the year. God does not want us to simply sit back, relax, and take it easy. We always need to be prepared to share the Gospel, working diligently until His return.

Our lives need to be bountiful harvests, pleasing to the Lord, making an impact on the world for Jesus. Seek His will for your life. He has work for you to do, for it is time for harvest! I pray God will give you wisdom and discernment, so you will hear His still, small voice. Take time to listen. Every delay could be a gift from God, saving you from harm as He protected me on the road, or leading you to victory as God led the Israelites when they conquered the city of Jericho. Follow the Lord's footsteps. Trust Him completely, and He will be with you everywhere you go!

Chapter Nineteen

Be the One

"For many are called, but few are chosen."' (Matt. 22:14 NLT)

When I was a young teenager, my dad was pastoring an Assembly of God church in my hometown. Although the congregation was small, we managed to do big things. Whether we were hosting a massive free chicken pilaf dinner with an outdoor gospel sing or bringing in vanloads of children for a summer Vacation Bible School, we never let anything stop us from reaching out to the lost and helping those in need, both in a physical and a spiritual sense. Still, one event would change the course of history, at least the history of my immediate family.

My dad had been in communication with a man by the name of Dwight Good. He and his twin brother ministered in song throughout the world. At the time, Dwight was traveling with General Boris Pyankov, a three-star Russian military general. He was visiting several churches in the United States, sharing his testimony of how God completely changed his life. The idea that he would take time out of his busy schedule to come to our church seemed unlikely, but my dad felt led to ask in faith.

A short time later, we received a phone call. The moment my dad answered the phone, I knew it would be good news. It was as if Jesus spoke to my heart in that moment, just as He did to the disciples, when "Jesus looked at them and said, 'With man this is impossible, but with God all things are possible'" (Matt. 19:26). The impossible became possible. Although our church was small, God brought this Russian general to the rural town of Live Oak,

Florida. Not only that, but he also spoke at a high school in a nearby county. Of course, my favorite aspect of his Florida itinerary was when he was a dinner guest in our home.

When this Russian military general sat down at the dinner table, he gave me the opportunity to experience several "firsts." One being the fact that this was the first time we ever had a Russian military general visit our home. Another was the fact that this was the first time we ever had an interpreter at our dinner table. Finally, this was the first time I ever made coffee. Aside from the fact that General Pyankov drank three cups and said it was delicious, this is not the real story. Nor is the fact that he blessed me with a special gift, a hand-painted tray from Russia. The real story is *his* story.

Baptized at the young age of four years old in the Russian Orthodox Church, General Pyankov grew up as an atheist, following the death of his Christian grandmother when he was only seven. He joined the military when he was eighteen years old. He rose through the ranks to become one of only twenty-six three-star generals in Russia's army and he became deputy secretary of defense in 1991. He served in the Russian military for more than four decades, earning seventeen medals.

Although he had never believed in God as an adult, God was certainly watching over him. During a mission, both of the engines in the helicopter he was flying in failed. The aircraft began spiraling out of control. In the midst of the calamity, he remembered the lessons he had learned from his grandmother. As he and the other communist and atheist passengers were plunging to certain death, they cried out to God in desperation. God heard their cries for help and miraculously spared their lives, allowing the aircraft to land safely in the tops of some trees. Rather than go back to the life he once lived, his mission became the invaluable task of putting a Bible in the hands of every Russian soldier. He made a commitment to God to share the Gospel of Jesus Christ all around the world.

Hearing his testimony was truly life changing. His stories from the battlefield, his experiences in the Soviet Union, and his close encounter with God were extraordinarily inspirational. It was humbling to know that God moved a figurative mountain, just to give us this experience. Sadly, many people missed such a wonderful opportunity. Countless people in our community told my parents and me they were busy and they would "catch him next time." What they did not realize was this was most likely a once-in-a-lifetime experience, for three-star Russian military generals who have committed their life to Christ seldom pass through this region.

I wonder, when Jesus returns to this earth, will some of them tell Him now is not a good time? Will they complain about the fact that they *have* to go to Heaven? While this notion seems ridiculous to my way of thinking, it is disconcerting to know some people may take this approach. The Lord even asked, "'When the Son of Man comes, will he find faith on the earth?'" (Luke 18:8). Likewise, Jesus encountered individuals who had little faith, even in His hometown (Mark 6:4-6). Many individuals seek to fulfill their own wants and desires, with little regard for anything or anyone else. Their self-centeredness often prevents them from helping their fellow man or even from receiving a blessing from God above. Yet God has not called us to serve ourselves, but to serve others.

God has not called us to serve ourselves, but to serve others.

When General Pyankov spoke at our church, Dwight Good sang a song titled, "Be the One." Dave Clark, Al Denson, and Don Koch wrote the song, but hearing Dwight sing this song was my first time hearing this song. The lyrics of this song beckon the listener to ponder whether he or she will answer the call of God.

In Mark 16:15, Jesus told the disciples, "'Go into all the world and preach the gospel to all creation.'" He is calling you and me to do the same. We must go forth and share the Gospel with the world. People are dying daily, some without the saving knowledge of Jesus Christ. Others are living in darkness, looking for a glimpse of hope in all of the wrong places. Jesus has called us to be the light. He said, "'You are the light of the world'" (Matt. 5:14). Will you boldly go forth in this dark world and shine your light for Jesus Christ?

Standing Out

Through the years, my dad and I have occasionally sung a song titled, "I'll Stand for Jesus," written by Franklin Walden. The lyrics of this song ring truer now than ever before, as we must all take a stand for Jesus Christ, even if making a stand for Christ puts us in harm's way. Around the world, one in twelve Christians experience persecution for their faith, according to the list published by Open Doors USA, a nonprofit organization devoted to serving persecuted Christians.[1]

In recent years, there have been numerous targeted attacks on Christians. Consider the Syrian refugees, for example. Thousands of Christians have fled from their homes in Syria and surrounding regions. Militant groups continually seek to isolate Christians in an effort to eradicate them from the earth. In some regions, two-thirds of the Christians have had to move to another city or even a different country. In spite of these tragic occurrences, the majority of Christians are standing strong in the Lord, not allowing these radicalized groups to destroy their faith in the one true God.

One such pastor has stayed with his family in Syria, struggling to make ends meet. Devoted to the call God has placed on his life, he is caring for his dwindling congregation, a daughter who is ill, children in an orphanage, and over two hundred families whom he helps through the support of Open Doors USA. Most of the doctors and other professionals have fled the country, leaving little assistance behind. Amid the calamity, he said, "'God is in control, He controls everything. Sometimes [H]e does this from behind a curtain; we don't see Him working. Time will come when we will understand that He was always there. . . . God is moving and doing great things around us, many are being saved.'"[2] Instead of looking at his situation, he is keeping his eyes on his Savior.

Stories like this help put things into perspective. For many people, their greatest concerns when they get up in the morning are having fresh coffee to drink and hoping their car will start when they head off to work. While minor inconveniences in life may annoy us, these types of trivial circumstances do not even compare to the major challenges that millions of people face on a daily basis. Some Christians are tortured and murdered because of their faith. Others wake up every day wondering if they will have clean, safe water to drink or ultimately die of thirst. While many people are contemplating what to have for dinner, other people around the globe are wondering if they will have dinner at all, or even be able to live to see another sunrise, due to malnourishment, disease, and other life-threatening conditions.

There have been tens of millions of Christian martyrs throughout history, with nearly one hundred thousand individuals still losing their lives to martyrdom each year. With all of the violence in the world, what should Christians do to cope with such hatred? Jesus imparted wisdom on how to handle such situations: "'You will be hated by everyone because of me, but the one who stands firm to the end will be saved'" (Matt. 10:22). Even when people come against us and our lives may be in danger, we must stand firm in our faith.

If you find yourself in a situation where someone asks you to renounce Jesus Christ, stand firm. Do not deny Christ, as the apostle Peter did three times in a row (Luke 22:54–62). Instead, be quick to affirm your relationship with Christ in the presence of other people. Jesus said, "'Whoever acknowledges me before others, I will also acknowledge before my Father in heaven. But whoever disowns me before others, I will disown before my Father in heaven'" (Matt. 10:32–33). When we acknowledge our Lord and Savior publicly, we make our Heavenly Father proud. When we fail to recognize Him, He will disown us. Let us all make the important decision to proclaim the name of Jesus everywhere we go, no matter the cost.

Consider the story of the young girl who professed her faith during the Columbine High School massacre in 1999. Reportedly, the shooter asked if she believed in God. When she said, "Yes," the perpetrator took her life. While the Columbine shooting was one of the first school shootings to gain widespread coverage, especially in regards to the martyrdom of one or more students, this was not the first occurrence of people being martyrs for Christ. Theologians consider Stephen to be one of the earliest Christian martyrs. Accused of blasphemy, he delivered a lengthy speech denouncing the authorities and their beliefs, taking a stand for Christ. Even though his life was ended abruptly, his testimony likely helped change the life of Saul of Tarsus, who was a witness to the stoning of Stephen (Acts 7:58). Perhaps seeing someone so strong in their faith was what began to soften Saul's heart, as he later became the apostle Paul, a prolific writer and follower of Christ.

When we take a stand for Jesus, it is almost certain that someone else is watching. Besides the bystanders who surround us, we can have assurance that God is watching. He will give us strength to endure the persecution. He will place people in our path who need to hear the Gospel. We will never know the impact our actions will have on other people. We have no idea how God will use us. We do not have to traverse the battlefield alone, for He will be our shield and defender. He has already prevailed over all evil on this earth and will place our enemies under our feet (Ps. 110:1).

In John 16:33, Jesus said we do not have to be concerned about the troubles of this world, for He has already overcome the entire world. There are so many promises like this one in God's Word, yet many people fail to realize what Jesus is actually telling us. Instead, they live their lives in fear, whether it is fear of failure, fear of tomorrow, or fear of life itself. We do not have to be afraid when God is on our side. No matter how difficult a situation may seem, He is greater than every single trial we face.

We can gain strength from this scripture, even in the midst of turmoil: "Greater is he that is in you, than he that is in the world" (1 John 4:4 KJV). When we have complete faith that God is greater than anything this world throws our way, then we can surmount every valley and every mountain. As Paul wrote in the book of Ephesians, "Be strong in the Lord and in his mighty power. Put on the full armor of God, so that you can take your stand against the devil's schemes" (Eph. 6:10–11). If we trust the Lord to give us strength and protect us, we will be able to stand up against the vilest forces of evil.

Standing up for Christ is very unpopular in our society today, even across social media channels. Recently, I posted a scripture on Twitter. Much to my dismay, dozens of people sent hateful replies, including expletives and highly inappropriate content. My "offensive" post included the following scriptural paraphrase: "Every knee will bow and every tongue confess that Jesus Christ is Lord" (Phil. 2:10–11). Yet some people referred to this as a "fairy tale." I pray they will come to know the truth and accept Jesus Christ as their Lord and Savior before it is too late. For one day, they will discover the truth and realize my tweet was entirely non-fiction.

Through my online ministry, I often encounter people who are adamantly against the Gospel. Whether I am talking about the love of Jesus or the healing power of God, I often receive backlash concerning my *Be Encouraged* webcast. From criticizing my appearance to throwing out vulgarities, some people will stop at nothing when they are trying to discredit God's Word. In all honesty, the negative comments often bothered me in the beginning. Here I was, simply trying to provide encouragement to people all around the world, yet this was how some people showed their appreciation. Now, though, God has helped me realize they are not attacking me personally, but instead, they are attacking the Gospel message.

People even persecuted Jesus and His disciples when they shared the Good News. Jesus said in Matthew 5:11–12, "'Blessed are you when people insult you, persecute you and falsely say all kinds of evil against you because of me. Rejoice and be glad, because great is your reward in heaven, for in the same way they persecuted the prophets who were before you.'" As Jesus so eloquently reminded us, we should rejoice when someone persecutes us.

Let us boldly declare the Gospel of Jesus Christ, even if we have to stand alone.

While I am saddened when I see such hostile responses to my posts online, I rejoice in the fact that thousands of people are hearing about Jesus, maybe even for the very first time. It is humbling to know God could use a video I create in my own home to take the Gospel message to so many different nations. I pray God will use my posts to plant a seed in the hearts of individuals who may not otherwise darken the door of a church. I pray they will believe Jesus Christ is Lord, for if they come to know the truth, the truth will set them free (John 8:32): free from counterfeit religions, free from false doctrines, and free from every attack of the enemy. There is true freedom found through Jesus Christ alone!

Sadly, many people have heard this message and still do not

believe. Many others have not even heard the message of the Gospel. God's Word says, "How, then, can they call on the one they have not believed in? And how can they believe in the one of whom they have not heard? And how can they hear without someone preaching to them?" (Rom. 10:14). It is up to us to go forth and share the Gospel. Even amid persecution, we must answer the call. There are times when being the *one* literally means being *the one*. Yet when God has given us a desire in our heart to share the Gospel of Jesus Christ, then nothing can stop us from being a light. Let us boldly declare the Gospel of Jesus Christ, even if we have to stand alone.

When God Calls

Even before I was born, my parents were involved in many different aspects of ministry. From pastoring churches and traveling on the evangelistic field, to ministering in music and organizing children's ministry events, they continually strived to "be the one." Gratefully, God instilled within me the same desire to listen earnestly to God's still, small voice. For more than thirty years now, I have endeavored to follow God's will for my life. My purpose on this planet is to share the love of Jesus Christ with others. That is why God raised me to life when I was born. Whether my dad and I have the opportunity to sing at a prison, lead worship at a local church, or go on a mission overseas, our greatest desire is to share the Gospel. Every door God opens is important. Every person we minister to matters. Every moment spent in ministry is sacred and precious, a gift from God above.

As a young person, I realized early on that not everyone in ministry had come to this conclusion, nor did these individuals share the same ideals as my parents and me. I quickly learned the harsh realities of being in full-time or even part-time ministry. For those on the outside looking in, ministry is not all coming up roses, as the old adage says. There are times when professed

Christians get outraged over the color of the drapery, the uncomfortable nature of the pews, the temperature of the sanctuary, and so many other insignificant matters. They worry about the possibility of another church member wearing the same dress as them on Sunday morning, while there are members of the community whose entire wardrobe consists of the tattered clothes on their back. Others express their dissatisfaction if the church potluck dinner does not feature the same number of proteins as last month, even though there are people living on the streets who have not had a hot meal in years. Since when have we lost touch with reality? Ministry is about ministering to people in need, not nitpicking over the trivial shortcomings of the church.

Frankly, I am grateful for the opportunity to have an "inside look" at ministry in general. Not because I want to contribute to the negativity often lurking behind the scenes, but instead, so I can strive to be an even greater positive influence within the ministry God has given me. My experiences have molded and shaped me to the point where I know precisely why I minister. I do not share the Gospel with others out of obligation. I tell people about Jesus Christ, desiring God to find me faithful in His sight. I minister not to please the sons of men, but to please the Son of Man.

Although there have been some peculiar experiences associated with ministry, such as the church I recall that had lots and lots of curtains, I have also enjoyed many sweet times of fellowship and worship on this journey as well. I will always have fond memories of singing at Brother Apperson's church. One of the things I remember most is that he always gave me a fresh apple when we sang at his church. I have been fishing with preacher's kids, petted preacher's cats (which made me feel at home, since cats are my favorite animal and my cat Morris is very special to me), and helped preacher's wives clean up the kitchen after a delicious meal. Through these times spent traveling with my parents, I developed a keen awareness for the concept of the family of God. For I soon discovered that family is not restricted to blood relatives. Many times, a pastor and his family became an extension of our own family.

One summer, my dad was preaching revivals throughout the Cumberland Gap region of Virginia, Tennessee, and Kentucky. My dad and I sang, my dad delivered a message from God's Word, and my mom provided a special program for the children. On one such occasion, we stayed with a pastor and his family in their parsonage. The fact that they had a daughter who was close to my age made it extra exciting. When we were not in church or enjoying a scrumptious meal together, she and I played every game you could imagine. From playing school to cooking pretend food, we had a blast and made many special memories together.

My parents nurtured friendships with her parents as well, all of us sharing God's love for one another. We all loved our families, and we all appreciated a delightful meal. To this day, I still make several recipes given to us by the pastor's wife. She was the first one to share the indulgent flavors of muddy buddies and chocolate éclair cake with us. My taste buds are forever grateful. Yet

I minister not to please the sons of men, but to please the Son of Man.

the greatest bond we shared was not one founded upon food or family, but it was one grounded in the solid Rock, Jesus Christ. We shared a common bond of ministry, which is our life's calling.

Regardless of where God leads us on this path of ministry, one thing is always constant. God is the One who is leading us. We could never open the doors He swings wide open. From hosting a Russian general in a small rural community church to singing in places like Bucharest, Romania, with my dad, only God could arrange these opportunities. That is why I want to follow the advice of the Psalmist David who wrote, "Be still before the LORD and wait patiently for him" (Ps. 37:7). We will not always understand where God is leading us. Sometimes, we must sit still and wait for God to move in our lives. He may call us into ministry right away, but He may want to prepare us first. Either way, His timing is impeccable.

Simultaneously, we need to be ready and willing to answer His call, even when we least expect it. I recall a time when the pastor asked me to pray at a very large church, with no advanced warning. As I walked toward the platform, the words of the apostle Paul came to mind: "Preach the word; be prepared in season and out of season; correct, rebuke and encourage—with great patience and careful instruction" (2 Tim. 4:2). I am always prepared to share the Gospel or to pray and talk to our Heavenly Father. How humbling it was to know in my heart that God chose me for this special opportunity. God may call us to pray, share our testimony with a colleague or friend, visit a local homeless shelter, or even embark on the mission field. No matter what He calls us to do, we need to be eager to go forth and fulfill His call.

You may be wondering if God has truly called you into the ministry. If you have placed your trust in Jesus Christ, then the answer to this question is a resounding yes. God has called all of us to tell others about His saving grace: "But you are a chosen people, a royal priesthood, a holy nation, God's special possession, that you may declare the praises of him who called you out of darkness into his wonderful light" (1 Pet. 2:9). The world may be full of darkness. Other Christians may even seek to bring you down at times, but God has made provision to call us out of darkness. He wants to bring us into His wonderful light. We do not have to stay in the blinding darkness. With Jesus Christ, our Cornerstone, we can walk in light. He will light the way, so we may share His light with others along life's journey.

Just as General Pyankov was knocking at death's door as his

helicopter fell from the sky, you may find yourself in what seems like a hopeless situation. You may feel as if you have plunged into a dark cavern of despair, not knowing how to escape. Years of regret, sorrow, or disappointment may have overwhelmed you to the point where you cannot see a single ray of hope. Take heart! You do not have to live in darkness any longer. The same God who brought General Pyankov safely to the ground will bring you to safety as well. Call on the name of the Lord, and you shall be saved (Acts 2:21).

God wants to use you for His glory. Just as the General's testimony encourages people even today, you need to share your story. God will place people in your life, so you can encourage them with your testimony. Will you follow His leading? Will you share the Gospel? Will you answer when God calls?

Chapter Twenty

Qualifying the Called

"It is not that we think we are qualified to do anything on our own. Our qualification comes from God." (2 Cor. 3:5 NLT)

Before I was even born, my parents had a call on their lives to lift up the precious name of Jesus Christ. They traveled and ministered all over the United States and Canada, proclaiming the Good News. Having parents who were so dedicated to the Lord's work, I grew up with the notion that everyone was involved in some aspect of ministry and that weekends were all about going to church. I would not have wanted it any other way, for it was a blessing to grow up sharing the Gospel!

As an adult, I have sadly discovered that countless Christians are not involved in ministry at all. Many churchgoers consider going to church to be a spectator sport. They sit in the pew on Sunday, counting down the minutes until the service ends, in anticipation of a delectable dinner followed by their favorite sporting event as viewed from their comfortable easy chair. For some individuals, church is like checking off a box one day a week, never to think about it the other six days of the week. In reality, there is little purpose in hearing the Gospel, while failing to share this marvelous message throughout the week.

I firmly believe everyone who has put their trust in Jesus Christ has a call on their life to share the Gospel. We should all be involved in some facet of ministry, whether it is for five people or an audience of five thousand. God has work for all of us to do. Look around you. Your pastor cannot speak to every single person you see each day. It is up to you and me to share the knowledge of salvation through Jesus Christ with them while we still can. Christ will return one day soon, and then the door of opportunity to share the Gospel will close. We cannot afford to miss even one opportunity.

Thanks to the godly influence of my parents, I have always understood the importance of walking through every door God opens. We sang at churches and held revivals throughout the southeast as I was growing up. For several years, my dad also served as the pastor of Christ Fellowship Community Church. We took every opportunity to share the love of Jesus Christ with the local community. Of course, none of the wonderful outreaches we offered happened automatically. My dad, mom, and I, along with several members of the church, were the ones who made it all happen. Whether it was someone to pick up the neighborhood children in the church van, someone to teach Sunday school classes, or someone to supervise the church nursery, volunteers stepped up to the plate to ensure everything ran smoothly.

We do not have to have perfect pitch, but a propensity to honor our Heavenly Father in all we do.

Through the ministry God allowed us to lead, we served as a lighthouse in the middle of our town. People often came for assistance, but left with something far greater, the knowledge of the only living God who loves them unconditionally. It was not about growing a mega church or having the fanciest building in town. Our primary goal was to tell others about Jesus Christ.

There is more to ministry than being the most sought-after evangelist or a chart-topping vocalist. The aim of ministry should be following the call God has placed on our lives. The way we live our lives should reflect our desire to please the Lord in all we do. Psalm 19:14 (NLT) says, "May the words of my mouth and the meditation of my heart be pleasing to you, O LORD, my rock and my redeemer." We should pray every single day that every word, which comes from our lips, would be pleasing to the Lord.

We are not on this earth to please men, but to please God. Revelation 4:11 (KJV) tells us, "Thou art worthy, O Lord, to receive glory and honour and power: for thou hast created all things, and for thy pleasure they are and were created." God has created us for His delight, so we might worship Him and honor Him. He wants us to sing praises to His name and glorify Him forevermore. Perhaps you are getting a bit nervous about this notion of singing praises, since you may not be able to carry a tune in a bucket. That is perfectly okay. The Bible says we are simply to praise the Lord. We do not have to have perfect pitch, but a propensity to honor our Heavenly Father in all we do. Remember, worship is not entertainment; God shares His glory with no one.

Several years ago, my dad and I visited a church in Cherokee, North Carolina. During the service, one of the members of the congregation sang a special song. This elderly gentleman poured his heart into every single note. Although it may not have been a performance deemed "good enough" to grace many prominent stages in the world, it was something I will always remember. The zeal and love for our Lord that he expressed through this single song embodied a greater message than a month of sermons could convey. His aim was not to please the congregation, but to please his Lord and Savior, Jesus Christ. As he sang, he held nothing back. He passionately sang of his anticipation of seeing Christ. He gave everything he could to the delivery of this song, so that it might be pleasing to our Heavenly Father. Through his ministry, I know God used him to touch people's hearts. How do I know? I know because his song touched my own heart in a special way.

Ministry is more than being qualified for the task. Having a Master of Science degree in English education is not what makes me a good schoolteacher; having the desire to make a positive impact on my students is what makes me an effective educator. Likewise, ministry begins with a passion to serve the Lord. If God calls you, He will qualify you. When God places a calling on your life, all He needs is a willing vessel. We need to give our all for the cause of Christ. Once we take the first step, God will use us in ways we could never imagine.

Be Encouraged!

On April 27, 2014, I recorded the very first episode of my *Be Encouraged* webcast. As I sat down in our home with my Bible in one hand and my camera in the other, I prayed God would use the video to encourage at least one person. Fifty-seven people originally watched that first video. From that moment on, I felt in my spirit that God was placing a call on my life more than ever to speak about His love.

I have always enjoyed speaking to others. As a young person, I competed in many public speaking competitions, even at the state level. In recent times, I have spoken at state and national education conferences. Although the idea of speaking on camera did not even make me flinch, I wondered how I was qualified to share a message based on God's Word. I have not gone to seminary or earned a degree in theology. I am not a pastor or an evangelist. How could I possibly teach others about the Scriptures? Why would God choose me for this great responsibility?

While many reservations circled through my mind, I knew then and know now deep within my heart that I only need to absolutely trust God. Why do I feel this way? The answer is simple. God does not call the qualified; He qualifies the called. With this in mind, I faithfully proclaim the Good News through my webcast, prayerfully striving to encourage people around the world. The majority of videos now have several thousand views within the first few days they are available online. It is nothing I have done, but what God has done through me. Even though I initially felt inadequate for the calling God placed on my life, God has helped me realize that He is the One who has given me the qualifications I need to reach out to the lost and to those who are discouraged through this ministry.

Of course, I am not the first person who felt a little out of their league in answering God's call. Moses is the prime example of someone whose calling was to do something that seemed beyond his limitations. God commanded him to speak to Pharaoh, the king of Egypt. While this might be a tremendous opportunity for an eloquent speaker who seeks a prominent stage on which to pontificate, Moses was not a public speaker. He even told the Lord, "'Pardon your servant, LORD. I have never been eloquent, neither in the past nor since you have spoken to your servant. I am slow of speech and tongue'" (Exod. 4:10). Some theologians believe Moses may have had a speech impediment. Either way, he obviously did not feel qualified to speak on the Lord's behalf. Still, the Lord called him to speak, and the Lord knew he was able.

God does not call the qualified; He qualifies the called.

In fact, the Lord seemed perplexed that Moses would even hint at being unable to accomplish this charge. The Lord questioned, "'Who gave human beings their mouths? Who makes them deaf or mute? Who gives them sight or makes them blind? Is it not I, the LORD? Now go; I will help you speak and will teach you what to say'" (Exod. 4:11–12). Moses was concerned he would not have the words to speak. God reassured him that He would provide the message, if Moses agreed to be the Lord's messenger. Moses was extremely apprehensive and still asked God to send someone else instead (Exod. 4:13). At the end of the day, Moses probably would have rather given this mission to someone more qualified, as opposed to taking on such a great task himself.

When I think about this passage, I am somewhat surprised that Moses would have the same tendencies we have today. Of course, Moses was a real human being like you and me. He likely experienced fatigue and often desired for more time for rest as opposed to more work. How many times do we try to put a task in the hands of someone else? Even in our places of work, we may try to lasso someone else with a tedious duty we would prefer to avoid, such as preparing a lengthy report, organizing a daunting stack of papers, or giving a momentous presentation. No matter the job, we could always think of someone more capable. Yet when we receive the assignment, would it not be best if we forged ahead? We should just put our head down, put our best foot forward, and strive to win the race, rather than quit before the starter even waves the green flag.

While Moses may not have had someone giving him a pep talk to encourage him to give this speaking engagement a good old college try, he had something far greater. The Lord told him that he could do it! Nevertheless, Moses was afraid of failure. God became angry with Moses and told him to take Aaron, his brother. The Lord said, "And thou shalt speak unto him, and put words in his mouth: and I will be with thy mouth, and with his mouth, and will teach you what ye shall do. And he shall be thy spokesman unto the people: and he shall be, even he shall be to thee instead of a mouth, and thou shalt be to him instead of God" (Exod. 4:15–16 KJV). Even though Moses felt as if he could not handle this mission, God equipped him for the challenge by using Aaron, who collaborated with Moses so they could carry on this ministry together.

God may ask us to do what appears impossible, but He will always ensure we have the talents and tools we need, and maybe even some extra hands for the job. He will never throw us into the deep end without providing a life preserver. The Lord may gently push us out into deep waters, but He will always be there, watching over us. He will be the strength we need to replace our weaknesses. In the case of Moses, he did not have the public speaking talent, but Aaron was an effective speaker. Together, they delivered the Lord's message given to them through the Holy Spirit. Moses and Aaron listened to His still, small voice, and they delivered the word of the Lord.

When they gathered the Israelite elders, Aaron and Moses did exactly as the Lord instructed them to do. As soon as they had fulfilled their God-ordained tasks, the Israelites believed: "And when they heard that the LORD was concerned about them and had seen their misery, they bowed down and worshiped" (Exod. 4:31). It only took two willing vessels to bring about complete transformation among the Israelites.

As they spoke to the elders, Aaron and Moses found success. This was akin to getting their feet wet before confronting Pharaoh. When they approached his throne, they delivered the message of the Lord: "Let my people go, that they may hold a feast unto me in the wilderness" (Exod. 5:1 KJV). Unlike the response they received from the Israelites, Pharaoh was not so agreeable. Pharaoh said, "Who is the LORD, that I should obey his voice to let Israel go? I know not the LORD, neither will I let Israel go" (Exod. 5:2 KJV). Pharaoh likely thought he was too powerful to obey the word of the Lord. As a ruler, he certainly did not want to receive orders from anyone else, even the Lord Himself.

Imagine how Moses and Aaron felt. Here they had fulfilled the Lord's command, crossing every *t* and dotting every single *i*, only to come up against a proverbial brick wall. Like Moses and Aaron, we often face challenging tasks in our lives, and there may be times when we fail to complete these assignments successfully. While this may result in momentary dismay or even slight humiliation, nothing on this earth could ever compare to failing before the Almighty God. Moses had a crucial responsibility. In opposition, Pharaoh made life even more miserable for the Israelites. I am sure Moses was extremely disheartened, thinking they would never be able to get through to such an obstinate ruler. Yet in his heart, he must have known God would make a way. In spite of the discouraging valleys he had to walk through, Moses knew that God would prove faithful every time, if he kept his eyes on the Lord, devotedly pursuing God's call.

Who Has God Called?

In 2012, my dad and I decided we would do something completely different for the holidays. We had always listened to the anointed music of the Brooklyn Tabernacle Choir, so instead of purchasing gifts, we made plans to visit New York City for the very first time. The reason we traveled to this illustrious concrete jungle was not to view the sights or to eat at iconic restaurants. Instead, the main purpose for our journey to New York was to worship at the Brooklyn Tabernacle.

For several years, the Christmas season seemed lonely without my mom. The void of her not being with us left a major dent in our holiday plans. This was the first time I could remember being completely overjoyed in the Christmas season, since the last time my mom celebrated the holiday with us. I felt as if someone lifted a weight off my shoulders the moment I walked through the doors. When we walked into the foyer, we could immediately feel the presence of the Holy Spirit. Mere words cannot explain the way the Spirit of the Lord was so very real in the sanctuary. Peace filled my soul, and joy flooded my heart. It was certainly not a coincidence that the title of the Brooklyn Tabernacle Christmas program that year was, "Christmas Once Again." God will use all sorts of things to speak to us, even three simple words written on a church bulletin.

Since our first trip to New York, we have had the honor of visiting the Brooklyn Tabernacle many times. Now I consider this house of prayer to be my second home church. One of the most special portions of each service is when everyone in the sanctuary begins lifting their voices, worshiping God and thanking Him for His many blessings. Joining in with thousands of voices, singing praises to Jesus Christ, it feels like a taste of our worship in Heaven. Just imagine the

God will use all sorts of things to speak to us, even three simple words written on a church bulletin.

moment when we see Jesus Christ face-to-face, when we bow down to worship Him forevermore.

Sadly, not everyone will have the opportunity to be part of such a glorious celebration. Some people will not enter into Heaven's gates, even though God has extended an invitation to all who will believe. God invites every man and woman, and every boy and girl, to receive the gift of salvation, yet there are many who refuse to turn away from sin and receive His grace and forgiveness. Many do not believe in Jesus Christ. Still others have not even heard about Jesus.

You may suppose I am speaking of some remote village somewhere where they have never used a telephone or even had the luxury of electricity. On the other hand, you may picture a tribe of indigenous people living deep within a jungle rainforest. Your mind could even wander to someone living on the streets of a third world country, surrounded by inescapable poverty. While these circumstances certainly exist, there are also people in our very midst who have not heard the Good News of the Gospel.

I recently watched a video of someone who grew up in the

Jewish faith in New York City, but had never read the Bible. I sat on my sofa astounded. Living in such a metropolis, yet this individual had never read the most widely circulated book in the history of the world. Another person recently told me the same thing. Living in the United States of America, possessing several years of education and the ability to read, yet they could not remember a time when they had opened the pages of God's Word. Why had no one around them ever shared this wondrous book?

Jesus Christ commissioned the disciples to go forth and preach the Good News to all creation. He was not implying that only pastors or evangelists should preach the Good News. This directive extends to every single person who has put their trust in Jesus Christ. We are all supposed to tell others about the redeeming love of Jesus Christ. The time of Christ's return is drawing near. We must share the Good News with a sense of urgency while we still have the opportunity.

On one of our visits to the Brooklyn Tabernacle, Pastor Jim Cymbala spoke about the critical need to witness to others and how we should all be preachers of the Gospel.[1] In this modern era, the word *preacher* is misunderstood. People think of the minister as having a supreme status in the church hierarchy. Sometimes this means donning a long robe, sitting apart from the congregation, or even using a different tone of voice for delivering messages from the pulpit. Ultimately, though, a preacher is simply someone who tells others about Jesus.

Pastor Cymbala explained that the word *preach*, when translated from the Greek language, means "to declare, to publish, to talk about, to say, to share, to say something about."[1] Preaching is not something that requires an academic degree in theological studies or ordination from a high-ranking seminary. Every single one of us has the ability to speak, to share the Gospel of Jesus Christ, and to give testimony of our relationship with our Lord and Savior.

The book of Acts gives us a profound illustration of the freedom we all have to preach, no matter where we are located on the globe. Acts 8:1 tells us, "On that day a great persecution broke out against the church in Jerusalem, and all except the apostles were scattered throughout Judea and Samaria." When the church was persecuted, as it still is today in many countries, Christians could not stay in one location. Because of the dangers that existed in their hometowns, they had to flee to other villages. Even with the persecution, the disciples opted to stay put, ministering to the people in that region as best they could. During this time of persecution, multitudes of people accepted the gift of salvation.

The individuals who fled the city realized the necessity of sharing the message of the Gospel. As such, they did not rely on having the apostles with them to spread the Gospel. Acts 8:4 says, "Those who had been scattered preached the word wherever they went." These unnamed Christians, driven away from their homes and their workplaces, possibly torn apart from their families, continued to share the Good News. They had lost everything. Instead of blaming God or drifting into a depressed state, they kept their eyes focused on the one thing they still possessed: salvation through Jesus Christ. They preached the message of salvation everywhere they went because they understood the importance of introducing the world to Jesus Christ.

If the Christians who were in the midst of dire circumstances were willing and able to minister to others, what is our excuse? Many of us have comfortable homes, reliable vehicles, and steady jobs. Even if we are struggling financially, what does it cost to share the Good News? Does it cost anything to talk to our next-door neighbor, or to witness to someone at the local supermarket or the café down the street? Why do we refrain from sharing the greatest news we could ever give someone?

Think about your parents, grandparents, siblings, aunts,

uncles, cousins, friends, coworkers, neighbors—the list goes on. If they were standing on the edge of a cliff, would you help guide them to safety? As followers of Christ, we have the roadmap to eternal life. We can be the messenger to deliver life-saving news, but if we do not share this message, the people we see every day could very well end up in hell. Some people do not like to speak about this horrible place, but it is a real place of eternal fury.

Revelation 20:15 says, "Anyone whose name was not found written in the book of life was thrown into the lake of fire." The Book of Life includes the names of the individuals who have put their complete trust in Jesus Christ. You cannot buy a ticket to Heaven, nor can you accomplish enough good works to go there. An individual recently told me they did not feel "good enough" for God. According to God's Word, there is not one single person who is good enough. I am not good enough. You are not good enough. No one is good enough. Romans 3:23 says we have all sinned and fallen short of the glory of God. We do not deserve His unmerited favor, yet His grace is free to all who believe.

No one is worthy to stand before God's throne. We must all confess our sins and believe in the Lord Jesus Christ. Jesus said, "'I am the way and the truth and the life. No one comes to the Father except through me'" (John 14:6). He claimed absolute exclusivity.

Jesus is the only road to salvation. If you are traveling down a different road, turn around.

Jesus is the only road to salvation. If you are traveling down a different road, turn around. Look to God for direction. His Word will be the light to your path and a lamp unto your feet (Ps. 119:105).

Once you begin your journey down the narrow road that

leads to life everlasting, remember your mission does not stop there. We cannot claim to be Christians and simply live for ourselves. Being a Christian means living for Jesus. We need to be all in for Christ, proclaiming the Gospel of Jesus Christ everywhere we go. Jesus commissioned us for this very purpose. So let us remain faithful to the One who is forever faithful. May we forever pursue our calling as we share the Good News!

Chapter Twenty-One

Soar like an Eagle

"But those who hope in the LORD will renew their strength.
They will soar on wings like eagles; they will run and not grow
weary, they will walk and not be faint." (Isa. 40:31)

In our extensive travels, my dad and I often find ourselves boarding a regional jet, a Boeing 747, or even an Airbus, taking off for our next destination. We have taken the red-eye flight home from New York City on more than one occasion. Typically, the flight is smooth, and there are no problems. On one particular trip, this was certainly not the case. Following several delays, the airline ultimately canceled our flight. All hotels were booked solid because of the countless flight cancellations, due to both mechanical problems and weather-related incidents around the country. Our "bed" for the evening was a cold, hard metal bench in the baggage claim area.

Aside from the uncomfortable nature of the furniture, our primary concern was the fact that we were located right next to a construction zone. While I lacked x-ray vision to see through the wall, I am certain they must have been hosting the national jackhammer convention right there in the middle of the airport, on the other side of the wall, which sounded as if it was paper-thin. I have heard many things in my life, but words cannot quite describe the annoying reverberation of a loud, ear-piercing jackhammer blasting away all night long, especially when you are already experiencing a sleepless night.

To complicate matters, we had planned to get a quick bite to eat in the terminal before our flight. Of course, being that we were stuck in baggage claim, the only edible items were vending machine fare, along with a few snacks we had with us in our carry-on luggage. We tried to occupy our minds by listening to music (which was hard to hear above the sound of a full-fledged construction ensemble), or reading a book, but the situation was quite miserable.

Soon, an airline employee walked toward us. She came bearing gifts: blankets, pillows, bottles of water, and snacks. All with a smile on her face, apologizing as if she had single-handedly caused our terrible predicament. Of course, we knew she was not at fault whatsoever. We thanked her profusely, happy to have a respite from the mundane reality that would last for roughly five more hours. She was kind, with a gentle spirit. We never saw her again. Perhaps God sent her to ease the miserable nature of our circumstances.

That is just like God, to care about His children even when they are only in the midst of a tiny little hiccup on the road of life. Even though we were weary from sleep deprivation, I knew God had everything under control. While we would have rather been on our original flight at the scheduled time, I found solace in the notion that God knew which flight would be safe. He knew which plane was sound, which pilot was seasoned, and which flight path was clear. Sometimes, delays are God's way of synchronizing us with His perfect timing.

Thankfully, not every flight is such a burden. God has allowed us to soar above some amazing scenery, such as our trip to the Last Frontier. As we boarded a de Havilland Beaver floatplane in Juneau, the capital city of Alaska, I knew we were in for an awe-inspiring journey. In all of our airborne hours, this flight deserves the prize for being the most breathtaking and certainly the most memorable. We took an exhilarating sightseeing flight, soaring over towering treetops, brilliantly blue bodies of water, and ice-capped mountains. The highlight of the entire flight was gazing out at Taku Glacier, which is approximately thirty-six miles long and nearly four miles wide. Soon the floatplane soared over the entire width of the glacier, and then began flying along its length, dipping ever more closely to its rugged, yet stunningly beautiful surface.

Taku Glacier is the deepest and thickest alpine temperate glacier ever discovered in the world, covering 386 square miles. Oddly enough, it is the solitary advancing glacier among twenty glaciers situated in the Juneau Icefield. Even with its enormous mass, this glacier continues to inch forward each year. Indescribably heavy, yet moving ahead.

Unlike this glacier, human beings are not as prone to moving forward, especially if something is weighing us down. In fact, our first response may be to stop moving forward altogether because our burden is too difficult. Challenges in life often bring us to our knees, taking away our desire even to enjoy living life. Some people may turn into a pseudo recluse due to receiving a layoff notice at work, having their house burn to the ground, or worst

Sometimes, delays are God's way of synchronizing us with His perfect timing.

of all, losing someone they love. Sadly, some individuals eventually reach the point of giving up. Even getting out of bed in the morning becomes a chore.

I read a post on social media not too long ago where an individual said, "I cannot do this anymore," meaning they could not cope with life anymore. I quickly prayed that God would encourage them and send the Holy Spirit, the Comforter, to them in their moment of desperation. Even now, I pray they have found the everlasting love of Jesus Christ and are actively seeking to see God's master plan fulfilled in their life.

Do you identify with this individual? Are you at your breaking point? Does it seem as if you have exhausted all of your options? Do not give up. Second Corinthians 4:16–17 says, "Therefore we do not lose heart. Though outwardly we are wasting away, yet inwardly we are being renewed day by day. For our light and momentary troubles are achieving for us an eternal glory that far outweighs them all." The trials on this earth are not eternal, but the glory awaiting us in Heaven will last forever. In the meantime, we need to take comfort in the fact that God will renew our strength every day, helping us overcome the trials we face in life.

I can tell you from personal experience that disappointments are a part of life. Even Jesus said we would face difficulties in this world, but you can rest assured that Jesus Christ will walk with you through every single trial. Even in the moments when you feel like throwing in the towel, remember Jesus Christ is sitting at the right hand of the Father, intercede on your behalf (Rom. 8:34). He will always be your strength when you are weary. Jesus will carry your burden, helping you place one foot in front of the other, gradually inching forward like those legendary glaciers.

> Jesus will carry your burden, helping you place one foot in front of the other, gradually inching forward like those legendary glaciers.

Isaiah 40:31 says if we put our hope in the Lord, we will run and not grow weary. When we put our hope in Jesus Christ, He will replenish our strength, just as a fatigued marathon runner finds refreshment from drinking a bottle of cool spring water and placing a cold towel around their neck. Only instead of a temporary reprieve, the Lord will renew our spirits continually.

When we trust in the Lord completely, He will be our strength. He will give us courage to face each new day with a smile on our face and a song in our heart, no matter how challenging our circumstances may seem. Regardless of how many miles we have to run, we do not have to forfeit the race. With Christ on our side, we can run and not become weary. We can walk and not feel faint. Just like the airplanes, on which I have had the pleasure of flying, we can soar on wings like eagles!

Looking to Jesus

God's creation is one of magnificence and grandeur, from the sparkling azure waters of the ocean to the delicate, vibrant blooms of flowers in the springtime. While I stand amazed at the splendor of God's handiwork, one of the geographical features that makes my heart sing are the lofty peaks of mountains rising toward the heavens. It does not matter if I am looking at the subtle rolling hills in Tennessee or the towering glacier-covered vistas in the Alps; I always marvel at the astounding beauty, which God has so beautifully created.

On one trip to Europe, we had the opportunity to stay in a chalet overlooking the Matterhorn. The name *Matterhorn* essentially means "peak in the meadows."[1] The view surrounding this popular peak is overwhelmingly gorgeous. What a rare opportunity to be able to sit on the chalet's balcony, admiring this colossal mountain landscape. Words cannot quite articulate how I felt the moment I laid eyes on this iconic peak. I was in awe that God would create something so majestic. One glimpse of such a scene and it seemed my worries drifted away. Of course, the mountains were not the source of my solace; God is the One who provided the peace to fill my soul. Yet I must admit that mountains do provide a beautiful backdrop for receiving this unprecedented peace.

While traveling through mountainous regions brings much

inspiration and comfort, I can also recall a time when a trip to the mountains was anything but consoling. On August 2, 2008, my parents and I were camping at River Valley Campground in Cherokee, North Carolina. That afternoon, we attended an anniversary party for two fellow campers. Upon returning to our camper, we sat out on our deck, enjoying the soothing sounds of the water. Tragically, this peaceful day ended with a living nightmare.

Jesus Christ will never leave nor forsake us. He will help us. He will give us hope. He is hope.

That night, my mom went to be with the Lord. As we stood outside of our camper, we called family and friends to tell them the heartrending news. While my heart was broken into a million pieces, I vividly recall looking up at the silhouette of the ridge high above us. In that moment of desperation, God placed a scripture in my heart and mind. Psalm 121:1–2 says, "I lift up my eyes to the mountains—where does my help come from? My help comes from the LORD, the Maker of heaven and earth." Even though my present circumstances seemed hopeless at the time, God used this verse to remind me that true, lasting hope only comes from the Lord. He is the One who helped my dad and me through this unimaginable trial.

In life, we cannot explain everything that happens. Yet even when life is spinning out of control, like a plane crashing to the ground, we can put our trust in the One who will never fail. Jesus Christ will never leave nor forsake us. He will help us. He will give us hope. He *is* hope. We must look unto the hills, keeping our eyes on Jesus Christ, for all of our help comes from the Lord.

Chapter Twenty-Two

Are You Prepared?

"'Therefore keep watch, because you do not know
on what day your Lord will come.'" (Matt. 24:42)

Floridians worked tirelessly to prepare for the arrival of Hurricane Irma in September 2017. From purchasing bottled water and batteries to filling up gas tanks and boarding up windows, everyone did what they could to ensure they would be ready to weather the storm. With the threat of a catastrophic hurricane aiming for the Sunshine State, none of us wanted the storm to catch us off guard.

As a native Floridian, it saddened me to think of the possible destruction and loss of life that could come upon our state. Watching people at the grocery store, stocking up on supplies, I actually became tearful when I thought about the reasons why they were clearing out the shelves. While some of them were simply restocking their pantry, others were purchasing items out of desperation. They were not buying eight boxes of cereal or two entire cases of canned Vienna sausages at a time because they were getting a bargain. They were attempting to use tangible items to ease their fear of the unknown.

Some individuals were uncertain as to how long they would be without power. Evacuees who stayed in shelters waited apprehensively, wondering if they would return home only to find no home at all. Still others were afraid they would not even survive to assess the damage found on their property. Although I had experienced many hurricane seasons before, I had never sensed such a feeling of doom among my fellow southerners. It seemed some people were preparing for the worst without even hoping for the best.

At our home, we prepared for the worst and prayed for God's protection. We boarded up our windows for the first time ever. Many people filled sandbags in an attempt to protect their homes and businesses from floodwaters. Based on the storm's path, there was a possibility it could come directly over us as a category three hurricane. The forecast was grim for nearly every inch of the Florida peninsula and the Florida Keys as well. Fear was contagious, especially with the mass destruction caused by Hurricane Harvey in Texas fresh in our minds.

As Hurricane Irma barreled up the west coast, all eyes were on the National Hurricane Center updates. When the hurricane made landfall, preparations had to cease. Everybody sought a secure location in which to ride out the storm, whether in homes, hotels, shelters, churches, or other structures. Time had run out. Irma unleashed her fury from coast-to-coast, bringing unprecedented devastation to much of the southeast.

Sadly, Hurricane Irma took the lives of dozens of people across the Caribbean and the state of Florida. Thousands of homes suffered extensive damage or even total destruction. Many homes remained uninhabitable for more than a year. According to the National Oceanic and Atmospheric Administration, the total cost of the storm damage was fifty billion dollars, making it one of the top five costliest U.S. hurricanes on record.[1]

One moment, everyone was living normal lives, going to work and school, visiting family and friends, and enjoying everyday activities. The next moment, normalcy became foreign. As the violent winds blew and the torrential rain fell, life changed. The power went out. Communities endured devastation. Lives were lost.

As I watched the news and observed the destruction firsthand in my hometown, I realized the close parallel between the necessity of preparing for a hurricane and the even more critical need to be prepared for eternity. Some people who went to bed the night Irma came through never woke up to see the aftermath of the storm. One moment they were living on this earth; the next moment they found themselves in either Heaven or hell. When someone's life on earth ends, there is no second chance to make a decision for Christ. Yet for those who choose to accept Jesus Christ as their personal Lord and Savior, eternity begins the moment they put their hope in Christ.

One day soon, a trumpet will sound. This is not a trumpet like the ones found in a symphony orchestra, but a trumpet blast heard around the world. Upon this trumpet call, the dead in Christ will rise first and those who have put their trust in Jesus Christ will be caught up to meet the Lord in the air (1 Thess. 4:16–17). The moment the trumpet sounds, Jesus Christ will victoriously return to take His children home. Christ could return today. Have you prepared for eternity?

Unlike a hurricane, there will be no meteorologists or newscasters warning people in advance. The newspaper headline will never read, "Christ Comes Back Tomorrow." Matthew 24:36 tells us, "'But about that day or hour no one knows, not even the angels in heaven, nor the Son, but only the Father.'" That is why we must be ready, prepared for His coming, every moment of every day. In the same way you would not want to be caught off guard in a horrific storm, you do not want to be unprepared when the Lord returns to this earth.

Perhaps you are reading this book, with the knowledge that your family or friends are saved, hoping that will count for something. Matthew 24:40–41 states, "'Two men will be in the field; one will be taken and the other left. Two women will be grinding with a hand mill; one will be taken and the other left.'" Simply knowing someone who knows Jesus as his or her personal Savior is not enough. You cannot rely on another person's salvation to be your ticket to Heaven.

You may be a good person. You may strive to do the right things. You may believe God will have mercy on you simply because of what you have done. According to the Bible, we have all sinned. Our sin brought spiritual death and separation from God. We can never be righteous on our own merit. Good deeds cannot save us. Coming from a well-respected family or having kindhearted friends cannot provide salvation. The Bible says, "For it is by grace you have been saved, through faith—and this is not from yourselves, it is the gift of God—not by works, so that no one can boast" (Eph. 2:8–9). Nothing we do on our own can make us worthy of salvation. It is only by the grace of God that we can receive this priceless gift.

You cannot rely on another person's salvation to be your ticket to Heaven.

John 3:16 says, "For God so loved the world that he gave his one and only Son, that whoever believes in him shall not perish but have eternal life." God's Word also says, "Everyone has sinned; we all fall short of God's glorious standard" (Rom. 3:23 NLT). The only way to receive redemption for our sins is through the blood Jesus Christ shed on the cross of Calvary. Confess your sins today. Believe in Jesus Christ. Call on the name of the Lord and you shall be saved (Acts 2:21).

There is no need to purchase a special stock of supplies. Boarding up windows is useless. There is only one way to prepare for Christ's return. Jesus said, "'I am the way and the truth and the life. No one comes to the Father except through me'" (John 14:6). Jesus Christ is the only way to obtain salvation. Jesus is the only way to receive everlasting life. Receive the unending love of Jesus Christ today.

When Christ returns, there will be no emergency alert appearing on the screen of your smartphone. God's Word says,

"'So you also must be ready, because the Son of Man will come at an hour when you do not expect him'" (Matt. 24:44). No one knows the day when Christ will return, except God Himself (Matt. 24:36).

Unlike weather alerts informing you of an approaching storm, there will be no warning concerning the return of Christ. Once Jesus Christ returns, the window of opportunity to receive the gift of salvation will close. Your opportunity is now. Make the most vital preparation of your life. Repent of your sins. Ask Jesus Christ to be the Lord of your life today.

The Lost Is Found

On one particular trip to central Florida, my parents and I set out to celebrate my birthday. During our trip, I lost one of my favorite sweatshirts. As someone who is very warm-natured, I often find myself carrying sweatshirts and jackets more than I ever wear them. Instead of carrying my purple sweatshirt around in my arms all day, my mom invited me to put it around the arm of her electric wheelchair. Unfortunately, somewhere in the midst of our travels, my sweatshirt was lost.

It was a long shot, but my dad took us over to the lost and found department. Much to my surprise, an employee had picked up my sweatshirt and deposited it in this designated location for lost items. Yes, it was only a sweatshirt, but what a blessing to find my lost garment.

When I was a very young girl, losing things seemed to be a regular occurrence. I can recall at least two times when I absentmindedly set my purse down in a store or mall, never to see it again. As I have matured, I have thankfully learned the importance of holding on to things. Sometimes, though, things now seem to run away from me: earrings fall off, necklaces come unclasped. Yet I have always managed to find them before they are missing forever, even when I once lost an earring along the sandy shoreline at the beach! Although I have become more competent at finding things, it still sends me in a flurry of disappointment when I discover something is missing, no matter how insignificant the item may be.

Have you ever lost something? Maybe you misplaced a cell phone, a wallet, or a set of keys. Many things in life are easily lost. Small objects roll underneath furniture, items fall between the sofa cushions, and important papers become lost in the shuffle of incoming mail. Children may even find themselves lost in a large crowd of people until they find their parents or guardians, alleviating the panic and distress caused by the unexpected separation of parent and child. Without doubt, inexplicable joy ensues when someone finds someone or something that is lost!

One time, I found a signed paycheck in a storefront parking lot. I am grateful God allowed me to find the paycheck, instead of someone who might cash the check and spend this hardworking family's much-needed income. Although I did not have the phone number for the payee, I was able to contact the local farm, which had issued the check. When the individual who lost the check came to our home to pick it up, the man brought his wife and children, all dressed in their Sunday best. To show their appreciation, they blessed us with two flats of fresh brown eggs, all because I found something they had lost.

Even the Bible tells stories of people losing things. A shepherd left ninety-nine sheep behind just to find one lost lamb. One woman lost one of her silver coins, and after she found it, called her friends and neighbors over for a celebration. The prodigal son spent all of his money on prostitutes and wild living. He reached the point where he even craved a meal of pig's food, due to lack of food during famine. Finally, he returned home. He asked his dad to make him a servant because he no longer felt worthy to be his son. Instead of showing anger, his dad said, "'Bring the fattened calf and kill it. Let's have a feast and celebrate. For this son of mine was dead and is alive again; he was lost and is found"' (Luke 15:23–24). What a wonderful story of forgiveness, reminding us that we, too, can return to the loving arms of our Heavenly Father, even if we have strayed away from His mercy and grace.

Just as the shepherd, the woman, and the father rejoiced at finding what was lost, the angels in Heaven rejoice when an individual gives his or her life to Christ. The Bible says, "'There will be more rejoicing in heaven over one sinner who repents than over ninety-nine righteous persons who do not need to repent'" (Luke 15:7). When someone makes the decision to serve the Lord with all of their heart, they become a child of God. Unlike the children who may find themselves lost in a sea of strangers, those who put their hope in Jesus Christ will never be lost.

Amid so much separation in this world, nothing can separate us from the unconditional love of Jesus Christ. Romans 8:38–39 says, "For I am convinced that neither death nor life, neither angels nor demons, neither the present nor the future, nor any powers, neither height nor depth, nor anything else in all creation, will be able to separate us from the love of God that is in Christ Jesus our Lord." What an amazing promise! Nothing on earth, not even life or death, can separate us from our Lord's compassion, if we put our trust in Him. Even when storms or other calamities surround us, we are inseparable from the amazing love of Jesus Christ.

Amid so much separation in this world, nothing can separate us from the unconditional love of Jesus Christ.

My dad occasionally tells the story of one stormy night when I was quite young. We lived in a mobile home during the early years of my life, until my dad built our beautiful brick home. On this particular night, tornadoes were in the area, and the storms were growing very intense, so my dad wrapped me up in several layers of blankets and quilts to protect me from any flying debris outdoors. My mom grabbed some family photos and my three favorite stuffed animals. These plush toys, affectionately known as "The Big Three," or Baby Bear, Dado, and Cupcake, went with me everywhere when I was a little girl! We quickly scrambled to the car, with me in my dad's arms, and we all headed to my grandparent's house across the field. I do not remember too much about this frightening ordeal, but I thank God for the blessing of parents who kept me safe. My grandparent's house might have been the physical safe haven, but I know God was the One who was our refuge from the storm.

In the midst of every circumstance life throws our way, Jesus will send His angels to encamp around us, protecting us from harm. Why would He do this for us? Because that is how much He loves us. First John 3:16 says, "This is how we know what love is: Jesus Christ laid down his life for us." Love is more than a word. It is an action. Christ did not die on the cross to gain notoriety nor to prove a point. Jesus died to cleanse our sins, to redeem us, and to give us life everlasting in Heaven.

> If you had been the only person on this earth, Jesus still would have given His life for you.

If you had been the only person on this earth, Jesus still would have given His life for you.

Here in the southeastern United States, we have a saying of going out of your way to help someone. Jesus is the ultimate example of this, for He truly went out of His way to save you and me. My dad wrote a song titled, "He Went Out of His Way," that expresses the magnitude of the sacrifice Jesus made for us.

The Savior left His throne;
In a stable He was born.
He came to bring salvation to the sinner.
To seek and save the lost,
Give His life to pay the cost.
Like no one ever did,
He went out of His way.

Chorus:
He went out of His way,
For the soul who was astray.
Our ransom He would pay;
He went out of His way.
He died upon the tree
To set the captive free.
To ransom you and me,
He went out of His way.

A friend who's always there,
The One who hears my prayer.
No one ever cared for me like Jesus.
I can always count on Him;
He is my closest friend.
To help me day by day,
He went out of His way.[2]

Jesus went out of His way for you because of His great love for you. No matter where you are today, you are not out of the reach of the love of Jesus Christ. You can never be lost from God's sight. You may be in a prison, a hospital, or even a war-torn village. Wherever you are, Jesus Christ loves you. Jesus died to save you. He rose again on the third day, and now He is sitting at the right hand of the Father (Rom. 8:34). If you are looking for everlasting hope, a constant friend, and help in times of trouble, pray these words from your heart:

Dear Jesus,

Thank You for loving me unconditionally. I believe You died on the cross and rose again. Please forgive me of my sins. Come into my heart and make me a new creation. I want to live for You. Help me share Your love with others.

In Your Precious Name, Jesus,
Amen.

Do not wait until tomorrow to pray this prayer, for it may be too late. The individuals who lost their lives during the 2017 hurricane season had no idea they were nearing the final seconds of their life. There was no warning. One minute, they were bracing for a catastrophic storm. The next moment, their life on this earth ended. There is no guarantee that we will still be on this earth tomorrow. Even so, God has promised us an eternal home in Heaven if we prepare ahead of time.

If you were to breathe your last breath on earth this very moment, do you know with full assurance that your heart is prepared? Ask Jesus Christ to come into your heart today. It is the most important decision you will ever make. Stop living your life, feeling as if you are lost in a sea of despair. There is eternal hope found in Jesus Christ alone. Jesus came to seek and save the lost. Receive the gift of salvation. Your life will change forever when God transforms your life from lost to found!

Chapter Twenty-Three

Sunshine Awaits

"The city does not need the sun or the moon to shine on it, for the glory of God gives it light, and the Lamb is its lamp." (Rev. 21:23)

On the sun-soaked island of Santorini, Greece, the main city of Thira sits above the jagged, towering cliffs, which are remnants of a volcanic caldera. The volcanic eruption occurred in 1650 BC, leaving behind a group of smaller islands known collectively as the Cyclades. Due to the harsh terrain surrounding the island, there are only five methods of getting to this precariously positioned vacation destination. If you are not flying in to the only airport on the island or sailing in on a seaworthy vessel, then you must choose to walk 580 steps, ride a donkey to the top via the zigzagging walking path, or ride in a cable car boasting a mesmerizing view. At its highest point, the cable car ascends to 220 meters above the gleaming blue water and unique volcanic rock faces below. My dad and I chose the cable car. As someone who absolutely loves heights, I can attest to the fact that the view of the striking seascape below was truly fabulous.

The entire day seemed as if we were driving our rental car within the confines of a movie set. The island landscapes were spectacular, offering photogenic panoramas in every direction. The highlights of the day were soaking in the warm waters of the Aegean Sea at Perissa Beach and enjoying Greek pastries at a small bakery we stumbled upon on our drive back into town. As we rode the cable car back down to sea level, I reflected on how this was an experience we would always remember, for it was one of those priceless days, which only God could coordinate.

Much like this picturesque isle offers a choice of transportation to travel to the main island's central hub; there are many other choices in life. When we sit down at a restaurant, we commonly receive a menu. We can choose anything we like, ranging from our favorite appetizer and entrée to our choice dessert and beverage. In many countries, individuals have the freedom to choose which church to attend, which school to send their children to, and which home to live in. From the style of clothing we want to wear to the make and model of car we prefer to drive, the choices we have on this earth are seemingly endless.

An infinite number of choices, yet only one choice on this earth will make a difference for all eternity. The decision to accept Jesus Christ as your personal Lord and Savior is the most important decision you will ever make. The only way to receive salvation is through Jesus Christ alone. Jesus said, "'I am the way and the truth and the life. No one comes to the Father except through me'" (John 14:6). You cannot buy salvation, nor can you earn it through kindheartedness or charitable acts. This world may offer many alternatives, but "'salvation is found in no one else, for there is no other name under heaven given to mankind by which we must be saved'" (Acts 4:12). Jesus Christ is the only way to salvation. He is the Son of the only true and living God. Jesus is the only source of eternal hope.

Perhaps you are adrift in a sea of hopelessness. You may feel unloved or unwanted. It may seem as if you are in the middle of a never-ending sunset with no dawn in sight. Regardless of your current circumstances, Jesus Christ loves you unconditionally. He accepts you just the way you are, with all of your battle scars and even the innermost secrets you keep hidden inside your heart. He wants to wash your sins away and give you a new beginning. All things become new through Jesus Christ (2 Cor. 5:17).

The terrible mistakes you have made, the guilt-ridden regret, your past that haunts you—all of these things will be forgiven and forgotten forever when you confess your sins and make Jesus Christ the Lord of your life. Micah 7:19 (ESV) says, "He will again have compassion on us; he will tread our iniquities underfoot. You will cast all our sins into the depths of the sea." God will cast all of your sins into the sea of forgetfulness, giving you the gift of eternal life, complete with a fresh start.

I want to encourage you to call on Jesus Christ. Do not wait until tomorrow. Make today the day of salvation. In the past year alone, I have seen young children lose their lives in horrific accidents. I have lost dear friends unexpectedly due to cancer and other health problems. Terrorist attacks, roadside bombs, school shootings, and many other calamities are prevalent throughout the land. The world is in great turmoil. Many people are hurting, some are fighting for their lives, and still others are grieving. Yet even when the sorrows of life seem hard to bear, God's Word says we should "not grieve like the rest of mankind, who have no hope" (1 Thess. 4:13). This verse does not mean that we will not grieve. Instead, it means we should always remember the eternal hope we have in Jesus Christ.

The decision to accept Jesus Christ as your personal Lord and Savior is the most important decision you will ever make.

In 2014, I wrote a song titled, "Follow Hope." This song has become an anthem for me, especially when I am facing a trial. No matter how dark a situation seems, the Lord will be our strength, moment by moment, day by day. When we follow Jesus, we are following the one true source of eternal hope. I pray God uses the first verse and chorus of this song to remind you to follow Jesus, for He will always be with you in the sunshine and the rain.

Life is like a tunnel
Where I cannot see the end.
Circumstances blind my eyes
'Till only darkness wins.
That's when I call on Jesus' name;
He gives me strength day by day.
He's like the sunshine after rain;
That's why I can say.

Chorus:
I'm following my best friend;
I'm following God's Son.
Every step that I take,
He has already done.
He gives me hope tomorrow;
He gives me hope today.
I'll always follow Jesus,
The truth, the life, the way.[1]

In my own personal life, I have experienced a tremendous amount of joy, but I have also endured much sorrow. Although I can testify concerning many answered prayers, there have been times when it seemed God was silent. Having lost all three of my siblings as premature infants, my precious mom, as well as three grandparents and numerous friends and relatives, I have attended more funerals than weddings. The loss has been devastating at times. I can recall one particular time when I purchased four sympathy cards in one single day. Yet even in the midst of these heartbreaking experiences, I knew my help would come from the Lord, as God's Word promises in Psalm 121:2. Jesus said, "'Surely I am with you always, to the very end of the age'" (Matt. 28:20). Jesus will never fail us, even when life is uncertain.

For the residents of Haiti and the Dominican Republic, they sadly realized the fragile nature of life when Hurricane Matthew brought deadly destruction upon these island nations. This category four hurricane pounded them for approximately forty-eight hours, bringing life-threatening wind, rain, floods, and mudslides. For many islanders, life changed forever. Two photographs stood out to me. One showed a distraught woman receiving consolation from her loved ones; she lost two of her children in the storm. Another showed a man pushing all of the worldly possessions he now owned in a small wheelbarrow, attempting to make it to an emergency shelter before the floodwaters rose any higher.

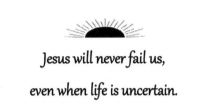

Jesus will never fail us, even when life is uncertain.

A cataclysmic storm like this helps put things in perspective. It reminds us what is truly important in life. Life is a dangerous place, with no promise of tomorrow. We are only here by the grace of God. He is the One who shields us from the raging storms of life, both literal and figurative. He wants to be the place of safety in which we can abide, if we will listen to His voice. God will not drag us along like a young child having a temper tantrum. It is up to us to choose whether we will follow His leading. We need to follow His steps, trusting Him as a child trusts their mother and father.

When we completely trust our Heavenly Father, He will help keep us from harm. A rescheduled appointment could be the difference between life and death. Traffic delays could inevitably prevent you from totaling your car and landing yourself in a hospital bed. Every day, God orders our steps. Psalm 119:133–134 says, "Direct my footsteps according to your word; let no sin rule over me. Redeem me from human oppression." There will be times when we get off track, led by our sinful nature. Certain individuals and organizations may seek to discourage us. Friends and family could disappoint us. Instead of allowing others to determine the course of our lives, we need to keep our eyes on Jesus, for He will never let us down. We need to follow His footsteps in all we do. God knows what is best for our lives.

Does this mean that no one who follows His steps will ever encounter obstacles on the road of life? Definitely not, for life will indeed have its share of challenges. The apostle Paul would doubtless agree. He experienced attacks on every side. One day, he encountered a woman possessed by a "spirit by which she predicted the future" (Acts 16:16). Paul cast out the spirit when he said, "'In the name of Jesus Christ I command you to come out of her!' At that moment the spirit left her" (Acts 16:18). While it seems this would be a miraculous event, her owners were enraged because their business venture would no longer be viable, since the spirit's evil powers provided a significant income. Upon finding out what happened, they took Paul to the authorities, where "the crowd joined in the attack against Paul and Silas, and the magistrates ordered them to be stripped and beaten with rods. After they had been severely flogged, they were thrown into prison, and the jailer was commanded to guard them carefully" (Acts 16:22–23).

Paul's mission was to share the Gospel of Jesus Christ. He simply cast out an evil spirit, just as God had given him authority to do, yet he narrowly escaped death because of this action. Yet even with all of the hardships Paul endured, he never gave in to his human weakness. He did not abandon the Lord Jesus. He stayed strong in his faith. In fact, God's Word says, "About midnight Paul and Silas were praying and singing hymns to God, and the other prisoners were listening to them" (Acts 16:25). Their time in jail is a wonderful example of God working all things together for good. Because of their faithfulness to God, they continued to praise Him, even in the middle of the night.

Paul and Silas were beaten to the point where they were likely unrecognizable. Surely, they must have been writhing in pain, attempting to nurse their wounds. Despite their condition, they did not sit idly by, saying, "Woe is me." They sought no pity. They simply gave thanks to God and glorified the name above all names by singing praises to Him. At that moment, "There was such a violent earthquake that the foundations of the prison were shaken. At once all the prison doors flew open, and everyone's chains came loose" (Acts 16:26). The jailer frantically came to the cells, assuming everyone had escaped, but all of the prisoners were still inside the prison. That night, the jailer and his entire household dedicated their lives to Christ. If we could speak to Paul today, I am sure he would tell us that every scar was worth it after all. He was dedicated to the cause of Christ, fully aware of the eternal value of his ministry, something far greater than anything this world could offer.

Similar to Paul and Silas, millions of Christians are suffering because of the wickedness that abounds. Many of them endure persecution and imprisonment. Some of them lose their lives because of their faith. Even amid the hatred in the world, we cannot live in fear. We need to be redeeming the time, for the coming of the Lord is at hand. We must go forth and proclaim the name of Jesus Christ to everyone we meet before it is too late. Sadly, approximately 150,000 people die every twenty-four hours. How many of them die without knowing the marvelous grace of Jesus Christ? It is devastating to think of the number of people who are dying and going to an eternal hell. It is truly heartbreaking. Like our Heavenly Father, I do not want anyone to perish without having a relationship with Christ (2 Pet. 3:9).

If you were to die tonight, do you know with absolute confidence where you would go? Would you hear our Heavenly Father say, "Well done, thou good and faithful servant," or would you hear the words, "Depart from me" (Matt. 25:21, 41 KJV)? Only you know what the outcome would be. No one else can answer this question for you. Your parent's salvation cannot save you. The wealth you may have accumulated cannot provide an escape. You must answer honestly, for God knows your heart. The time to answer is now, while you still have the opportunity to choose eternal life through Jesus Christ.

God loved the world so much that He gave His only Son to die on a cross for the forgiveness of our sins (John 3:16). Because of love, He paved the way for us to receive redemption: "But God demonstrates his own love for us in this: While we were still sinners, Christ died for us" (Rom. 5:8). Jesus Christ was not looking for fame or fortune. So why did He give His life for you and me? Jesus gave His life for us because of love (1 John 3:16). He rose again on the third day and is sitting at the right hand of God, continually interceding on our behalf. You may wonder why He would go to such great lengths for you. You may struggle with the notion that the King of kings would make such a great sacrifice. It is because of God's great love for humankind.

The Bible says we have all sinned and fallen short of the glory of God (Rom. 3:23). Every single person is in dire need of salvation. If a person is sick, they must seek medical care, so they can get well. Jesus said, "'It is not the healthy who need a doctor, but the sick'" (Matt. 9:12). In like manner, the souls of every single person on earth are sick. They are full of sin. The only anecdote for sin is the shed blood of Jesus Christ, the spotless Lamb of God. He alone can save us from our sins. He is the only way to have our souls cleansed. He is the only way to receive salvation (John 14:6). He is the only way to eternal life in Heaven.

The Wedding Day

A few summers ago, my dad and I had the opportunity to see a marvelous piece of artwork in Paris, France. This enormous painting, aptly named, *The Wedding at Cana*, depicts Jesus' first miracle. Hanging at twenty-two feet high and thirty-two feet long, this lavish piece of art created by Italian artist Paolo Veronese dwarfs every other painting in the room where it currently hangs in the Louvre Museum. Even though it is quite grand, the most eye-catching aspect of this work of art is the fact that there are over one hundred figures depicted in the painting, but only one seems to be looking at the viewer of the painting. The eyes of Jesus Christ are staring straight ahead, looking at those who behold this artistic image. What a testament to the grace of God, for a biblical message to have a prominent position, even amid a primarily secular collection.

When I think of this beautiful painting, it brings to mind a special event in March 2017, when I witnessed the marriage of a dear friend of mine, Evelyn. The wedding was outdoors, under a cluster of oak trees in a rural area. Family and friends were in place, and the music began to play as the bride made her way down the aisle. The gown my friend wore was beautiful, the fresh flowers gracing the tables had a sweet aroma, and the open-air setting was serene. Even so, one of the most memorable parts of the wedding was the minister's sermon. He spoke about the first miracle Jesus performed at the wedding at Cana.

During the marriage celebration, they ran out of wine. Jesus' mother encouraged Him to assist. Jesus directed the servants to fill the jars with water, and then draw some out and give it to the host of the banquet (John 2:7–8). A moment later, "The master of the banquet tasted the water that had been turned into wine. He did not realize where it had come from, though the servants who had drawn the water knew. Then he called the bridegroom aside and said, 'Everyone brings out the choice wine first and then the cheaper wine after the guests have had too much to drink; but you have saved the best till now'" (John 2:9–10).

Jesus performed this miracle to make known His glory and to encourage His disciples to believe in Him. John 2:11 says, "What Jesus did here in Cana of Galilee was the first of the signs through which he revealed his glory; and his disciples believed in him." Although the first miracle Jesus performed was a pivotal moment in His ministry, the most momentous occasion will be when He returns to this world. One day soon, a trumpet will sound, and everyone who believes in Him will be ushered into the presence of the Lord for the Marriage Supper of the Lamb.

Revelation 19:9 says, "'Blessed are those who are invited to the wedding supper of the Lamb!'"

When we enter into Heaven's gates, there will be no more goodbyes. We will be together with the Lord for eternity.

Beyond the confines of this earth and all of life's disappointments, God is preparing an eternal home for us in Heaven. The sorrow we have endured will fade away. The tears we have cried will be no more. The moment Jesus steps out on the clouds, the world will change eternally. God's Word says, "For the Lord himself will come down from heaven, with a loud command, with the voice of the archangel and with the trumpet call of God, and the dead in Christ will rise first. After that, we who are still alive and are left will be caught up together with them in the clouds to meet the Lord in the air. And so we will be with the Lord forever. Therefore encourage one another with these words" (1 Thess. 4:16–18). The coming of Christ is closer than it has ever been before. Let us comfort others with this glorious news, so they may ready their hearts for His return.

Even today, we could hear the trumpet's blast, sounding loud above the hustle and bustle of this world. The graves will open and those who have accepted Jesus Christ as their Lord and Savior will rise to meet Christ in the air. Then, all Christians who are alive will join them in the clouds. Our human minds cannot quite conceive how all of this will happen, yet I can assure you, it will happen just as God's Word says. I especially love God's promise that we will be with the Lord forever in Heaven.

Traveling is one of my favorite things to do, yet I find one aspect of travel to be bittersweet. Along the way, I grow close to new friends and saying goodbye is difficult, such as the time my dad and I sang at Grace Ministries International in Montréal, Québec, Canada. We made so many friends there. What a rare gift that a strong bond can form so quickly within the family of God, just as it did between the church's congregation and my dad and me. Walking out the door of the church, tears fell from my eyes, not knowing when I would see them again. I must admit, saying goodbye is not one of my strengths, but one day we will have said our last goodbye. When we enter into Heaven's gates, there will be no more goodbyes. We will be together with the Lord for eternity.

If the thought of leaving this earthly dwelling in exchange for a heavenly city is unsettling to you, think about the place God has been preparing for us. Our Heavenly Father has been building a place for us over the course of more than two thousand years. The earthly home we have here cannot compare to the one we will have in Heaven. Unlike this earth, where we have a sun and a moon to give us light, the Bible says Heaven does not need either celestial body as its light source, "for the glory of God gives it light, and the Lamb is its lamp" (Rev. 21:23). Jesus Christ will be the One to give radiant light to our eternal home in Heaven.

Heaven Awaits

When I travel to a new location, it only takes a matter of minutes for me to acclimate to my new surroundings. Whether I am ministering in a foreign land or sightseeing close to home, it does not take long before I am ready to settle down and stay a while. I grow attached to the endearing people, the striking scenery, and even the delectable food. Although it is a blessing to feel at home most everywhere I roam, it makes leaving all the more difficult. Once I am home, I then find it hard to pack up and leave. As I frequently tell people, I am a homebody who just so happens to love traveling the world. One day, though, I will be taken to a brand new home, unlike any place I have ever seen, living forevermore with Jesus Christ, my Lord and Savior.

What will Heaven be like? Although I cannot fully answer this question, I can tell you that Heaven is more beautiful than the most talented artist on earth could ever attempt to illustrate. Through the centuries, individuals have attempted to paint a picture of what Heaven is like, yet the Bible says no one could imagine what the Father has prepared for those who love Him (1 Cor. 2:9). Heaven is not like going to another city, another state, or another country. Heaven is God's House.

Jesus said, "'In my Father's house are many rooms. If it were not so, would I have told you that I go to prepare a place for you? And if I go and prepare a place for you, I will come again and will take you to myself, that where I am you may be also. And you know the way to where I am going'" (John 14:2–4 ESV). God has prepared a place for us, so we can live with Him. Jesus said that we know the way to Heaven, for there is only one method of getting there. You cannot get there via a plane, automobile, or metro system. Jesus Christ is the only way to reach Heaven. Will you accept the invitation to live in Heaven with Jesus?

Some people determine in their hearts that they will call on Jesus at a more convenient time. Perhaps they will stop to pray next week, next month, or next year. Nevertheless, the Bible tells us there is no guarantee of tomorrow. James 4:14 says, "Why, you do not even know what will happen tomorrow. What is your life? You are a mist that appears for a little while and then vanishes." We have no idea whether we will wake up to see another sunrise or if today will be our last day on earth. Life is extremely fragile.

We are here for a moment and gone the next, just as the morning fog rolls in and soon disappears. Even though our lives are very brief, God has made a way for us to live forever.

In reality, there are very few, if any, forever things on this earth. Beautiful flowers bloom, only to wilt and decay. Likewise, people are born as precious little infants, only to grow old and frail. I recently saw a commercial where they captured the majority of a person's life span in a matter of thirty seconds, beginning with their birth. I remarked to my dad how the commercial was a true representation of the way life quickly passes by. Even so, God offers every single person the opportunity to live eternally. The world will pass away, "but whoever does the will of God lives forever" (1 John 2:17).

Perhaps the idea of living forever seems rather difficult at this time in your life. Instead of brilliant sunshine, you only notice the sun setting all around you, so the idea of living even one more day may be daunting. I want to encourage you not to lose hope. The sunset you find yourself in right now is temporary. Call on Jesus Christ, and you shall be saved (Rom. 10:13). Jesus Christ will bring you to safety as a lighthouse guides a ship safely into the harbor. He will give

Heaven is not like going to another city, another state, or another country. Heaven is God's House.

you peace that passes all understanding (Phil. 4:7). He is the source of our strength. Receive His unconditional love today.

When you make Jesus Christ the Lord of your life, you will still experience sorrow at times. Life will not be picture-perfect, but Jesus will be there to help you climb every mountain and cross every valley. Jesus said, "'In this world you will have trouble. But take heart! I have overcome the world'" (John

16:33). Jesus has already triumphed over all of the trials we face. With Him by our side, there is no task too difficult for us to accomplish. We can do all things through Christ (Phil. 4:13).

Like you, I have experienced some dark days, but Jesus has always been my light amid the darkness. Even as a little girl, I experienced the loss of my two baby brothers. In my young mind, I did not quite understand why God would take away my only siblings. Even now, I would love the chance to be a big sister to my brothers, Kenneth Lee, Jr. and Kenneth Nathaniel, and a little sister to my third sibling whom I never even had the opportunity to meet. Nevertheless, I trust in God's master plan. When I was a child, I knew God was in control. I had full confidence that He would shine forth His light even when the circumstances were so dark that I could not see my hand in front of my face. Still today, I remain completely certain that God will never fail. He always lights the way in the midst of every single trial, no matter how dim the situation may seem.

Each evening the sun sets, we are one day closer to our eternal home. For even in the sunset, there is sunshine awaiting you and me.

God will do the same for you. You do not have to stumble around in the dark like someone searching for a flashlight when the power goes out unexpectedly due to a sudden storm. Jesus said, "'Whoever follows me will never walk in darkness, but will have the light of life'" (John 8:12). Make the decision to follow Jesus Christ. He will be your light. He will replace your despair with hope. He will take away your sorrow and restore your joy. Put your trust in Jesus, the giver of life, the Savior of your soul, the source of eternal light.

Until the moment when Christ returns, keep your eyes on Him. The momentary troubles in life will fade away when you place your focus on Jesus Christ, the One who loves you more than you could ever truly imagine.

Be encouraged, for this fragile world of darkness is only our temporary dwelling place. The glory of Heaven awaits us. Each evening the sun sets, we are one day closer to our eternal home. For even in the sunset, there is sunshine awaiting you and me.

*"I will fulfill my vows to you, O God,
and will offer a sacrifice of thanks for your help.
For you have rescued me from death;
you have kept my feet from slipping.
So now I can walk in your presence, O God,
in your life-giving light."*

—Ps. 56:12–13 NLT

Acknowledgements

"And whatever you do, whether in word or deed, do it all in the name of the Lord Jesus, giving thanks to God the Father through him." (Col. 3:17)

Writing my first book has been one of the most fulfilling experiences of my life. What a joy it is to share part of my story through the composition of written words. I truly love writing, and I am already working on my second book.

Although God allowed me to write, edit, and design this book myself, I could not have completed this labor of love without my dad's wisdom and guidance. He encouraged me every step of the way, and he even proofread my entire manuscript. Then, he went another step further and wrote a beautiful foreword, for which I am truly humbled.

Thank you, Daddy, for writing such a kindhearted foreword and for everything you do to make me feel special. You always bring out the best in me. You inspire me in so many ways. You exemplify the unconditional love of Jesus. I love you, Daddy!

Additionally, I would like to express my sincere appreciation to the dear friends who contributed such heartfelt testimonials for my first literary endeavor. I treasure your constant encouragement and your steadfast friendship.

Above all, I want to thank my Heavenly Father, Jesus Christ. No words could convey my gratitude for everything the Lord has done for me. May my life be a living testimony of God's grace, as I continue to proclaim the glorious message of salvation through Jesus Christ!

Thank You, Jesus, for bringing me out of the sunset and into the sunshine. I owe my life to You, for You are the One who has given me life. I love You, Jesus, my Savior and my Lord.

Notes

Introduction

1. Campbell, Jennifer, "Thank You, Lord," 2015,
   http://www.cwrmusic.org.

Chapter Two: Shine His Light

1. Nave, Orville J., s.v. "Spikenard," in *Nave's Topical Bible*
   (Lincoln, NE: Topical Bible Publishing Company. 1903),
   1299.

Chapter Three: The Music in Me

1. Campbell, Jennifer, "He Will Stand By You," 1998,
   http://www.cwrmusic.org.
2. Ravenhill, Leonard, "The Judgment Seat of Christ,"
   Ravenhill, http://www.ravenhill.org/judgment.htm.

Chapter Four: All for Jesus

1. "The Bill of Rights: A Transcription," The U.S. National
   Archives and Records Administration,
   https://www.archives.gov/founding-docs/bill-of-rights-
   transcript.

Chapter Five: Expanding Borders

1. Operation Christmas Child Shoebox Recipient, email
   message to Jennifer Campbell, April 23, 2012.

2. Mason, Colin, and Stephen Mosher, "Earth Day: Abortion Has Killed 1-2 Billion Worldwide in 50 Years," Life Site News, http://www.lifenews.com/2011/04/21/earth-day-abortion-has-killed-1-2-billion-worldwide-in-50-years.

Chapter Six: Stuck in the Sunset

1. Campbell, Jennifer, "There's Sunshine Awaiting You," 2000, http://www.cwrmusic.org.

Chapter Seven: Mayday!

1. *Encyclopaedia Britannica*, s.v. "Distress signal," http://www.britannica.com/technology/distress-signal.
2. Huber, Chris, Heather Klinger, and Kristy J. O'Hara, "2017 Hurricane Harvey: Facts, FAQS, and how to help," World Vision, https://www.worldvision.org/disaster-relief-news-stories/hurricane-harvey-facts.
3. "Katrina's Storm Surge," Weather Underground, https://www.wunderground.com/education/Katrinas_surge_contents.asp.

Chapter Ten: Mountains of Faith

1. "Paradise Inn," Rainier Guest Services, https://mtrainierguestservices.com/accommodations/paradise-inn.
2. Campbell, Ken, "Speak His Name," 2014, http://www.cwrmusic.org.
3. "Upper Suwannee River and Springs," Suwannee River Water Management District, http://www.srwmd.state.fl.us/index.aspx?NID=116.

4. "Groundwater Modeling," South Florida Water Management District, https://www.sfwmd.gov/science-data/gw-modeling.

Chapter Eleven: Jesus Gave His Life for Love

1. Campbell, Jennifer, "Jesus Gave His Life for Love," 2013, http://www.cwrmusic.org.
2. Oakeley, Frederick and John Francis Wade. "O Come, All Ye Faithful." In *Sing His Praise*, 420. Springfield, MO: Gospel Publishing House. 1991.
3. Oxford Dictionaries, s.v. "adore," https://en.oxforddictionaries.com/definition/adore.

Chapter Twelve: Life Is a Mission Field

1. Morgan, Robert J., "Beyond the Sunset," in *Then Sings My Soul: 150 of the World's Greatest Hymn Stories* (Nashville, TN: Thomas Nelson, Inc. 2003), 293.

Chapter Thirteen: Be Still

1. Misachi, John, "Which Countries Border the Red Sea?" WorldAtlas, https://www.worldatlas.com/articles/which-countries-border-the-red-sea.html.
2. Strong, James, s.v. "raphah," in *A Concise Dictionary of the Words in the Hebrew Bible* (New York, NY: Abingdon-Cokesbury Press 1890), 110.
3. Bradbury, WM. B. and Anna B. Warner. "Jesus Loves Me." In *Tabernacle Hymns: Number Four*, 307. Chicago, IL: Tabernacle Publishing Company. 1953.

Chapter Fifteen: Heaven Ever After

1. Bradbury, William B. and Edward Mote. "The Solid Rock." In *Sing His Praise*, 116. Springfield, MO: Gospel Publishing House. 1991.
2. Weinberger, Lael, "Evolution in American Education and the Demise of Its Public School System," Answers in Genesis, https://answersingenesis.org/public-school/evolution-in-us-education-and-demise-of-its-public-school-system.
3. "Induced Abortion Worldwide," Guttmacher Institute, https://www.guttmacher.org/fact-sheet/induced-abortion-worldwide.
4. *Merriam-Webster Dictionary*, s.v. "Babel," https://www.merriam-webster.com/dictionary/Babel.
5. "Drunk Driving," National Highway Traffic Safety Administration, https://www.nhtsa.gov/risky-driving/drunk-driving.

Chapter Seventeen: When Opportunity Knocks

1. "Famous Quotations from Thomas Edison," Edison Innovation Foundation, https://www.thomasedison.org/edison-quotes.
2. Campbell, Ken, "Christ Will Return," 2015, http://www.cwrmusic.org.

Chapter Nineteen: Be the One

1. "Christian Persecution," Open Doors USA, https://www.opendoorsusa.org/christian-persecution.
2. Pease, Joshua, "Syrian Pastor Fights to Keep the Church Strong in a Dangerous Region," Open Doors USA, https://www.opendoorsusa.org/christian-

persecution/stories/syrian-pastor-fights-keep-church-strong-dangerous-region.

Chapter Twenty: Qualifying the Called

1. Cymbala, Jim. "Witness." Sermon at the Brooklyn Tabernacle, Brooklyn, NY, July 9, 2017.

Chapter Twenty-One: Soar like an Eagle

1. *Encyclopaedia Britannica*, s.v. "Matterhorn," https://www.britannica.com/place/Matterhorn-mountain-Europe.

Chapter Twenty-Two: Are You Prepared?

1. "Hurricane Costs," NOAA Office for Coastal Management, https://coast.noaa.gov/states/fast-facts/hurricane-costs.html.
2. Campbell, Ken, "He Went Out of His Way," 2005, http://www.cwrmusic.org.

Chapter Twenty-Three: Sunshine Awaits

1. Campbell, Jennifer, "Follow Hope," 2014, http://www.cwrmusic.org.

About the Author

J ennifer Joy Campbell was born and raised in the Sunshine State of Florida, where she and her father, Ken, share a home on their small family farm with their orange and white tabby cat, Morris. She also enjoys spending time with her Grandma Lucille.

Jennifer is a talented writer, speaker, web designer, and host of the *Be Encouraged* webcast, viewed each week by thousands of people representing all parts of the globe.

Jennifer is a graduate of Florida Gateway College (Lake City, Florida), the University of Florida (Gainesville, Florida), and Nova Southeastern University (Fort Lauderdale, Florida). She completed her Master of Science degree in English education with a 4.0 GPA. She has been teaching public school for thirteen years, following in her dad's footsteps.

Her dad, Ken, is a high school and college mathematics instructor, having thirty-five years' experience in the field of education. In the summer of 2019, he will be retiring from public education to devote more time to the ministry.

In addition to being educators, this father-daughter team enjoys cooking and baking. They are always experimenting with new creations in the kitchen, both sweet and savory, from fresh-baked cookies and cakes to homemade pasta and artisan bread.

Jennifer and her dad are involved in a worldwide missionary outreach, Christ Will Return Ministries. The focus of this ministry is to call attention to the return of Jesus Christ, to proclaim the Gospel to those who are lost, and to encourage believers to share the love of Christ boldly.

Ken and Jennifer are both gifted songwriters and accomplished pianists. They produce their recordings in-house using a large number of acoustic instruments as well as sampled orchestral notes from the Vienna Symphonic Library.

Jennifer and her dad have also written many Gospel tracts, a number of which have been translated into approximately twenty languages. They frequently travel to various parts of the world to share the Gospel and sing of His love. They consider it a blessing to have visited more than fifty countries and territories around the world. God has been with them each step of the way.

Ken and Jennifer make their Gospel articles, Jennifer's *Be Encouraged* webcast, and a number of their songs freely available online for the widest possible distribution worldwide at www.christwillreturn.org. For one day soon, Christ will return.

Contact Jennifer:

Website: www.jennifercampbell.net
Facebook: facebook.com/jenniferjoycampbell
Twitter: @JenJoyCampbell
Email: jennifer@jennifercampbell.net

Free Music Download

Visit **www.cwrmusic.org** for a free MP3 download of Jennifer's song titled, "There's Sunshine Awaiting You." May God use this song to encourage you today!

Made in the USA
Columbia, SC
20 November 2023

26551997R00190